SUPER 10

CBSE Class 12

Chemistry

2023 Exam Sample Papers

with 2021-22 Previous Year Solved Papers, CBSE Sample Paper & 2020 Topper Answer Sheet

DISHA™
Publication Inc

DISHA Publications Inc.
45, 2nd Floor, Maharishi Dayanand Marg,
Corner Market, Malviya Nagar, new Delhi -110017
Tel: 49842349/ 49842350

Edited By
Apurva Mishra
Soumi De

Typeset By
DISHA DTP Team

Write To Us At
feedback_disha@aiets.co.in

Contents

Latest Syllabus Issued by CBSE for Academic Year (2022-2023)

CHEMISTRY (CODE NO. 043)

CLASS XII (2022-23) (THEORY)

Time: 03 Hours **Max. Marks: 70**

S.NO.	TITLE	NO. OF PERIODS	MARKS
1.	Solutions	15	7
2.	Electrochemistry	18	9
3.	Chemical Kinetics	15	7
4.	d -and f -Block Elements	18	7
5.	Coordination Compounds	18	7
6.	Haloalkanes and Haloarenes	15	6
7.	Alcohols, Phenols and Ethers	14	6
8.	Aldehydes, Ketones and Carboxylic Acids	15	8
9.	Amines	14	6
10.	Biomolecules	18	7
	Total	**160**	**70**

Unit II: Solutions 15 Periods

Types of solutions, expression of concentration of solutions of solids in liquids, solubility of gases in liquids, solid solutions, Raoult's law, colligative properties - relative lowering of vapour pressure, elevation of boiling point, depression of freezing point, osmotic pressure, determination of molecular masses using colligative properties, abnormal molecular mass, Van't Hoff factor.

Unit III: Electrochemistry 18 Periods

Redox reactions, EMF of a cell, standard electrode potential, Nernst equation and its application to chemical cells, Relation between Gibbs energy change and EMF of a cell, conductance in electrolytic solutions, specific and molar conductivity, variations of conductivity with concentration, Kohlrausch's Law, electrolysis and law of electrolysis (elementary idea), dry cell-electrolytic cells and Galvanic cells, lead accumulator, fuel cells, corrosion.

Unit IV: Chemical Kinetics 15 Periods

Rate of a reaction (Average and instantaneous), factors affecting rate of reaction: concentration, temperature, catalyst; order and molecularity of a reaction, rate law and specific rate constant, integrated rate equations and half-life (only for zero and first order reactions), concept of collision theory (elementary idea, no mathematical treatment), activation energy, Arrhenius equation.

Unit VIII: d and f Block Elements 18 Periods

General introduction, electronic configuration, occurrence and characteristics of transition metals, general trends in properties of the first-row transition metals – metallic character, ionization enthalpy, oxidation states, ionic radii, colour, catalytic property, magnetic properties, interstitial compounds, alloy formation, preparation and properties of $K_2Cr_2O_7$ and $KMnO_4$.

Lanthanoids – Electronic configuration, oxidation states, chemical reactivity and lanthanoid contraction and its consequences.

Actinoids - Electronic configuration, oxidation states and comparison with lanthanoids.

Unit IX: Coordination Compounds 18 Periods

Coordination compounds - Introduction, ligands, coordination number, colour, magnetic properties and shapes, IUPAC nomenclature of mononuclear coordination compounds. Bonding, Werner's theory, VBT, and CFT; structure and stereoisomerism, the importance of coordination compounds (in qualitative analysis, extraction of metals and biological system).

Unit X: Haloalkanes and Haloarenes 15 Periods

Haloalkanes: Nomenclature, nature of C–X bond, physical and chemical properties, optical rotation mechanism of substitution reactions.

Haloarenes: Nature of C–X bond, substitution reactions (Directive influence of halogen in monosubstituted compounds only). Uses and environmental effects of - dichloromethane, trichloromethane, tetrachloromethane, iodoform, freons, DDT.

Unit XI: Alcohols, Phenols and Ethers 14 Periods

Alcohols: Nomenclature, methods of preparation, physical and chemical properties (of primary alcohols only), identification of primary, secondary and tertiary alcohols, mechanism of dehydration, uses with special reference to methanol and ethanol.

Phenols: Nomenclature, methods of preparation, physical and chemical properties, acidic nature of phenol, electrophilic substitution reactions, uses of phenols.

Ethers: Nomenclature, methods of preparation, physical and chemical properties, uses.

Unit XII: Aldehydes, Ketones and Carboxylic Acids 15 Periods

Aldehydes and Ketones: Nomenclature, nature of carbonyl group, methods of preparation, physical and chemical properties, mechanism of nucleophilic addition, reactivity of alpha hydrogen in aldehydes, uses.

Carboxylic Acids: Nomenclature, acidic nature, methods of preparation, physical and chemical properties; uses.

Unit XIII: Amines 14 Periods

Amines: Nomenclature, classification, structure, methods of preparation, physical and chemical properties, uses, identification of primary, secondary and tertiary amines.

Diazonium salts: Preparation, chemical reactions and importance in synthetic organic chemistry.

Unit XIV: Biomolecules 18 Periods

Carbohydrates - Classification (aldoses and ketoses), monosaccharides (glucose and fructose), D-L configuration oligosaccharides (sucrose, lactose, maltose), polysaccharides (starch, cellulose, glycogen); Importance of carbohydrates.

Proteins - Elementary idea of - amino acids, peptide bond, polypeptides, proteins, structure of proteins - primary, secondary, tertiary structure and quaternary structures (qualitative idea only), denaturation of proteins; enzymes.
Hormones - Elementary idea excluding structure.

Vitamins - Classification and functions.

Nucleic Acids: DNA and RNA.

Note:
The content indicated in NCERT textbooks as excluded for the year 2022-23 is not to be tested by schools.

CBSE SAMPLE QUESTION PAPER (THEORY)

SESSION : 2022-2023

Time : 3 Hours **Max. Marks : 70**

General Instructions

Read the following instructions carefully

(a) *There are 35 questions in this question paper with internal choice.*

(b) *SECTION A consists of 18 multiple-choice questions carrying 1 mark each.*

(c) *SECTION B consists of 7 very short answer questions carrying 2 marks each.*

(d) *SECTION C consists of 5 short answer questions carrying 3 marks each.*

(e) *SECTION D consists of 2 case- based questions carrying 4 marks each.*

(f) *SECTION E consists of 3 long answer questions carrying 5 marks each.*

(g) ***All questions are compulsory.***

(h) ***Use of log tables and calculator are not allowed.***

SECTION-A

The following questions are multiple-choice questions with one correct answer. Each question carries 1 mark. There is no internal choice in this section.

1. The major product of acid catalysed dehydration of 1-methylcyclohexanol is:

(a) 1-methylcyclohexane (b) 1-methylcyclohexene

(c) 1-cyclohexylmethanol (d) 1-methylenecyclohexane

2. Which one of the following compounds is more reactive towards S_N1 reaction?

(a) $CH_2=CHCH_2Br$ (b) $C_6H_5CH_2Br$ (c) $C_6H_5CH\,(C_6H_5)Br$ (d) $C_6H_5CH(CH_3)\,Br$

3. $KMnO_4$ is coloured due to:

(a) d-d transitions (b) charge transfer from ligand to metal

(c) unpaired electrons in d orbital of Mn (d) charge transfer from metal to ligand

4. Which radioactive isotope would have the longer half-life ^{15}O or ^{19}O? (Given rate constants for ^{15}O and ^{19}O are $5.63 \times 10^{-3}\ s^{-1}$ and $k = 2.38 \times 10^{-2} s^{-1}$ respectively.)

(a) ^{15}O (b) ^{19}O

(c) Both will have the same half-life (d) None of the above, information given is insufficient

5. The molar conductivity of CH_3COOH at infinite dilution is 390 Scm^2/mol. Using the graph and given information, the molar conductivity of CH_3COOK will be:

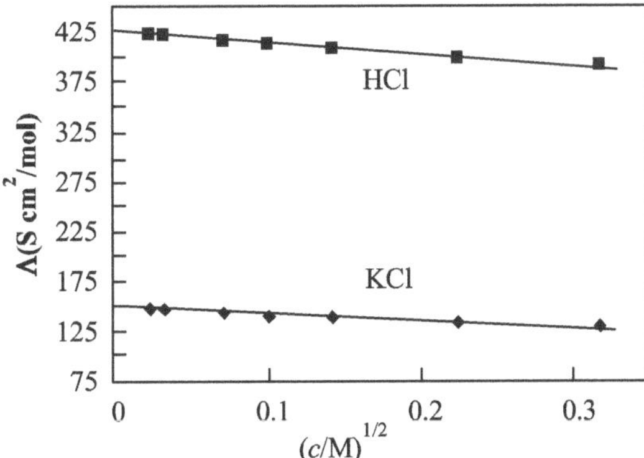

(a) 100 Scm^2/mol (b) 115 Scm^2/mol (c) 150 Scm^2/mol (d) 125 Scm^2/mol

***FOR VISUALLY CHALLENGED LEARNERS**

***5.** What is the molar conductance at infinite dilution for sodium chloride if the molar conductance at infinite dilution of Na^+ and Cl^- ions are 51.12×10^{-4} Scm^2/mol and 73.54×10^{-4} Scm^2/mol respectively?

(a) 124.66 Scm^2/mol (b) 22.42 Scm^2/mol (c) 198.20 Scm^2/mol (d) 175.78 Scm^2/mol

6. For the reaction, $A + 2B \rightarrow AB_2$, the order w.r.t. reactant A is 2 and w.r.t. reactant B. What will be change in rate of reaction if the concentration of A is doubled and B is halved?

(a) increases four times (b) decreases four times (c) increases two times (d) no change

7. Arrange the following in the increasing order of their boiling points:
A : Butanamine, B: N,N-Dimethylethanamine, C: N-Etthylethanaminamine

(a) C<B<A (b) A<B<C (c) A<C<B (d) B<C<A

8. The CFSE of $[CoCl_6]^{3-}$ is 18000 cm^{-1} the CFSE for $[CoCl_4]^-$ will be:

(a) 18000 cm^{-1} (b) 8000cm^{-1} (c) 2000 cm^{-1} (d) 16000 cm^{-1}

9. What would be the major product of the following reaction?
$C_6H_5—CH_2—OC_6H_5 + HBr \rightarrow A + B$

(a) $A=C_6H_5CH_2OH$, $B=C_6H_6$ (b) $A=C_6H_5CH_2OH$, $B= C_6H_5Br$
(c) $A=C_6H_5CH_3$, $B=C_6H_5Br$ (d) $A=C_6H_5CH_2Br$, $B=C_6H_5OH$

10. Which of the following statements is not correct for amines?

(a) Most alkyl amines are more basic than ammonia solution.
(b) pK_b value of ethylamine is lower than benzylamine.
(c) CH_3NH_2 on reaction with nitrous acid releases NO_2 gas.
(d) Hinsberg's reagent reacts with secondary amines to form sulphonamides.

11. Which of the following tests/reactions is given by aldehydes as well as ketones?

(a) Fehling's test (b) Tollen's test (c) 2,4 DNP test (d) Cannizzaro reaction

12. Arrhenius equation can be represented graphically as follows:

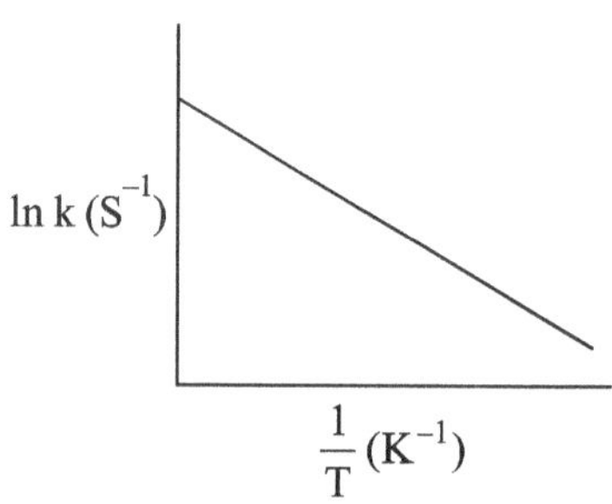

The (i) intercept and (ii) slope of the graph are:

(a) (i) ln A (ii) E_a/R (b) (i) A (ii) E_a (c) (i) ln A (ii) $-E_a/R$ (d) (i) A (ii) $-E_a$

***FOR VISUALLY CHALLENGED LEARNERS**

***12.** The unit of rate constant for the reaction
$2A + 2B \rightarrow A_2B_2$
which has rate = k $[A]^2[B]$ is:

(a) mol $L^{-1}s^{-1}$ (b) s^{-1} (c) mol L^{-1} (d) mol^{-2} L^2 s^{-1}

13. The number of ions formed on dissolving one molecule of $FeSO_4 \cdot (NH_4)_2SO_4 \cdot 6H_2O$ in water is:

(a) 3 (b) 4 (c) 5 (d) 6

14. The oxidation of toluene to benzaldehyde by chromyl chloride is called

(a) Etard reaction (b) Riemer-Tiemann reaction (c) Stephen's reaction (d) Cannizzaro's reaction

15. Given below are two statements labelled as Assertion (A) and Reason (R)

Assertion (A): An ether is more volatile than an alcohol of comparable molecular mass.
Reason (R): Ethers are polar in nature.

Select the most appropriate answer from the options given below:

(a) Both A and R are true and R is the correct explanation of A
(b) Both A and R are true but R is not the correct explanation of A.
(c) A is true but R is false.
(d) A is false but R is true.

16. Given below are two statements labelled as Assertion (A) and Reason (R)
Assertion (A): Proteins are found to have two different types of secondary structures viz alpha-helix and beta-pleated sheet structure.
Reason (R): The secondary structure of proteins is stabilized by hydrogen bonding.
Select the most appropriate answer from the options given below:
(a) Both A and R are true and R is the correct explanation of A
(b) Both A and R are true but R is not the correct explanation of A.
(c) A is true but R is false.
(d) A is false but R is true.

17. Given below are two statements labelled as Assertion (A) and Reason (R)
Assertion (A) : Magnetic moment values of actinides are lesser than the theoretically predicted values.
Reason (R) : Actinide elements are strongly paramagnetic.
Select the most appropriate answer from the options given below:
(a) Both A and R are true and R is the correct explanation of A
(b) Both A and R are true but R is not the correct explanation of A.
(c) A is true but R is false.
(d) A is false but R is true.

18. Given below are two statements labelled as Assertion (A) and Reason (R)
Assertion (A): Tertiary amines are more basic than corresponding secondary and primary amines in gaseous state.
Reason (R): Tertiary amines have three alkyl groups which cause +I effect.
Select the most appropriate answer from the options given below:
(a) Both A and R are true and R is the correct explanation of A
(b) Both A and R are true but R is not the correct explanation of A.
(c) A is true but R is false.
(d) A is false but R is true.

SECTION-B

This section contains 7 questions with internal choice in two questions. The following questions are very short answer type and carry 2 marks each.

19. A first-order reaction takes 69.3 min for 50% completion. What is the time needed for 80% of the reaction to get completed? (Given: log 5 =0.6990, log 8 = 0.9030, log 2 = 0.3010)

20. Account for the following:
(a) There are 5 OH groups in glucose
(b) Glucose is a reducing sugar

OR

What happens when D-glucose is treated with the following reagents
(a) Bromine water
(b) HNO_3

21. Give reason for the following:
(a) During the electrophilic substitution reaction of haloarenes, para substituted derivative is the major product.
(b) The product formed during S_N1 reaction is a racemic mixture.

OR

(a) Name the suitable alcohol and reagent, from which 2-Chloro-2-methyl propane can be prepared.
(b) Out of the Chloromethane and Fluoromethane, which one is has higher dipole moment and why?

22. The formula $Co(NH_3)_5CO_3Cl$ could represent a carbonate or a chloride. Write the structures and names of possible isomers.

23. Corrosion is an electrochemical phenomenon. The oxygen in moist air reacts as follows:
$O_2(g) + 2H_2O(l) + 4e^- \rightarrow 4OH^-$ (aq).
Write down the possible reactions for corrosion of zinc occurring at anode, cathode, and overall reaction to form a white layer of zinc hydroxide.

24. Explain how and why will the rate of reaction for a given reaction be affected when
(a) a catalyst is added
(b) the temperature at which the reaction was taking place is decreased

25. Write the reaction and IUPAC name of the product formed when 2-Methylpropanal (isobutyraldehyde) is treated with ethyl magnesium bromide followed by hydrolysis.

SECTION-C

This section contains 5 questions with internal choice in two questions. The following questions are short answer type and carry 3 marks each.

26. Write the equations for the following reaction:
(a) Salicylic acid is treated with acetic anhydride in the presence of conc. H_2SO_4
(b) Tert butyl chloride is treated with sodium ethoxide.
(c) Phenol is treated with chloroform in the presence of NaOH

27. Using Valence bond theory, explain the following in relation to the paramagnetic complex $[Mn(CN)_6]^{3-}$
(a) type of hybridization
(b) magnetic moment value
(c) type of complex – inner, outer orbital complex

28. Answer the following questions:
(a) State Henry's law and explain why are the tanks used by scuba divers filled with air diluted with helium (11.7% helium, 56.2% nitrogen and 32.1% oxygen)?
(b) Assume that argon exerts a partial pressure of 6 bar. Calculate the solubility of argon gas in water. (Given Henry's law constant for argon dissolved in water, K_H = 40kbar)

29. Give reasons for **any 3** of the following observations:
(a) Aniline is acetylated before nitration reaction.
(b) pK_b of aniline is lower than the m-nitroaniline.
(c) Primary amine on treatment with benzenesulphonyl chloride forms a product which is soluble in NaOH however secondary amine gives product which is insoluble in NaOH.
(d) Aniline does not react with methyl chloride in the presence of anhydrous $AlCl_3$ catalyst.

30. (a) Identify the major product formed when 2-cyclohexylchloroethane undergoes a dehydrohalogenation reaction. Name the reagent which is used to carry out the reaction.
(b) Why are haloalkanes more reactive towards nucleophilic substitution reactions than haloarenes and vinylic halides?

OR

(a) Name the possible alkenes which will yield 1-chloro-1-methylcyclohexane on their reaction with HCl. Write the reactions involved.
(b) Allyl chloride is hydrolysed more readily than n-propyl chloride. Why?

SECTION-D

The following questions are case-based questions. Each question has an internal choice and carries 4 (1+1+2) marks each. Read the passage carefully and answer the questions that follow.

31. Strengthening the Foundation: Chargaff Formulates His "Rules"

Many people believe that James Watson and Francis Crick discovered DNA in the 1950s. In reality, this is not the case. Rather, DNA was first identified in the late 1860s by Swiss chemist Friedrich Miescher. Then, in the decades following Miescher's discovery, other scientists–notably, Phoebus Levene and Erwin Chargaff--carried out a series of research efforts that revealed additional details about the DNA molecule, including its primary chemical components and the ways in which they joined with one another. Without the scientific foundation provided by these pioneers, Watson and Crick may never have reached their groundbreaking conclusion of 1953: that the DNA molecule exists in the form of a three-dimensional double helix.

Chargaff, an Austrian biochemist, as his first step in this DNA research, set out to see whether there were any differences in DNA among different species. After developing a new paper chromatography method for separating and identifying small amounts of organic material, Chargaff reached two major conclusions:

(i) the nucleotide composition of DNA varies among species.

(ii) Almost all DNA, no matter what organism or tissue type it comes from maintains certain properties, even as its composition varies. In particular, the amount of adenine (A) is similar to the amount of thymine (T), and the amount of guanine (G) approximates the amount of cytosine (C). In other words, the total amount of purines (A + G) and the total amount of pyrimidines (C + T) are usually nearly equal. This conclusion is now known as "Chargaff's rule."

Chargaff's rule is not obeyed in some viruses. These either have single- stranded DNA or RNA as their genetic material.

Answer the following questions:

(a) A segment of DNA has 100 adenine and 150 cytosine bases. What is the total number of nucleotides present in this segment of DNA?

(b) A sample of hair and blood was found at two sites. Scientists claim that the samples belong to same species. How did the scientists arrive at this conclusion?

(c) The sample of a virus was tested and it was found to contain 20% adenine, 20% thymine, 20 % guanine and the rest cytosine. Is the genetic material of this virus (a) DNA- double helix (b) DNA-single helix (c) RNA? What do you infer from this data?

OR

How can Chargaff's rule be used to infer that the genetic material of an organism is double- helix or single- helix?

32. Henna is investigating the melting point of different salt solutions. She makes a salt solution using 10 mL of water with a known mass of NaCl salt. She puts the salt solution into a freezer and leaves it to freeze. She takes the frozen salt solution out of the freezer and measures the temperature when the frozen salt solution melts. She repeats each experiment.

S.No.	Mass of the salt used in g	Melting point in °C	
		Readings Set 1	Reading Set 2
1	0.3	−1.9	−1.9
2	0.4	−2.5	−2.6
3	0.5	−3.0	−5.5
4	0.6	−3.8	−3.8
5	0.8	−5.1	−5.0
6	1.0	−6.4	−6.3

Assuming the melting point of pure water as 0°C, answer the following questions:

(a) One temperature in the second set of results does not fit the pattern. Which temperature is that? Justify your answer.

(b) Why did Henna collect two sets of results?

(c) In place of NaCl, if Henna had used glucose, what would have been the melting point of the solution with 0.6 g glucose in it?

OR

What is the predicted melting point if 1.2 g of salt is added to 10 mL of water? Justify your answer.

SECTION-E

The following questions are long answer type and carry 5 marks each. Two questions have an internal choice.

33. (a) Why does the cell voltage of a mercury cell remain constant during its lifetime?

(b) Write the reaction occurring at anode and cathode and the products of electrolysis of aq KCl.

(c) What is the pH of HCl solution when the hydrogen gas electrode shows a potential of –0.59 V at standard temperature and pressure?

OR

(a) Molar conductivity of substance "A" is 5.9×10^3 S/m and "B" is 1×10^{-16} S/m. Which of the two is most likely to be copper metal and why?

(b) What is the quantity of electricity in Coulombs required to produce 4.8 g of Mg from molten $MgCl_2$? How much Ca will be produced if the same amount of electricity was passed through molten $CaCl_2$? (Atomic mass of Mg = 24 u, atomic mass of Ca = 40 u).

(c) What is the standard free energy change for the following reaction at room temperature? Is the reaction spontaneous?
$Sn(s) + 2Cu^{2+}(aq)$ à $Sn^{2+}(aq) + 2Cu^{+}(s)$

34. A hydrocarbon (A) with molecular formula C_5H_{10} on ozonolysis gives two products (B) and (C). Both (B) and (C) give a yellow precipitate when heated with iodine in presence of NaOH while only (B) give a silver mirror on reaction with Tollen's reagent.

(a) Identify (A), (B) and (C).

(b) Write the reaction of B with Tollen's reagent

(c) Write the equation for iodoform test for C

(d) Write down the equation for aldol condensation reaction of B and C.

OR

An organic compound (A) with molecular formula $C_2Cl_3O_2H$ is obtained when (B) reacts with Red P and Cl_2. The organic compound (B) can be obtained on the reaction of methyl magnesium chloride with dry ice followed by acid hydrolysis.

(a) Identify A and B
(b) Write down the reaction for the formation of A from B. What is this reaction called?
(c) Give any one method by which organic compound B can be prepared from its corresponding acid chloride.
(d) Which will be the more acidic compound (A) or (B)? Why?
(e) Write down the reaction to prepare methane from the compound (B).

35. Answer the following:
(a) Why are all copper halides known except that copper iodide?
(b) Why is the $E^{o}_{(V^{3+}/V^{2+})}$ value for vanadium comparatively low?
(c) Why HCl should not be used for potassium permanganate titrations?
(d) Explain the observation, at the end of each period, there is a slight increase in the atomic radius of d block elements.
(e) What is the effect of pH on dichromate ion solution?

SOLUTIONS

Q.1 to 18 each correct answer 1 mark

1. **(b)** 1-methylcyclohexene
According to Saytzeff rule i.e highly substituted alkene is major product. Here dehydration reaction takes place, alkene is formed due to the removal of a water molecule.

2. **(c)** $C_6H_5CH(C_6H_5)Br$
$C_6H_5CH(C_6H_5)^+$ carbocation formed is more stable

3. **(b)** charge transfer from ligand to metal
The Mn atom in $KMnO_4$ has +7 oxidation state with electron configuration $[Ar]3d^0 4s^0$ Since no unpaired electrons are present, d–d transitions are not possible. The molecule should, therefore, be colourless.
Its intense purple due to L→M (ligand to metal) charge transfer 2p(L) of O to 3d(M) of Mn.

4. **(a)** ^{15}O
The rate constant for the decay of O-15 is less than that for O-19. Therefore , the rate of decay of O-15 will be slower and will have a longer half life .

5. **(b)** 115 Scm^2/mol
$\Lambda^\circ CH_3COOK = \Lambda^\circ CH_3COOH + \Lambda^\circ KCl - \Lambda^\circ HCl = 390 + 150 - 425 = 115\ Scm^2/mol$

5* (For visually challenged learners)
(a) $124.66 \times 10^{-4}\ Sm^2mol^{-1}$
Molar conductance of NaCl $= \lambda^+_{Na} + \lambda^+_{Cl}$
$= 51.12 \times 10^{-4} + 73.54 \times 10^{-4}$
$= 124.66 \times 10^{-4}\ Sm^2mol^{-1}$

6. **(a)** increases 4 times
Rate = $[A]^2$
If [A] is doubled then Rate' = $[2A]^2 = 4[A]^2$ = 4 Rate

7. **(d)** B<C<A
In primary amine intermolecular association due to H-bonding is maximum while in tertiary it is minimum.

8. **(b)** 8000 cm^{-1}
$\Delta t = (4/9) \times 18000 cm^{-1} = 8000\ cm^{-1}$

9. **(d)** A.=$C_6H_5CH_2Br$, B = C_6H_5OH,
$C_6H_5CH_2OC_6H_5$ H+ $C_6H_5CH_2OC_6H_5$

10. **(c)** CH_3NH_2 on reaction with nitrous acid releases NO_2 gas
Wrong statement. The evolution of nitrogen gas takes place.

11. **(c)** 2,4 DNP test
Fehling's, Tollen's and Cannizzaro reaction is shown by alcohols only.

12. **(c)** (i) ln A (ii) - E_a/R

12* (For visually challenged learners)
(d) $mol^{-2}\ L^2\ s^{-1}$ since the order of reaction is 3.

13. **(c)** 5
$1Fe^{2+}$, 2 SO_4^{2-} and 2 NH_4^+ ions

14. A Etard reaction

15. **(b)** Both A and R are true but R is not the correct explanation of A. A and R are two different statements about ethers The correct reason is that hydrogen bonding does not exist amongst ether molecules.

16. **(b)** Both A and R are true but R is not the correct explanation of A.

17. **(b)** Both A and R are true but R is not the correct explanation of A.
The magnetic moment is less as the 5f electrons of actinides are less effectively shielded which results in quenching of orbital contributions , they are strongly paramagnetic due to presence of unpaired electrons.

18. **(a)** Both A and R are true and R is the correct explanation of A.

19. Half life $t_{1/2} = 0.693/k$
k= 0.693/69.3 = 1/100 = 0.01 min^{-1} (1/2 mark)
For first order reaction

$$k = \frac{2.303}{t}\log\frac{[Ro]}{[R]}$$ (1 mark)

$$t = \frac{2.303}{0.01}\log\frac{100}{20}$$

$t = 230.3\log 5$ (log 5 =0.6990)
$t = 160.9$ min (1/2 mark)

20. (a) Acetylation of glucose with acetic anhydride gives glucose pentaacetate which confirms the presence of five –OH groups. Since it exists as a stable compound, five –OH groups should be attached to different carbon atoms.
(1 mark)

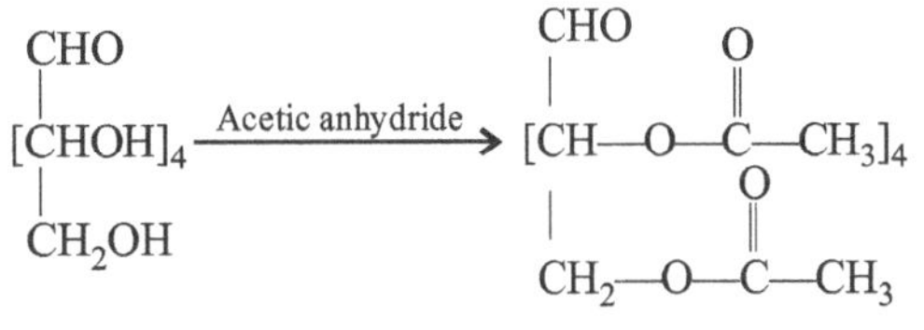

$$\begin{array}{l} CHO \\ | \\ [CHOH]_4 \\ | \\ CH_2OH \end{array} \xrightarrow{\text{Acetic anhydride}} \begin{array}{l} CHO \\ | \\ [CH-O-\overset{O}{\overset{\|}{C}}-CH_3]_4 \\ | \\ CH_2-O-\overset{O}{\overset{\|}{C}}-CH_3 \end{array}$$

(b) Glucose reduces Fehlings reagent

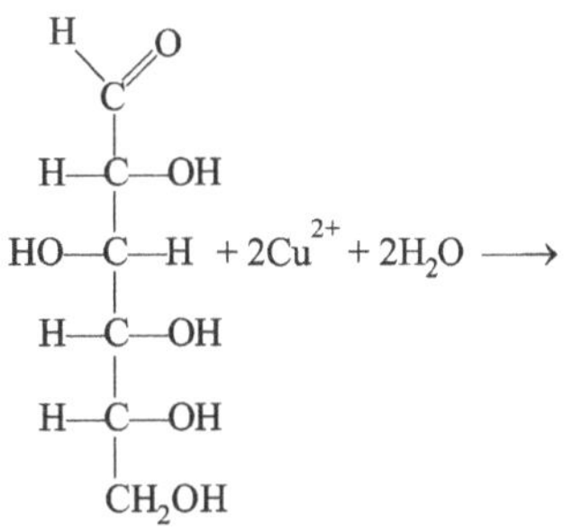

$$\begin{array}{c} H\diagdown\ \ \diagup\!\!\!\diagup O \\ C \\ | \\ H-C-OH \\ | \\ HO-C-H \\ | \\ H-C-OH \\ | \\ H-C-OH \\ | \\ CH_2OH \end{array} + 2Cu^{2+} + 2H_2O \longrightarrow$$

HO O
C
H—C—OH
HO—C—H $+ Cu_2O + 4H^+$ (1 mark)
H—C—OH
H—C—OH
CH_2OH

OR

(a) $CHO-[CHOH]_4-CH_2OH \xrightarrow{Br_2\ water} COOH-[CHOH]_4-CH_2OH$ (1 mark)

Gluconic acid

(b) $CHO-[CHOH]_4-CH_2OH \xrightarrow{Oxidation} COOH-[CHOH]_4-COOH \xleftarrow{Oxidation} COOH-[CHOH]_4-CH_2OH$

Saccharic acid Gluconic acid

(1 mark)

21. (a) At the ortho position, higher steric hindrance is there, hence para isomer is usually predominate and is obtained in the major amount. (1 mark)

(b) During the S_N1 mechanism, intermediate carbocation formed is sp^2 hybridized and planar in nature. This allows the attack of nucleophile from either side of the plane resulting in a racemic mixture. (1 mark)

OR

(a) Tert butyl alcohol or 2-methyl propan-2-ol using Lucas reagent , mixture of conc. HCl and $ZnCl_2$ the reaction will follow the S_N1 pathway. (1 mark)

(b) Chloromethane is having higher dipole moment. Due to smaller size of fluorine the dipole moment of flouromethane is comparatively lesser. (1 mark)

22. $[Co(NH_3)_5CO_3]Cl$ and $[Co(NH_3)_5Cl]CO_3$ (1/2+1/2 = 1 mark)

Pentaaminecarbonatocobalt(III)chloride (1/2 mark)

Pentaaminechloridocobalt(III)carbonate (1/2 mark)

23. Anode: $Zn\ (s) \rightarrow Zn^{2+}\ (aq) + 2\ e^-$ (1/2 mark)

Cathode: $O_2(g) + 2H_2O(l) + 4e^- \rightarrow 4OH^-\ (aq)$. (1/2 mark)

Overall: $2\ Zn\ (s) + O_2(g) + 2H_2O(l) \rightarrow 2\ Zn^{2+}(aq) + 4OH^-\ (aq)$

$2\ Zn(s) + O_2(g) + 2H_2O(l) \rightarrow 2\ Zn(OH)_2$ (ppt) (1 mark)

24. (a) The rate of reaction will increase. The catalyst decreases the activation energy of the reaction therefore the reaction becomes faster. (1/2+1/2 = 1 mark)

(b) The rate of reaction will decrease. At lower temperatures the kinetic energy of molecules decreases thereby the collisions decrease resulting in a lowering of rate of reaction. (1/2+1/2 = 1 mark)

25. $(CH_3)_2CHCHO + C_2H_5MgBr \xrightarrow{dry\ ether} (CH_3)_2CHCH(C_2H_5)(OMgBr)$ (1mark)

$(CH_3)_2CHCH(C_2H_5)(OMgBr) \xrightarrow{H^+/H_2O} (CH_3)_2CHCH(C_2H_5)(OH)$ (1 mark)

2-Methylpentan-3-ol

26. (i) Aspirin is formed

Salicylic acid (COOH, OH) $+ [CH_3CO]_2O \xrightarrow{H^+}$ Acetylsalicylic acid [Aspirin] (COOH, $OCOCH_3$) $+ CH_3COOH$ (1 mark)

(ii) $(CH_3)_3CCl \xrightarrow{sodium\ ethoxide} (CH_3)_2C{=}CH_2$

2methylpropene

(1 mark)

(iii) o-hydroxybenzaldehyde will be formed (1 mark)

Phenol (OH) $\xrightarrow[3\ KOH]{CHCl_3}$ o-hydroxybenzaldehyde (OH, CHO)

27. $[Mn(CN)_6]^{3-}$

Mn = [Ar] $3d^54s^2$

Mn^{3+} = [Ar] $3d^4$

Mn (ground state)

↑	↑	↑	↑	↑		⇅				

Mn in +3 state

↑	↑	↑	↑							

Mn in $[Mn(CN)_6]^{3-}$

⇅	↑	↑	××	××		××		××	××	××

d^2sp^3 hybridisation

xx are electrons donated by ligand CN^-

Type of hybridization – d^2sp^3 (1 mark)

Magnetic moment value – $\sqrt{n(n+2)} = \sqrt{(2(2+2))} = 2.87$ BM

(n= no. of unpaired electrons) (1 mark)

Type of complex – inner orbital (1 mark)

28. (a) Henry's law: the partial pressure of the gas in vapour phase (p) is proportional to the mole fraction of the gas (x) in the solution. (1 mark)

The pressure underwater is high, so the solubility of gases in blood increases. When the diver comes to surface the pressure decreases so does the solubility causing bubbles of nitrogen in blood, to avoid this situation and maintain the same partial pressure of nitrogen underwater too, the dilution is done. (1 mark)

(b) $p = K_H x$
mole fraction of argon in water $x = p/k = 6/40 \times 10^3$
$= 1.5 \times 10^{-4}$ (1 mark)

29. (a) Aniline is acetylated, before nitration reaction in order to avoid formation of tarry oxidation products and protecting the amino group, so that p-nitro derivative can be obtained as major product. (1 mark)
(b) pK_b of aniline is lower than the m-nitro aniline. The basic strength of aniline is more that m-nitroaniline. pk_b value is inversely proportional to basic strength. Presence of Electron withdrawing group decrease basic strength. (1 mark)
(c) Due to the presence of acidic hydrogen in the N-alkylbenzenesulphonamide formed by the treatment of primary amines. (1 mark)
(d) Aniline does not react with methylchloride in the presence of $AlCl_3$ catalyst , because aniline is a base and $AlCl_3$ is Lewis acid which lead to formation of salt. (1 mark)

30. (a) The major product formed when 2-cyclohexylchloroethane undergoes dehydrohalogenation reaction is 1-cyclohexylethene. The reagent which is used to carry out the reaction is ethanolic KOH. (1+1 = 2 marks)
(b) Haloalkanes are more reactive than haloarenes and vinylic halides because of the presence of partial double bond character C-X bond in haloarenes and vinylic halides. Hence they do not undergo nucleophilic reactions easily. (1 mark)

OR

(a) Methylenecyclohexane

CH_2 (=cyclohexane) $\xrightarrow{HCl}$ 1-chloro-1-methylcyclohexane (Cl, CH_3) (1/2+1/2 = 1 mark)

1-Methylcyclohexene

CH_3 (cyclohexene) $\xrightarrow{HCl}$ 1-chloro-1-methylcyclohexane (Cl, CH_3) (1/2+1/2 = 1 mark)

(b) Allyl chloride shows high reactivity as the carbocation formed in the first step is stabilised by resonance while no such stabilisation of carbocation exists in the case of n-propyl chloride. (1 mark)

31. (a) A = 100 so T = 100
C=150 so G = 150
Total nucleotides = 100+100+150+150 =500 (1 mark)
(b) They studied the nucleotide composition of DNA. It was the same so they concluded that the samples belong to same species. (1 mark)
(c) A = T = 20%
But G is not equal to C so double helix is ruled out. (1/2 mark)
The bases pairs are ATGC and not AUGC so it is not RNA (1/2 mark)
The virus is a single helix DNA virus (1 mark)

OR

According to Charagaff rule, all double helix DNA will have the same amount of A and T as well as C will be same amount as G. If this is not the case then the helix is single stranded. (2 marks)

32. The melting point of ice is the freezing point of water. We can use the depression in freezing point property in this case.
(a) 3rd reading for 0.5 g there has to be an increase in depression of freezing point and therefore decrease in freezing point so also decrease in melting point when amount of salt is increased but the trend is not followed on this case. (1 mark)
(b) two sets of reading help to avoid error in data collection and give more objective data. (1 mark)
(c) $\Delta T_f(\text{glucose}) = 1 \times K_f \times \dfrac{0.6 \times 1000}{180 \times 10}$ ....(1) (1/2 mark)

$\Delta T_f(\text{NaCl}) = 2 \times K_f \times \dfrac{0.6 \times 1000}{58.5 \times 10}$ (1/2 mark)

$3.8 = 2 \times K_f \times \dfrac{0.6 \times 1000}{58.5 \times 10}$ ....(2)

Divide equation 1 by 2

$\dfrac{\Delta T_f\ (\text{glucose})}{3.8} = \dfrac{58.5}{2 \times 180}$ (1/2 mark)

ΔT_f (glucose = 0.62 Freezing point or Melting point = – 0.62 °C (1/2 mark)

OR

depression in freezing point is directly proportional to molality (mass of solute when the amount of solvent remains same) (1 mark)
0.3 g depression is 1.9 °C
0.6 g depression is 3.8 °C
1.2 g depression will be 3.8 × 2 = 7.6 °C (1 mark)

33. The cell potential remains constant during its life as the overall reaction does not involve any ion in solution whose concentration can change during its life time. (1 mark)
(b) KCl (aq) à K^+ (aq) + Cl^- (aq)

cathode: $H_2O(l) + e^-$ à $\frac{1}{2}H_2$ (g) + OH^- (aq) (1/2 mark)

anode: Cl^- (aq) à $\frac{1}{2}Cl_2$ (aq) + e^-(1/2 mark)

net reaction:

KCl (aq) + H_2O (l) à K^+ (aq) + OH^- (aq) + $\frac{1}{2}H_2$ (g) + $\frac{1}{2}Cl_2$ (g) (1 mark)

(c) Given, potential of hydrogen gas electrode = –0.59 V
Electrode reaction: $H^+ + e^- \rightarrow 0.5\ H_2$

Applying Nernst equation,

$E(H^+/H_2) = E°(H^+/H_2) - \frac{0.059}{n}\log\frac{[H_2]^{1/2}}{[H^+]}$ (1 mark)

$E°(H^+/H_2) = 0$ V
$E(H^+/H_2) = -0.59$ V
$n = 1$
$[H_2] = 1$ bar
$-0.59 = 0 - 0.059(-\log[H^+])$ (1/2 mark)
$-0.59 = -0.059pH$
$\therefore$ pH = 10 (1/2 mark)

OR

(a) "A" is copper, metals are conductors thus have high value of conductivity. (1 mark)
(b) $Mg^{2+} + 2e^- $ à Mg
1 mole of magnesium ions gains two moles of electrons or 2F to form 1 mole of Mg
24 g Mg requires 2 F electricity
4.8 g Mg requires 2 × 4.8/24 = 0.4 F = 0.4 × 96500 = 38600C (1 mark)
$Ca^{2+} + 2e^- \rightarrow Ca$
2 F electricity is required to produce 1 mole =40 g Ca
0.4 F electricity will produce 8 g Ca (1 mark)
(c) F = 96500C, n=2,
$Sn^{2+}(aq) + 2e^- \rightarrow Sn(s) - 0.14V$
$Cu^{2+}(aq) + e^- \rightarrow Cu^+(aq)\ 0.15$ V
E°cell = E°cathode – E°anode
= 0.15 – (–0.14) = 0.29V (1 mark)
$\Delta G° = -nFE^o_{cell}$
= –2 × 96500 × 0.29 = 55970 J/mol (1 mark)

34. A is an alkene
B is an aldehyde with $-CH_3$ group
C is a methyl ketone
$CH_3CHO + [Ag(NH_3)_2]^+ + OH^- \longrightarrow CH_3COO^- + Ag + NH_3 + H_2O$ (1/2 mark)
$CH_3COCH_3 + NaOH + I_2 \longrightarrow CHI_3 + CH_3COONa$ (1/2 mark)
A : $CH(CH_3)=C(CH_3)_2$, B: CH_3CHO, C: $O=C(CH_3)_2$
(1.5 = 1/2 mark each)

$CH_3COCH_3 + CH_3CHO$
$\downarrow Ba(OH)_2$
$(CH_3)_2C(OH)CH_2COCH_3 + CH_3CH(OH)CH_2CHO + (CH_3)_2C(OH)CH_2CHO + CH_3CH(OH)CH_2COCH_3$
$\downarrow$ heat
$(CH_3)_2C{=}CHCOCH_3 + CH_3CH{=}CHCHO + (CH_3)_2C{=}CHCHO + CH_3CH{=}CHCOCH_3$
(2.5 = 1/2 mark for each product, ½ for the reaction)

OR

(a) (A): CCl_3COOH, (B): CH_3COOH (1 mark)
(b) $CH_3COOH \xrightarrow[\text{(ii) } H_2O]{\text{(i) Red P/}Cl_2} CCl_3COOH$,
Hell Volhard Zelinsky reaction (1/2 +1/2 = 1 mark)
(c) $CH_3COCl \xrightarrow{H_2O} CH_3COOH$ (1 mark)
(d) A will be more acidic due to presence of 3 Cl groups (electron withdrawing groups) which increase acidity of carboxylic acid. (1 mark)
(e) $CH_3COOH \xrightarrow{\text{(i) NaOH, CaO (ii) heat}} CH_4 + Na_2CO_3$ (1 mark)

35. (a) Cu^{2+} oxidizes iodide ion to iodine. (1 mark)
(b) The low value for V is related to the stability of V^{2+} (half-filled t_{2g} level) (1 mark)
(c) Permanganate titrations in presence of hydrochloric acid are unsatisfactory since hydrochloric acid is oxidised to chlorine.
(d) The d orbital is full with ten electrons and shield the electrons present in the higher s-orbital to a greater extent resulting in increase in size.
(e) The chromates and dichromates are interconvertible in aqueous solution depending upon pH of the solution. Increasing the pH (in basic solution) of dichromate ions a colour change from orange to yellow is observed as dichromate ions change to chromate ions.

All India 2022
CBSE Board Solved Paper
Term-II

Time Allowed : 2 Hours ***Maximum Marks : 35***

General Instructions:

Read the following instructions carefully and strictly follow them.

(i) This question paper contains **12** questions. All questions are compulsory.

(ii) This question paper is divided into **three** Sections – Section **A**, **B** and **C**.

(iii) Section-A, Q. Nos. **1** to **3** are very short answer type questions carrying **2** marks each.

(iv) Section-B, Q. Nos. **4** to **11** are short answer type questions carrying **3** marks each.

(v) Section-C, Q. No. **12** is case based question carrying **5** marks.

(vi) Log tables and calculators are NOT allowed.

SECTION - A

1. An organic compound (A) with molecular formula C_3H_7NO on heating with Br_2 and KOH forms a compound (B). compound (B) on heating with $CHCl_3$ and alcoholic KOH produces a foul smelling compound (C) and on reacting with $C_6H_5SO_2Cl$ forms a compound (D) which is soluble in alkali. Write the structures of (A), (B), (C) and (D).

2. Write the products formed when benzaldehyde reacts with the following reagents (Any two) :

(i) CH_3CHO in presence of dilute NaOH

(ii) N_2N-OH in presence of weak acid

(iii) Tollen's reagent

3. The conductivity of 0.001M acetic acid is 7.8×10^{-5} S cm^{-1}. Calculate its degree of dissociation of $\Lambda°m$ for acetic acid is 390 S cm^2 mol^{-1}.

SECTION - B

4. (i) Why are melting points of transition metals high?

(ii) Why the transition metals generally form coloured compounds?

(iii) Why E° value for Mn^{3+}/Mn^{2+} couple is highly positive?

5. (a) (i) Which acid of the following pair would you expect to be stronger?

$F-CH_2-COOH$ or CH_3-COOH

(ii) Arrange the following compounds in increasing order of their boiling points :

$CH_3CH_2OH, CH_3-CHO, CH_3-COOH$

(iii) Give simple chemical test to distinguish between Benzaldehyde and Acetophanone.

OR

(b) (i) Which will undergo faster nucleophilic addition reaction?

Acetaldehyde or Propanone

(ii) What is the composition of Fehling's reagent?

(iii) Draw structure of the semicarbazone of Ethanal.

6. Give reasons :

(i) Ammonolysis of alkyl halides is not a good method to prepare pur primary amines.

(ii) Aniline does not give Friedel-Crafts reaction.

(iii) Although $-NH_2$ group is o/p directing in eletrophilic substitution reactions, yet aniline on nitration gives good yield of *m*-nitroaniline.

7. (a) What happens when

(i) Propanone is treated with CH_3MgBr and then hydrolysed?

(ii) Ethanal is treated with excess ethanol and acid?

(iii) Methanal undergoes Cannizzaro reaction?

OR

(b) Write the main product in the following reactions:

(i) $2CH_3COCl + (CH_3)_2Cd \rightarrow$

(ii) $CH_3CH_2CHO \xrightarrow{Zn(Hg)/conc.\ HCl}$

(iii) $C_6H_{11}-COONa + NaOH \xrightarrow[\Delta]{CaO}$

8. (a) Differentiate between the following :

(i) Adsorption and Absorption

(ii) Lyophobic Sol and Lyophilic Sol

(iii) Multimolecular Colloid and Macromolecular colloid

OR

(b) (I) Define the following terms :

(i) Zeta Potential

(ii) Coagulation

(II) Why a negatively charged sol is obtained when $AgNO_3$ solution is added to KI solution?

9. Define transition metals. Why Zn, Cd and Hg are not called transition metals ? How is the variability in oxidation states of transition metals different from that of *p*-block elements?

10. (a) Using valence bond theory, predict the hybridization and magnetic character of the complex : $[Ni(CO)_4]$ (Atomic number : Ni = 28)

(b) Write IUPAC name of $[Pt(NH_3)_2 Cl(NO_2)]$

(c) Why $[Co(en)_3]^{3+}$ is a more stable complex than $[Co(NH_3)_6]^{3+}$?

11. (a) Calculate $\Delta_r G°$ and long Kc for the following cell :

$$Ni(s) + 2\,Ag^+(aq) \rightarrow Ni^{2+}(aq) + 2Ag(s)$$

Given that E° cell = 1.05V, IF = 96,500 $Cmol^{-1}$.

OR

(b) Calculate the e.m.f. of the following cell at 298K :

$Fe(s) \mid Fe^{2+}$ (0.001 M) $\parallel H^+$ (0.01M) $\mid H_2(g)$ (1 bar) $\mid$ Pt(s)

Given that E°cell = +0.44 V

[log 2 = 0.3010 log 3 = 0.4771 log 10 = 1]

SECTION - C

12. Read the following passage and answer the questions that follow :

The rate of reaction is concerned with decrease in concentration of reactants or increase in the concentration of products per unit time. It can be expressed as instantaneous rate at a particular instant of time and average rate over a large interval of time. A number of factors such as temperature, concentration of reactants, catalyst affect the rate of reaction. Mathematical representation of rate of a reaction is given by rate law :

$$Rate = k[A]^x [B]^y$$

x and y indicate how sensitive the rate is to the change in concentration of A and B. Sum of $x + y$ gives the overall order of a reaction.

When a seqeuence of elementary reactions gives us the products, the reactions are called complex reactions. Molecularity and order of an elementary, reaction are same. Zero order reactions are relatively uncommon but they occur under special conditions. All natural and artificial radioactive decay of unstable nuclei take place by first order kinetics.

(a) What is the effect of temperature on the rate constant of a reaction?

(b) For a reaction A + B → Product, the rate law is given by, Rate = $k[A]^2 [B]^{1/2}$. What is the order of the raction?

(c) How order and molecularity are different for complex reactions ?

(d) A first order reaction has a rate constant $2 \times 10^{-3} s^{-1}$. How long will 6g of this reactant take to reduce to 2g ?

OR

The half life for radioactive decay of ^{14}C is 6930 years. An archaeological artifact containing wood had only 75% of the ^{14}C found in a living tree. Find the age of the sample. [log 4 = 0.6021 log 3 = 0.4771 log 2 = 0.3010 log 10 = 1]

Solutions

1. $CH_3CH_2CONH_2$ (A) $\xrightarrow[KOH]{Br_2}$ $CH_3CH_2NH_2$ (B) $\xrightarrow[KOH]{CHCl_3/\Delta}$ CH_3CH_2NC (C) Foul smelling compound

(A) $\xrightarrow{C_6H_5SO_2Cl}$ $CH_3CH_2-NH-SO_2-C_6H_5$ (D) Soluble in alkali **(2 Marks)**

2. (i) Reaction of benzaldehyde with CH_3CHO in presence of NaOH

$$C_6H_5CHO + CH_3CHO \xrightarrow{dil.NaOH} C_6H_5-CH(OH)-CH_2-CHO$$ **(1 Mark)**

3-Hydroxy 3 phenyl propanal (Aldol)

> **Note**
>
> *Aldols readily lose water on heating and give α-β unsaturated carbonyl compounds.*
>
> $$C_6H_5-CH(OH)-CH_2-CHO \xrightarrow[-H_2O]{\Delta} C_6H_5-CH=CH-CHO$$

(ii) Reaction of benzaldehyde with H_2N-OH in presence of weak acid

$$C_6H_5CHO + H_2N-OH \xrightarrow{H^+} C_6H_5-CH=N-OH + H_2O$$ **(1 Mark)**

(iii) Reaction of benzaldehyde with Tollen's reagent

$$C_6H_5CHO + 2[Ag(NH_3)_2]^+ + 3OH^- \longrightarrow C_6H_5COO^- + 2Ag + 2H_2O + 4NH_3$$ **(1 Mark)**

3. $$\lambda_m = \frac{K}{c} = \frac{7.8\times10^{-5}Scm^{-1}}{0.001mol\ L^{-1}}\times\frac{1000cm^3}{L} = 78.05\ cm^2\,mol^{-1}$$

$$\alpha = \frac{\lambda_m}{\lambda_m^0} = \frac{78.0\ Scm^2mol^{-1}}{390\ Scm^2mol^{-1}} = 0.2$$ **(2 Marks)**

4. (i) Transition metals have high melting point due to presence of unpaired electrons which are responsible for high strength of metallic bond. **(1 Mark)**

(ii) Transition metals generally form coloured compounds due to absorption of radiation from visible light region to excite the electrons from its one position to another position in *d*-orbitals. **(1 Mark)**

(iii) The outer electronic configuration in case of Mn^{3+} is $3d^4$ while in case of Mn^{2+} is $3d^5$ which is more stable as compare to $3d^4$ due to which it shows highly positive E° value for Mn^{3+}/Mn^{2+}. **(1 Mark)**

5. (a) (i) Acidity is directly proportional to the –I effect which means electron withdrawing group increases the acidic character. **(1 Mark)**

In case of $F-CH_2-COOH$, flourine shows–I effect due to which acidic character of this compound increases.

(ii) The compounds which have strongest hydrogen bonding between the molecules will show higher boiling point. **(1 Mark)**

CH_3COOH will have highest boiling point due to strong hydrogen bonding while CH_3CHO have lowest boiling point due to absence of hydrogen bonding.

Therefore; increasing order of boiling point is:

$CH_3CHO < CH_3CH_2CHO < CH_3COOH$

(iii) Benzaldehyde contains aldehydic functional group while Acetophenone contains ketonic functional group. Tollen's test is used to distinguish between benzaldehyde and acetophenone as it only respond in case of Aldehydes. Benzaldehyde reduces Tollen's reagent to give a red-brown precipitate of Cu_2O. **(1 Mark)**

OR

(b) (i) $CH_3-C(=O)-H$ (+I) Acetaldehyde $CH_3-C(=O)-CH_3$ (+I, +I) Propanone

propanone contains two CH_3 groups (i.e. +I effect) which makes carbonyl group less electron deficient due to which acetaldehyde show faster nucleophilic addition reaction. **(1 Mark)**

(ii) Fehling's reagent is composed by Fehling A and Fehling B. Fehling A is a blue-coloured aqueous solution of $CuSO_4$. Fehling B is colorless aqueous solution of potassium sodium tartrate ($KNaC_4H_4O_6.4H_2O$). **(1 Mark)**

> **Note**
>
> *Fehling reagent is used to test aldehydes. Ketones and aromatic aldehyde do not respond to Fehling's test.*

(iii) Structure of semicarbazone of ethanal

$$\underset{H}{\overset{CH_3}{}}\!\!>C=O + H_2N-NH-\overset{O}{\overset{\|}{C}}-NH_2 \longrightarrow NH-\overset{O}{\overset{\|}{C}}-NH_2$$

$$H_3C-\overset{H}{\overset{|}{C}}=N-NH-\overset{O}{\overset{\|}{C}}-NH_2$$
Semicarbazone

(1 Mark)

6. (i) Ammonolysis yields a mixture of primary, secondary, tertiary and quaternary salts. The separation of pure primary amines from ammonolysis of alkyl halide is a difficult process. **(1 Mark)**

(ii) Aniline does not give friedel-crafts reaction as it forms anilinium chloride salt which deactivates the ring for further acylation and alkylation reaction. **(1 Mark)**

(iii) $-NH_2$ group is electron donating group which activates the ring and gives ortho, para product but in case of nitration it will form anilinium ion in presence of acid and gives meta directing product. **(1 Mark)**

7. (a) (i) The reaction of propanone with grignard reagent

$$\underset{\text{propanone}}{CH_3-\overset{O}{\overset{\|}{C}}-CH_3} + CH_3MgBr \xrightarrow{H_2O} \underset{\text{2 methylpropan-2-ol}}{CH_3-\overset{OH}{\overset{|}{\underset{CH_3}{\underset{|}{C}}}}-CH_3}$$

(1 Mark)

(ii) When ethanal is reacted with excess ethanol and acid then acetal will form as a product.

$$\underset{\text{Ethanal}}{\underset{H}{\overset{CH_3}{}}\!\!>C=O} + C_2H_5OH \xrightarrow[-H_2O]{HCl} \underset{\text{Hemiacetal}}{\underset{H}{\overset{CH_3}{}}\!\!>C<\!\!\underset{OC_2H_5}{\overset{OH}{}}}$$

$$\xrightarrow[HCl,\ -H_2O]{C_2H_5OH} \underset{\text{Acetal}}{\underset{H}{\overset{H_3C}{}}\!\!>C<\!\!\underset{OC_2H_5}{\overset{OC_2H_5}{}}}$$

(1 Mark)

(iii) Methanal undergoes cannizzaro reaction

$$2\ \underset{\text{Methanal}}{\underset{H}{\overset{H}{}}\!\!>C=O} + \text{conc.KOH} \longrightarrow \underset{\text{Methanol}}{H-\overset{H}{\overset{|}{\underset{H}{\underset{|}{C}}}}-OH} + \underset{\text{Potassium methanoate}}{H-\overset{O}{\overset{\|}{C}}-OK}$$

(1 Mark)

Note

Cannizzaro reaction involves disproportionation i.e., self oxidation and self reduction of aldehydes which do not have alpha hydrogen. One molecule of aldehyde is reduced to alcohol and another is oxidised to carboxylic acid.

OR

(b) (i) $2CH_3COCl + (CH_3)_2Cd \longrightarrow CH_3-\overset{O}{\overset{\|}{C}}-CH_3$ **(1 Mark)**

(ii) $CH_3CH_2CHO \xrightarrow{Zn(Hg)/Conc.HCl} CH_3CH_2CH_3$ **(1 Mark)**

(iii)

$$C_6H_{11}-COONa + NaOH \xrightarrow[\Delta]{CaO} C_6H_{11}-H + Na_2CO_3$$

(1 Mark)

8. (a)

(i) **Adsorption**		**Absorption**
(a) The substance is only concentrated at the surface not in the bulk.	(a)	The substance is uniformly distributed throughout the bulk of solid.
(b) It is surface phenomenon.	(b)	It is bulk phenomenon.
(c) It is exothermic process.	(c)	It is endothermic process.
(d) It is temperature dependent.	(d)	It does not depend on the temperature. **(1 Mark)**

(ii) **Lyophobic sol**		**Lyophilic sol**
(a) Dispersed phase has no affinity for dispersion medium.	(a)	Dispersed phase has got affinity for dispersion medium.
(b) It is irreversible process.	(b)	It is reversible process.
(c) It is unstable.	(c)	It is stable.
(d) Colloidal particles are electrically charged.	(d)	Colloidal particles may or may not be charged. **(1 Mark)**

(iii) **Multimolecular colloid**		**Macromolecular colloid.**
(a) They are formed by the aggregation of a large number of atoms or molecules which generally have diameters less than 1nm.	(a)	They are molecules of large size.
(b) Examples-sols of gold and sulphur.	(b)	Examples-polymer like rubber, nylon, starch.
(c) They usually have lyophobic character.	(c)	They usually have lyophilic character.
(d) These are held by weak vander waals force.	(d)	These are flexible and can take any shape. **(1 Mark)**

OR

(b) (I) (i) Zeta potential: The potential difference between the fixed layer and the diffused layer of opposite charges is called the electrokinetic potential or zeta potential. **(1 Mark)**

The combination of the two layers of opposite charges around the colloidal particle is called Helmholtz double layer. The first layer of ions is firmly, held and is termed fixed layer while the second layer is mobile which is termed as diffused layer.

(ii) Coagulation: The process of settling of colloidal particles is called coagulation or precipitation of the Sol. **(1 Mark)**

(II) When $AgNO_3$ solution is added to KI solution, negatively charged Sol of AgI is formed due to selective adsorption of I^- ion from the dispersion medium. **(1 Mark)**

9. Those elements which have d subshell, partially filled with electrons and has ability to form cations with an incompletely filled d orbitals are known as Transition Metals.

Zn, Hg and Cd have completely filled orbitals in their ground state due to which they are not called as transition metals.

In case of *p*-block the lower oxidation states are favoured by the heavier members due to inert pair effect while in case of *d*-block the higher oxidation states are favoured by the heavier members. **(3 Marks)**

10. (a) Electronic configuration of Ni in ground state

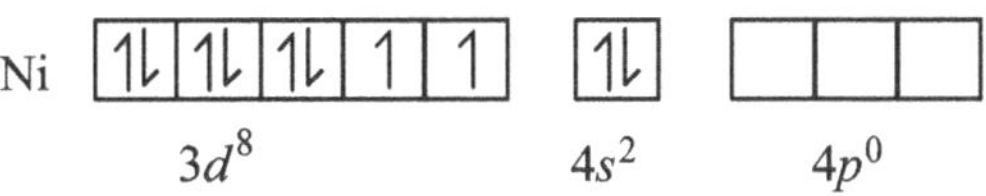

Electronic configuration of Ni atom in Ni $(CO)_4$

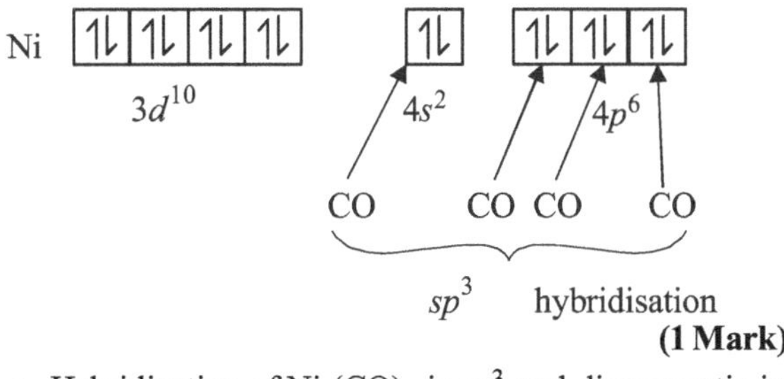

(1 Mark)

$\therefore$ Hybridisation of Ni $(CO)_4$ is sp^3 and diamagnetic in nature.

(b) IUPAC name of $[Pt(NH_3)_2Cl(NO_2)]$ is diamminechloridonitrito-N-platinum (II). **(1 Mark)**

(c) Ethylene diammine is a bidentate ligand and forms a stable chelate i.e. $[Co(en)_3]^{3+}$ chelating ligands form more stable complexes as compared to non-chelating ligands. Therefore; $[Co(en)_3]^{3+}$ is more stable complex than $[Co(NH_3)_6]^{3+}$. **(1 Mark)**

11. (a) $Ni(s) + 2Ag^+(aq) \longrightarrow Ni^{2+}(aq) + 2Ag(s)$

$\Delta G° = -n FE°cell$

$= -2 \times 96500 \times 1.05$

$= -202.650 \text{ kJ mol}^{-1}$ **(1 Mark)**

$\Delta G° = -RT \ln K_c$

$-202.650 = -8.314 \times 298 \times 2.303 \log K_c$ **(1 Mark)**

$\log K_c = 0.03552$

$K_c = 1.08$ **(1 Mark)**

OR

(b) $Fe(s) | Fe^{2+}(0.001M) || H^+ (0.01M) | H_2(g) (1 \text{ bar}) | Pt(s)$

$$E_{cell} = E°_{cell} - \frac{2.303 RT}{nF} \log \frac{[P]}{[R]}$$

$$= 0.44 - \frac{2.303 \times 8.314 \times 298}{2 \times 96500} \log \frac{[0.001]}{[0.01]}$$ **(1 Mark)**

$$= 0.44 + \frac{5705.85}{193000} \log [10]$$ **(1 Mark)**

$= 0.44 + 0.0296$

$E_{cell} = 0.469$ V **(1 Mark)**

12. (a) Rate constant depends on the temperature and directly proportional to each other. On increasing the temperature, the rate constant of reaction increases according to Arrhenius Equation.

$$K = Ae^{-E_a/RT}$$

As temperature increases, the exponential part of the equation becomes less negative and value of rate constant increases. **(1 Mark)**

(b) $A + B \longrightarrow$ Product

Rate $= k[A]^2 [B]^{1/2}$

$$\text{Order} = 2 + \frac{1}{2} = \frac{5}{2}$$ **(1 Mark)**

(c) For complex reaction, order is given by the slowest step and molecularity of the slowest step is same as the order of the overall reaction. **(1 Mark)**

(d) For first order reaction;

$$t = \frac{2.303}{k} \log \frac{[R]_0}{[R]}$$ **(1 Mark)**

$$= \frac{2.303}{2 \times 10^{-3}} \log \frac{[6]}{[2]}$$

$t = 550$ s **(1 Mark)**

OR

For first order reaction;

$$k = \frac{0.693}{t_{1/2}} = \frac{0.693}{6930} = 0.0001 \text{ years}^{-1}$$ **(1 Mark)**

It is known that,

$$t = \frac{2.303}{k} \log \frac{[R]_0}{[R]}$$

$$= \frac{2.303}{0.0001} \log \frac{100}{75}$$

$= 2875$ years **(1 Mark)**

All India 2022
CBSE Board Solved Paper
Term-I

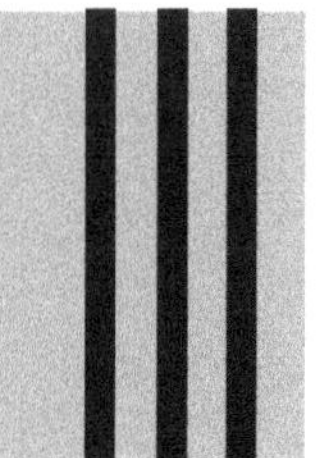

Time Allowed : 90 Minutes **Maximum Marks : 35**

General Instructions:

Read the following instructions very carefully and strictly follow them :

(i) This question paper contains **55** questions out of which **45** questions are to be attempted. **All** questions carry equal marks.

(ii) This question paper contains three Sections – Section A, B and C.

(iii) Section-A contains **25** questions. Attempt any **20** questions from Q. No. **01** to **25**.

(iv) Section-B contains **24** questions. Attempt any **20** questions from Q. No. **26** to **49**.

(v) Section-C contains **6** questions. Attempt any **5** questions from Q. No. **50** to **55**.

(vi) The first **20** questions attempted in **Section-A** & **Section-B** and first **5** questions attempted in **Section-C** by a candidate will be evaluated.

(vii) There is only one correct option for every multiple choice question (MCQ). Marks will not be awarded for answering more than one option.

(viii) There is no negative marking.

SECTION - A

This section consists of ***25*** *multiple choice questions with overall choice to attempt any* ***20*** *questions. In case more than desirable number of questions are attempted. ONLY first* ***20*** *questions will be considered for evaluation.*

1. Which one of the following pairs will form an ideal solution?

(a) Chloroform and acetone

(b) Ethanol and acetone

(c) *n*-hexane and *n*-heptane

(d) Phenol and aniline

2. Which of the following is known as amorphous solid ?

(a) Glass (b) Plastic

(c) Rubber (d) All of the above

3. The structure of pyrosulphuric acid is

(a) $HO-\overset{\overset{O}{\|}}{\underset{\underset{O}{\|}}{S}}-O-OH$

(b) $HO-\overset{\overset{O}{\|}}{\underset{\underset{O}{\|}}{S}}-OH$

(c) $HO-\overset{\overset{O}{\|}}{\underset{\underset{O}{\|}}{S}}-O-\overset{\overset{O}{\|}}{\underset{\underset{O}{\|}}{S}}-OH$

(d) $HO-\overset{\overset{O}{\|}}{\underset{\underset{O}{\|}}{S}}-O-O-\overset{\overset{O}{\|}}{\underset{\underset{O}{\|}}{S}}-OH$

4. The C – O – H bond angle in alcohol is

(a) slightly greater than 109°28′.

(b) slightly less than 109°28′.

(c) slightly greater than 120°.

(d) slightly less than 120°.

5. Consider the following reaction :

$$CH_3-CH=CH_2 \xrightarrow[\text{2. aq. KOH}]{\text{1. HBr}}$$

The major end product is

(a) $CH_3-\underset{\underset{OH}{|}}{CH}-CH_3$ (b) $CH_3-\underset{\underset{Br}{|}}{CH}-CH_3$

(c) $CH_3-CH_2-CH_2-OH$ (d) $CH_3-CH_2-CH_2-Br$

6. Nucleosides are composed of
   (a) a pentose sugar and phosphoric acid
   (b) a nitrogenous base and phosphoric acid
   (c) a nitrogenous base and a pentose sugar
   (d) a nitrogenous base, a pentose sugar and phosphoric acid

7. The oxidation state of – 2 is most stable in :
   (a) O (b) S
   (c) Se (d) Te

8. Which of the following is not a characteristic of a crystalline solid ?
   (a) A true solid
   (b) A regular arangement of constituent particles
   (c) Sharp melting point
   (d) Isotropic in nature

9. Which of the following formula represents Raoult's law for a solution containing non-volatile solute ?
   (a) $p_{solute} = p^0{}_{solute} \cdot x_{solute}$
   (b) $p = K_H.X$
   (c) $p_{total} = p_{solvent}$
   (d) $p_{solute} = p^0{}_{solvent} \cdot x_{solvent}$

10. An azeotropic solution of two liquids has a boiling point lower than either of the two when it
    (a) shows a positive deviation from Raoult's law.
    (b) shows a negative deviation from Raoult's law.
    (c) shows no deviation from Raoult's law.
    (d) is saturated.

11. Which of the following crystal will show metal excess defect due to extra cation ?
    (a) AgCl (b) NaCl
    (c) FeO (d) ZnO

12. Which of the following acids reacts with acetic anhydride to form a compound Aspirin ?
    (a) Benzoic acid (b) Salicylic acid
    (c) Phthalic acid (d) Acetic acid

13. Which of the following statements is wrong ?
    (a) Oxygen shows $p\pi - p\pi$ bonding.
    (b) Sulphur shows little tendency of catenation.
    (c) Oxygen is diatomic whereas sulphur is polyatomic.
    (d) O – O bond is stronger than S – S bond.

14. Amino acids which cannot be synthesized in the body and must be obtained through diet are known as
    (a) Acidic amino acids (b) Essential amino acids
    (c) Basic amino acids (d) Non-essential amino acids

15. Which one of the following halides contains $C_{sp^2} - X$ bond ?
    (a) Allyl halide (b) Alkyl halide
    (c) Benzyl halide (d) Vinyl halide

16. On mixing 20 mL of acetone with 30 mL of chloroform, the total volume of the solution is
    (a) < 50 mL (b) = 50 mL
    (c) > 50 mL (d) = 10 mL

17. Consider the following compounds :

    (cyclohexyl)–Cl, (cyclohexyl)–CH_2–Cl, (phenyl)–Cl
    I II III

    The correct order of reactivity towards S_N2 reaction
    (a) I > III > II (b) II > III > I
    (c) II > I > III (d) III > I > II

18. Which of the following forms strong $p\pi$–$p\pi$ bonding ?
    (a) S_2 (b) Se_2
    (c) Te_2 (d) O_2

19. F_2 acts as a strong oxidising agent due to
    (a) low $\Delta_{bond}H°$ and low $\Delta_{hyd}H°$
    (b) low $\Delta_{bond}H°$ and high $\Delta_{hyd}H°$
    (c) high $\Delta_{bond}H°$ and high $\Delta_{eg}H°$
    (d) low $\Delta_{hyd}H°$ and low $\Delta_{eg}H°$

20. Which of the following sugar is known as dextrose ?
    (a) Glucose (b) Fructose
    (c) Ribose (d) Sucrose

21. Cu reacts with dilute HNO_3 to evolve which gas ?
    (a) N_2O (b) NO_2
    (c) NO (d) N_2

22. Which of the following is a network solid ?
    (a) SO_2 (b) SiO_2
    (c) CO_2 (d) H_2O

23. Major product formed in the following reaction

    CH_3–C(CH_3)$_2$–Br + $NaOCH_3$ ⟶

    (a) CH_3–C(CH_3)$_2$–ONa (b) CH_3–C(CH_3)$_2$–OCH_3

    (c) 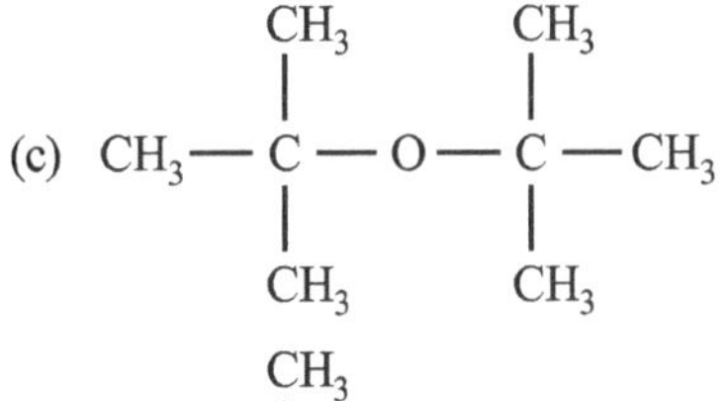

    (d) CH_3–C(CH_3)=CH_2

24. Chlorine reacts with cold and dilute NaOH to give
    (a) NaCl and $NaClO_3$ (b) NaCl and NaClO
    (c) NaCl and $NaClO_4$ (d) NaClO and $NaClO_3$

25. Elevation of boiling point is inversely proportional to
    (a) molal elevation constant (K_b)
    (b) molality (m)
    (c) molar mass of solute (M)
    (d) weight of solute (W)

SECTION - B

*This sections consists of **24** multiple choice questions with overall choice to attempt any **20** questions. In case more than desirable number of questions are attempted, ONLY first **20** questions will be considered for evaluation.*

26. An unknown gas 'X' is dissolved in water at 2.5 bar pressure and has mole fraction 0.04 in solution. The mole fraction of 'X' gas when the pressure of gas is doubled at the same temperature is
(a) 0.08 (b) 0.04
(c) 0.02 (d) 0.92

27. The base which is present in DNA but not in RNA, is
(a) Cytosine (b) Guanine
(c) Adenine (d) Thymine

28. In the following reaction

$CH_3-CH=CH-CH_2-OH \xrightarrow{PCC}$

the product formed is
(a) CH_3-CHO and CH_3CH_2OH
(b) $CH_3-CH=CH-COOH$
(c) $CH_3-CH=CH-CHO$
(d) $CH_3-CH_2-CH_2-CHO$

29. Enantiomers differ only in
(a) boiling point
(b) rotation of polarised light
(c) melting point
(d) solubility

30. The number of lone pairs of electrons in XeF_4 is
(a) zero (b) one
(c) two (d) three

31. Sulphuric acid is used to prepare more volatile acids from their corresponding salts due to its
(a) strong acidic nature
(b) low volatility
(c) strong affinity for water
(d) ability to act as a dehydrating agent

32. An element with density 6 g cm^{-3} forms a *fcc* lattice with edge length of 4×10^{-8} cm. The molar mass of the element is ($N_A = 6 \times 10^{23}\ mol^{-1}$)
(a) 57.6 g mol^{-1} (b) 28.8 g mol^{-1}
(c) 82.6 g mol^{-1} (d) 62 g mol^{-1}

33. In the reaction [cyclohexyl]–Br $\xrightarrow[\text{Dry ether}]{Mg}$ 'X' $\xrightarrow{H_2O}$ 'Y'

compound 'Y' is

(a)  (b) OMgBr

(c) (d) 

34. Which of the following is the weakest reducing agent in group 15 ?
(a) NH_3 (b) PH_3
(c) AsH_3 (d) BiH_3

35. The boiling point of a 0.2 m solution of a non-electrolyte in water is (K_b for water = 0.52 K kg mol^{-1})
(a) 100 °C (b) 100.52 °C
(c) 100.104 °C (d) 100.26 °C

36. Nucleic acids are polymer of
(a) amino acids (b) nucleosides
(c) nucleotides (d) glucose

37. Which of the following gas dimerises to become stable ?
(a) $CO_2(g)$ (b) $NO_2(g)$
(c) $SO_2(g)$ (d) $N_2O(g)$

38. In the following diagram point, 'X' represents

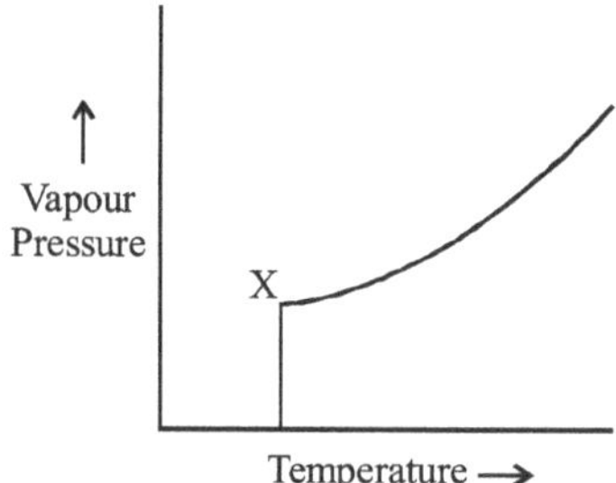

(a) Boiling point of solution
(b) Freezing point of solvent
(c) Boiling point of solvent
(d) Freezing point of solution

39. XeF_6 on reaction with NaF gives
(a) $Na^+[XeF_7]^-$ (b) $[NaF_2]^-[XeF_5]^+$
(c) $Na^+[XeF_6]^-$ (d) $[NaF_2]^+[XeF_5]^-$

40. Glucose on reaction with Br_2 water gives :
(a) Saccharic acid (b) Hexanoic acid
(c) Gluconic acid (d) Salicyclic acid

41. Which of the following is optically inactive ?
(a) (+)– Butan–2–ol (b) (–)– Butan–2–ol
(c) (±)– Butan–2–ol (d) (+)– 2 –Bromobutane

42. Which of the following is not a correct statement ?
(a) Halogens are strong oxidising agents.
(b) Halogens are more reactive than interhalogens.
(c) All halogens are coloured.
(d) Halogens have maximum negative electron gain enthalpy.

43. Which of the following has highest boiling point ?
(a) C_2H_5-F (b) C_2H_5-Cl
(c) C_2H_5-Br (d) C_2H_5-I

44. Which of the following isomer of pentane (C_3H_{12}) will give three isomeric monochlorides on photochemical chlorination ?

(a) 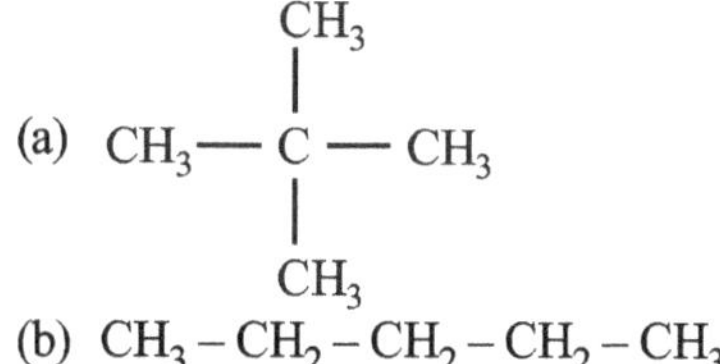

(b) $CH_3-CH_2-CH_2-CH_2-CH_3$
(c) $CH_3-CH(CH_3)-CH_2-CH_3$
(d) All of the above

DIRECTIONS (Qs. 45-49) : *Given below are the questions labelled as **Assertion (A)** and **Reason (R)**. Select the most appropriate answer from the options given below :*

(a) Both A and R are true and R is the correct explanation of A.
(b) Both A and R are true but R is not the correct explanation of A.
(c) A is true but R is false.
(d) A is false but R is true.

45. **Assertion (A) :** A raw mango placed in a saline solution loses water and shrivel into pickle.
Reason (R) : Through the process of reverse osmosis, raw mango shrivel into pickle.

46. **Assertion (A) :** H_2S is less acidic than H_2Te.
Reason (R) : H – S bond has more $\Delta_{bond} H^{\circ}$ than H–Te bond.

47. **Assertion (A) :** Chlorobenzene is less reactive towards nucleophilic substitution reaction.
Reason (R) : Nitro group in chlorobenene increases its reactivity towards nucleophilic substi-tution reaction.

48. **Assertion (A) :** Due to Schottky defect, there is no effect on the density of a solid.
Reason (R) : Equal number of cations and anions are missing from their normal sites in Schottky defect.

49. **Assertion (A) :** Fluorine forms only one oxoacid HOF.
Reason (R) : Fluorine atom is highly electronegative.

SECTION - C

*This section consists of **6** multiple choice questions with an overall choice to attempt any **5** questions. In case more than desirable number of questions are attempted, ONLY first **5** questions will be considered for evaluation.*

50. Match the following :

	Column-I		Column-II
(i)	Stoichiometric defects	(A)	Crystalline solids
(ii)	long range order	(B)	F-centres
(iii)	...ABC ABC ABC ...	(C)	Schottky and Frenkel defects
(iv)	Number of atoms per unit cell = 2	(D)	fcc structure
(v)	Metal excess defect due to anionic vacancies		

Which of the following is the best matched options ?
(a) (i) – (D), (ii) – (A), (iii) – (B), (iv) – (C)
(b) (i) – (C), (ii) – (A), (iii) – (D), (v) – (B)
(c) (i) – (C), (ii) – (A), (iii) – (D), (iv) – (B)
(d) (i) – (A), (ii) – (B), (v) – (C), (iv) – (D)

51. Which of the following analogies is correct ?
(a) XeF_2 : linear :: XeF_6 : square planar
(b) moist SO_2 : Reducing agent :: Cl_2 : bleaching agent
(c) N_2 : Highly reactive gas :: F_2 : inert at room temperature
(d) NH_3 : strong base :: HI : weak acid.

52. Complete the following analogy :
Curdling of milk : A :: α-helix : B
(a) A : Primary structure B : Secondary structure
(b) A : Denatured protein B : Primary structure
(c) A : Secondary structure B : Denatured protein
(d) A : Denatured protein B : Secondary structure

Case Study : (Qs. 53-55)

Alcohols and Phenols are acidic in nature. Electron withdrawing groups in phenol increase its acidic strength and electron donating groups decrease it. Alcohols undergo nucleophilic substitution with hydrogen halides to give alkyl halides. On oxidation primary alcohols yield aldehydes with mild oxidising agents and carboxylic acids with strong oxidising agents while secondary alcohols yields ketones. The presence of – OH groups in phenols activates the ring towards electrophilic substitution. Various important products are obtained from pheonol like salicylaldehyde, salicylic acid, picric acid etc.

53. Which of the following alcohols is resistant to oxidation ?
(a) $CH_3-C(CH_3)_2-OH$ (b) $CH_3-CH(CH_3)-OH$
(c) CH_3-CH_2-OH (d) CH_3-OH

54. Which of the following group increases the acidic character of phenol ?
(a) CH_3O- (b) CH_3-
(c) NO_2- (d) All of these

55. Consider the following reaction :

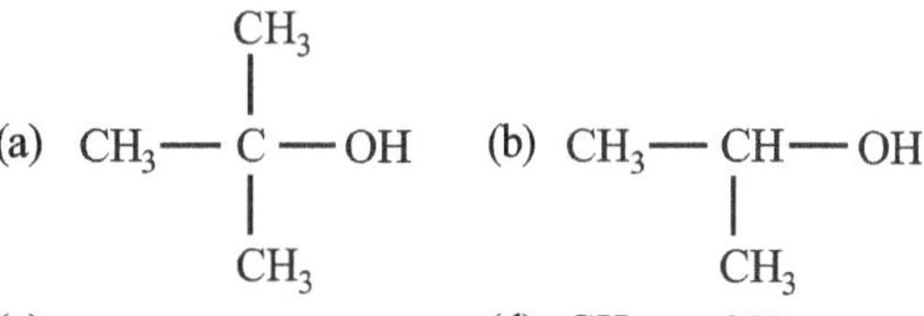

the products X and Y are

(a) X = (benzene ring with OH and COOH) Y = (benzene ring with CHO and OH)
(b) X = (benzene ring with OH and CHO) Y = (benzene ring with OH and COOH)
(c) X = (benzene ring with COOH and OH) Y = (benzene ring with OH and CHO)
(d) X = (benzene ring with OH and COOH) Y = (benzene ring with OH and CHO)

Solutions

1. **(c)** n-heptane and n-hexane obeys Raoult's law at all temperature and concentration. Hence; they will form an ideal solution.

2. **(d)** In amorphous solid, the constituent particles are not possess a regular three-dimensional arrangement. for example: Glass, Plastic, Rubber etc.

Like liquids, amorphous solids have a tendency to flow, though very slowly, therefore sometimes these are called pseudo solids or super cooled liquids.

3. **(c)** The formula of pyrosulphuric acid is $H_2S_2O_7$ and the structure is:

$$HO-\overset{\overset{O}{\|}}{\underset{\underset{O}{\|}}{S}}-O-\overset{\overset{O}{\|}}{\underset{\underset{O}{\|}}{S}}-OH$$

Both $H_2S_2O_8$ and $H_2S_2O_7$ contain same number of $S = O$ bonds i.e., 4 and $S - OH$ bond i.e., 2 but $H_2S_2O_8$ has peroxy linkage between two $S(S - O - O - S)$.

4. **(b)** The shape of alcohol is tetrahedral but due to presence of lone pair on oxygen atom, C—O—H bond angle decreases i.e. it will become less than 109°28′.

(Structure: CH_3–O–H with two lone pairs on O; bond angle 108.9°)

5. **(a) Step I:** Addition of HBr

$$CH_3-CH=CH_2 \xrightarrow{HBr} CH_3-\underset{\underset{Br}{|}}{CH}-CH_3$$

2-bromopropane

The product is formed according to markovnikov rule.

Step II: Reaction with aq. KOH

$$CH_3-\underset{\underset{Br}{|}}{CH}-CH_3 \xrightarrow{aq.\ KOH} CH_3-\underset{\underset{OH}{|}}{CH}-CH_3$$

The final product is formed by S_N2 reaction.

6. **(d)** Nucleosides are composed of a nitrogenous base, a pentose sugar and phosphoric acid.

7. **(a)** The most stable oxidation state of O is –2, S is +2, Se is +4 and Te is +4 and +6.

8. **(d)** Crystalline solids are anisotropic in nature, regular arrangement of constituent particles and have sharp melting point.

9. **(d)** Formula of Raoult's law for a non-volatile solute is:

$$P_{solute} = P^{\circ}_{solvent} \cdot \chi_{solvent}$$

10. **(a)** Azeotropes are of two types:

(i) The solution which shows large positive deviation from Raoult's law form minimum boiling azeotrope at a specific composition.

(ii) The solution which shows large negative deviation from Raoult's law form maximum boiling azeotrope at a specific composition.

11. **(d)** ZnO will show metal excess defect due to extra cation i.e. Zn^{2+} ion which will move to interstitial sites and the electrons to neighbouring interstitial sites.

When ZnO exhibits metal excess defect, its formula becomes $Zn_{1+x}O$.

12. **(b)** Salicylic acid + Acetic anhydride ⟶ Aspirin + Acetic acid

(Salicylic acid: benzene ring with COOH and OH; Acetic anhydride: $CH_3CO-O-COCH_3$; Aspirin: benzene ring with COOH and $O-\overset{O}{\overset{\|}{C}}-CH_3$; Acetic acid: CH_3COOH)

When salicylic acid reacts with acetic anhydride then aspirin will form as a final product.

13. **(b)** Sulphur has greater tendency for catenation as it exists in S_8 form. On heating these rings break and link jointly into long chains.

14. **(b)** The amino acids which are not synthesized in our body and obtained through diet are essential amino acids. For example: histidine, lysine, leucine etc.

15. **(d)** The vinyl halide contains ($C_{sp^2} - X$ bond)

$$H_2C=\underset{\underset{sp^2}{\downarrow}}{CH}-X$$

Vinyl halide

16. **(c)** The mixture of acetone and chloroform show negative deviation due to which the total volume of the solution will be less than 50.

17. **(c)** The order of reactivity towards S_N2 reaction is $1° > 2° > 3°$. Therefore, the correct order is II > I > III.

18. **(d)** Oxygen, being smaller in size can effectively form $p\pi - p\pi$ bonds with other atoms of itself. The other elements do not form $p\pi - p\pi$ bonds because of their relatively larger size.

19. **(b)** F_2 acts as a strong oxidising agent because of its low enthalpy of dissociation as F – F bond is weak due to electronic repulsion and high enthalpy of hydration.

20. **(a)** Glucose is a carbohydrate and act as a reducing sugar. It is also known as dextrose as it rotates the plane polarised light to the right.

21. **(c)** When copper reacts with dil. HNO_3, then nitric oxide gas is evolved.

$$\underset{\text{(dilute)}}{3Cu + 8HNO_3} \longrightarrow \underset{\text{Copper nitrate}}{3Cu(NO_3)_2} + 4H_2O + \underset{\text{(Nitric oxide)}}{2NO\uparrow}$$

22. **(b)** In SiO_2 molecule, each silicon atom is surrounded with the four bonds of oxygen atom and makes four Si – O bonds due to which it will form network solid like structure.

23. **(d)** $$CH_3-\overset{\overset{\large CH_3}{|}}{\underset{\underset{\large CH_3}{|}}{C}}-Br + NaOCH_3 \longrightarrow CH_3-\overset{\overset{\large CH_3}{|}}{C}=CH_2$$

The tertiary alkyl halides undergo elimination reaction to give alkenes.

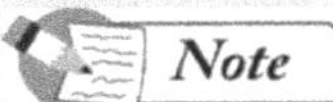

Note

A primary alkyl halide will prefers a S_N2 reaction, a secondary halide prefers S_N2 or elimination depending upon the strength of base/nucleophile. A tertiary alkyl halide prefers S_N1 or elimination depending upon the stability of carbocation or the more substituted alkene.

24. **(b)** When chlorine reacts with cold and dilute NaOH, then it will form sodium chloride and sodium chlorate as a product and it is a type of disproportionation reaction.

$2NaOH + Cl_2 \longrightarrow NaCl + NaOCl + H_2O$

25. **(c)** The formula of elevation in boiling point is:

$\Delta T_b = K_b \times m$

$$\Delta T_b = \frac{K_b \times W_A}{M_B \times W_B(Kg)}$$

$\therefore$ Elevation in boiling point is inversely proportional to molar mass of solute (M_B).

26. **(d)** We know that;

$$\frac{P_1}{P_2} = \frac{\chi_1}{\chi_2}$$

Here;

P_1 = initial pressure; P_2 = final pressure; χ = mole fraction

$$\frac{2.5}{5} = \frac{0.04}{\chi_2}$$

$\chi_2 = 0.08$

In a solution, $\chi_{solute} + \chi_{solvent} = 1$

$0.08 + \chi_{solute} = 1$

$\chi_{solute} = 1 - 0.08 \Rightarrow \chi_{solute} = 0.92$

27. **(d)** The bases which are present in RNA are adenine, uracil, guanine and cytosine.

28. **(c)** PCC act as an oxidising agent which converts 1° alcohol to aldehyde.

$$CH_3CH=CHCH_2OH \xrightarrow{PCC} CH_3CH=CH-CHO$$

29. **(b)** The compounds which are non-superimposable but have mirror images are known as enantiomers. They are differ only in optical activity i.e. rotation of polarised light.

30. **(c)** The structure of XeF_4 is

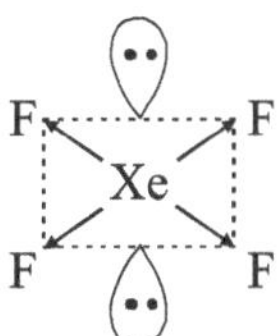

Therefore; the number of lone pairs of electrons in XeF_4 is two.

31. **(b)** Sulphuric acid is used to prepare more valatile acids from their corresponding salts due to its low volatility.

32. **(a)** As we know;

$$d = \frac{ZM}{N_A \times a^3}$$

for *fcc*, Z = 4

$$6\ g\ cm^{-3} = \frac{4 \times M}{6 \times 10^{23}\ mol^{-1} \times (4 \times 10^{-8}\ cm)^3}$$

$M = 57.6 g\ mol^{-1}$

33. **(a)**

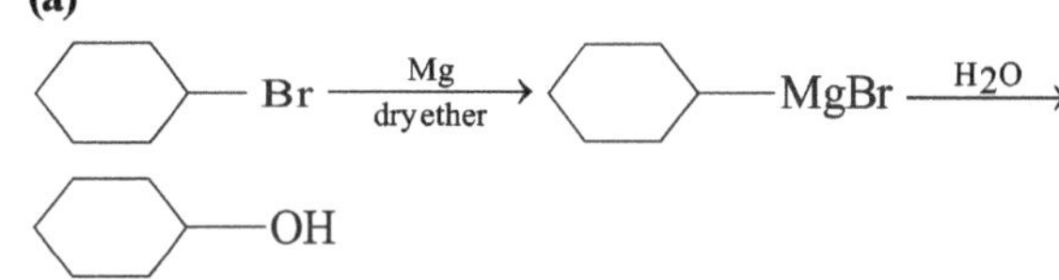

34. **(a)** The reducing agent of the dydrides increases down the group due to decrease in bond dissociation enthalpy. Therefore; NH_3 is the weakest reducing agent in group 15.

35. **(c)** $\Delta T_b = K_b \times m$

$= 0.52 \times 0.2$

$\Delta T_b = 0.104$

$T_b = T_b^\circ + \Delta T_b$

$= 100 + 0.104$

$T_b = 100.104°C$

36. **(c)** Nucleic acids are biological macromolecules which are polymers of repeating monomeric units called nucleotides.

37. **(b)** NO_2 is an odd electron species which contains one unpaired electron and tend to form a dimer by pairing the unpaired electrons. Therefore, NO_2 gas dimerises to become stable.

38. **(b)** The point 'X' represents the freezing point of solvent. The freezing point of a substance may be defined as the temperature at which the vapour pressure of the substance in its liquid phase is equal to the vapour pressure in the solid phase.

39. **(a)** The reaction between XeF_6 and NaF is

$XeF_6 + NaF \longrightarrow Na^+[XeF_7]^-$

40. **(c)**

$$\underset{\text{Glucose}}{\begin{array}{c}CHO\\|\\(CHOH)_4\\|\\CH_2OH\end{array}} + [O] \xrightarrow{Br_2/water} \underset{\text{Gluconic acid}}{\begin{array}{c}COOH\\|\\(CHOH)_4\\|\\CH_2OH\end{array}}$$

41. **(c)** (±) – butane-2-ol is a racemic mixture and behave as optically inactive.

42. **(b)** Interhalogens are more reactive than halogens as interhalogens are more likely to show hydrolysis and ionizes to give rise to polyatomic ions.

43. **(d)** On moving down the group, the size of halogen atoms and vander waals force of attraction increases due to which boiling point also increases. Therefore; $C_2H_5 - I$ has the highest boiling point.

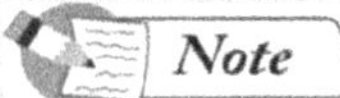

B. pt ∝ Strength of intermolecular forces
∝ Molar mass of compound
∝ Surface area

44. **(b)** *n*-Pentane will form three isomeric monochlorides on photochemical chlorination.

$\overset{a}{CH_3}—\overset{b}{CH_2}—\overset{c}{CH_2}—\overset{b}{CH_2}—\overset{a}{CH_3}$

$\xrightarrow[h\nu]{Cl_2}$
- $CH_3—CH_2—CH_2—CH_2—Cl$
- $CH_3—CH_2—CH_2—\underset{Cl}{\underset{|}{CH}}—CH_3$
- $CH_3—CH_2—\underset{Cl}{\underset{|}{CH}}—CH_2—CH_3$

45. **(c)** A is true but R is false. When raw mango is placed in a saline solution to prepare pickle the mango looses water due to osmosis and get shrivel. This event does not occur due to reverse osmosis.

In reverse osmosis the direction of osmosis is reversed by making pressure larger than the osmotic pressure and is applied to the solution side. In this, pure solvent flows outside of the conc. solution through a semipermeable membrane.

46. **(a)** H_2S is less acidic than H_2Te as the bond dissociation enthalpy of H – Te is lesser than H – S bond.

47. **(b)** Chlorobenzene is less reactive towards nucleophilic substitution reaction because the carbon atom on which halogen is attached is sp^2 hybridised and decreases the nucleophilic substitution whereas NO_2 group in chlorobenzene increases the reactivity by withdrawing or by making the ring deficient.

48. **(d)** In Schottky defect, the density of solid decreases and equal number of cations and anions are missing from their normal sites in Schottky defect.

49. **(a)** Fluorine forms only one oxoacid i.e. HOF due to small size of fluorine and highly electronegative atom.

50. **(b)**

(i) Schottky and Frenkel defects are the type of stoichiometric defects.

(ii) Crystalline solids have long range order which means there is a regular pattern of arrangement of particles which repeats itself over the entire crystals.

(iii) *fcc* structure show ...... ABC ABC ABC ...... type pattern.

(iv) Metal excess defect due to anionic vacancies is known as F-centres.

51. **(b)** Moist SO_2 act as a reducing agent due to evolution of nascent hydrogen. Cl_2 act as a bleaching agent due to its oxidising properties as it produce nascent oxygen.

52. **(d)** A : Denatured protein

B : Secondary protein

- Curdling of milk is due to denaturation of proteins.
- α-helix is an element of secondary structure in which the amino acid chain is arranged in a spiral.

53. **(a)** Tertiary alcohols, i.e., $CH_3—\underset{CH_3}{\overset{CH_3}{\overset{|}{\underset{|}{C}}}}—OH$ does not show oxidation.

In tertiary alcohols, tertiary C does not have hydrogen and it is bonded to another carbon. It is difficult to break C – C bond for the oxidation of C bonded to OH. Therefore it does not undergo oxidation.

54. **(c)** Electron withdrawing group increases the acidic character of alcohol. Therefore; $(–NO_2)$ group will increases the acidic character.

55. **(d)** Phenol (OH on benzene) $\xrightarrow[(ii)\ H^+]{(i)\ NaOH,\ CO_2}$ X (2-hydroxybenzoic acid: OH, COOH on benzene)

Phenol $\xrightarrow[(ii)\ H^+]{(i)\ CHCl_3 + aq.\ NaOH}$ Y (2-hydroxybenzaldehyde: OH, CHO on benzene)

CBSE TOPPER-2020
Answer Sheet

विषय कोड Subject Code : 043

परीक्षा का दिन एवं तिथि
Day & Date of the Examination : SATURDAY, 07/03/2020

उत्तर देने का माध्यम
Medium of answering the paper : ENGLISH

प्रश्न पत्र के ऊपर लिखे कोड को दर्शाएँ :
Write code No. as written on the top of the question paper :

Code Number	Set Number
56/5/1	● ② ③ ④

अतिरिक्त उत्तर-पुस्तिका (ओं) की संख्या
No. of supplementary answer-book(s) used: Nil

बेंचमार्क विकलांग व्यक्ति
Person with Benchmark Disabilities — हाँ / नहीं Yes / No: NO

विकलांगता का कोड
(प्रवेश पत्र के अनुसार)
Code of Disabilities
(as given on Admit Card): —

क्या लेखन – लिपिक उपलब्ध करवाया गया : हाँ / नहीं
Whether writer provided : Yes / No: NO

यदि दृष्टिहीन हैं तो उपयोग में लाए गये सोफ्टवेयर का नाम :
If Visually challenged, name of software used : —

*एक खाने में एक अक्षर लिखें। नाम के प्रत्येक भाग के बीच एक खाना रिक्त छोड़ दें। यदि परीक्षार्थी का नाम 24 अक्षरों से अधिक है, तो केवल नाम के प्रथम 24 अक्षर ही लिखें।

Each letter be written in one box and one box be left blank between each part of the name. In case Candidate's Name exceeds 24 letters, write first 24 letters.

कार्यालय उपयोग के लिए
Space for office use

SECTION-A

Ans1: Halogens have outer shell configuration ns^2np^5 and it is just short of one electron to attain a noble gas configuration. The electron gain enthalpy is the energy released (hence negative) when one electron is added to an atom.
As the halogens readily accept an electron to gain stability they release a large amount of energy and hence have maximum negative electron gain enthalpy in a period.

Ans2: Fluorine shows anomalous behaviour due to a number of reasons:
(1) very small size (smallest size in the group)
(2) absence of d-orbital and hence can't expand its octet
(3) maximum electronegativity in periodic table
(4) low bond dissociation energy of F_2 molecule

Ans3: Decreasing order of reducing characters of hydrogen halides
HI > HBr > HCl > HF. This trend is followed due to

increasing bond dissociation energies of the molecules HX
low bond dissociation energy means they can easily loose an H-atom and get oxidised to X2 and hence showing reducing character.

Ans4: Fluorine shows strong oxidising power (is stronger oxidising agent) than chlorine because of low bond dissociation enthalpy of F_2 molecule and high negative hydration enthalpy of F^-. Due to these F_2 tend to get reduced to F^- easily and hence show stronger oxidising power. Actually F_2 is the strongest oxidising agent.

Ans5: X – Bigger size as bigger halogen
X′ – Smaller size as lower halogen
Eg: ClF_3 where X = Cl and X′ = F

Ans6: Zinc-Amalgum (Mercury) cell is used in watches, hearing aids because their potential remains constant throughout their life.

A: $Zn(Hg) + H_2O \longrightarrow ZnO + 2e^- + 2H^+$

C: $HgO + 2e^- + 2H^+ \longrightarrow Hg + H_2O$

Cell Reaction: $Zn(Hg)_{(s)} + HgO_{(s)} \longrightarrow ZnO_{(s)} + Hg_{(l)}$

Ans7: $\overset{+7}{MnO_4^-} + 5e^- \longrightarrow Mn^{2+}$ charge required = 5F

5 moles e^- required to reduced 1 mole MnO_4^-

Ans8: $Kt = 2.303 \log \frac{[R_0]}{[R]}$: 1st order reaction

$\Rightarrow \log \frac{[R_0]}{[R]} = \left(\frac{K}{2.303}\right) \cdot t$

value of slope $= \frac{K}{2.303}$

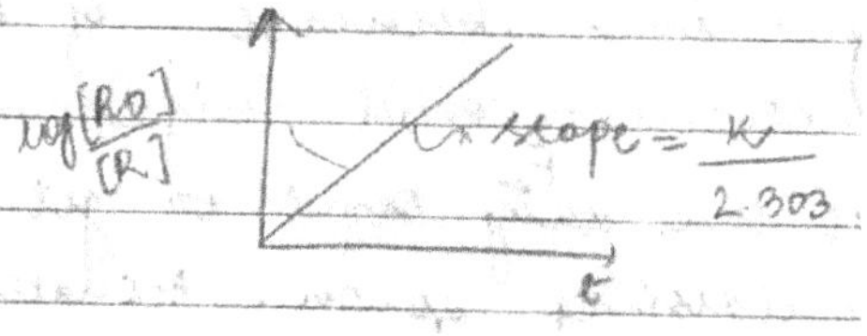

$\log \frac{[R_0]}{[R]}$; slope $= \frac{K}{2.303}$; t

Ans9: Sucralose

Ans10: Bakelite

Ans11: (c) CO

Ans12: (b) a substitution reaction

Ans13: (c) CH_3NH_2

Ans 14. (a) O

Ans 15: (c) Amphoteric

Ans 16: K ∝ C
A X R ✓ Ans : D Assertion wrong, Reason correct

Ans 17: slighty more A X
R ✓ Ans : D Assertion wrong, Reason correct

Ans 18: ~~AQ&B~~ Δt < P Ans : A Both correct, R is correct explanation

Ans 19: A ✓ R X Ans : C . A correct, R wrong

Ans 20: A X R ✓ Ans : D A wrong, R correct

SECTION-B

Ans 21: Raoult's law state that in a solution of volatile components, the partial pressure of each volatile component is directly proportional to their ~~partial~~ ~~pressure~~ mole fraction in the solution.

Let 2 volatile components be A and B
then, $p_A \propto x_A$ and $p_B \propto x_B$
$\Rightarrow p_A = p^0_A x_A$ $\Rightarrow p_B = p^0_B x_B$
p^0_A, p^0_B: proportionality constants.

On the other hand, Henry Law states that partial pressure of a (volatile) gas in a liquid is directly proportional to its molefraction.
$p \propto x \Rightarrow p = K_H x$
K_H = Henry's constant

By comparing the two equations, we see they are very similar and it seems as the Raolts Law is special case of Henry's Law in which $K_H = p^0$

Ans 22: (a) dil NaCN plays the role of converting Gold into a complex form so it can be easily freed from the impurities. NaCN don't react with the impurities and react only with gold.
$4Au + 8CN^- + O_2 + 2H_2O \rightarrow 4[Au(CN)_2]^-$ (Aurocyanide) $+ 4OH^-$
(b) CO is used for reduction of iron oxides (haemetite

or magnetite) to iron metal as CO is a strong reducing agent at high temperatures

$Fe_2O_3 + CO \rightarrow Fe_3O_4 + CO_2$

$Fe_3O_4 + CO \rightarrow FeO + CO_2$

$FeO + CO \rightarrow Fe + CO_2$
(iron metal.)

This process is carried out in a blast furnace at high temperatures.

Ans23: Brownian movement is the continuous and random zig-zag movement of colloidal particles in the dispersion medium. They are caused due to unbalanced bombardment of collodial particles with the particles of the dispersion medium.

When they collide, the exert a stirring effect on each other and hence prevents setting down of colloidal particles and hence accounts for its stability.

Brownian movement

Ans 24: (a) $[\overset{+3}{Fe}(CN)_6]^{3-}$

IUPAC: Hexacyanidoferrate (III) ion

hybridization:

$Fe_{26} = [Ar]^{18}\ 4s^2\ 3d^6$

$Fe^{3+} = [Ar]^{18}\ 4s^0\ 3d^5$

as CN^- is a strong field ligand and causes pairing up of ē

3d: | 1L | 1L | 1 | | | ; 4s: | | ; 4p: | | | |

↑ 6 CN^-

↓

3d: | 1L | 1L | 1 | xx | xx | ; 4s: | xx | ; 4p: | xx | xx | xx |

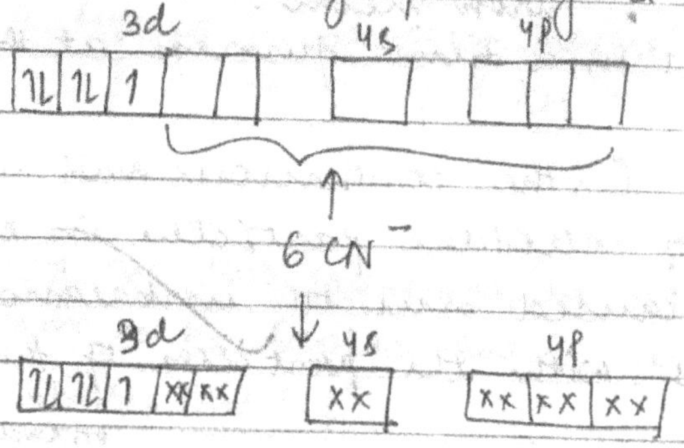

Hence its hybridisation is d^2sp^3

shape: Octahedral.

(b) Ambidentate ligand: Ligands having two different atoms through which it can act as a ligand.

For eg: $CN^{\ominus}$: $\overset{\leftarrow \ominus}{C} \equiv N$ or $\ddot{C} = \ddot{N}: \rightarrow$
cyanido - C cyanido - N

whereas,
chelating ligand are polydentate ligands and act as ligands with 2 or more of its atoms and hence form a ring like structure called chellate
for eg: ethane-1,2-diamine $CH_2 - CH_2$ NH_2 NH_2 : bidentate ligand
chelating complexes are more stable

Ans 25: Antiseptics are antimicrobials that are applied on living tissues like wounds to inhibit growth of pathogens. They can't be ingested in human body.
Disinfectants are antimicrobials that are applied on inanimate (non-living) objects like floors, tiles to prevent growth of microbes. They have higher concentrations than antiseptics.
0.2% phenol solution act as an antiseptic and its 1% solution acts as a disinfectant.

Ans26: i) Ethylene glycol + Phthalic acid

$HO-CH_2-CH_2-OH + HOOC-C_6H_4-COOH$

↓

$[O-CH_2-CH_2-O-\overset{O}{\overset{\|}{C}}-C_6H_4-\overset{O}{\overset{\|}{C}}-O]_n$

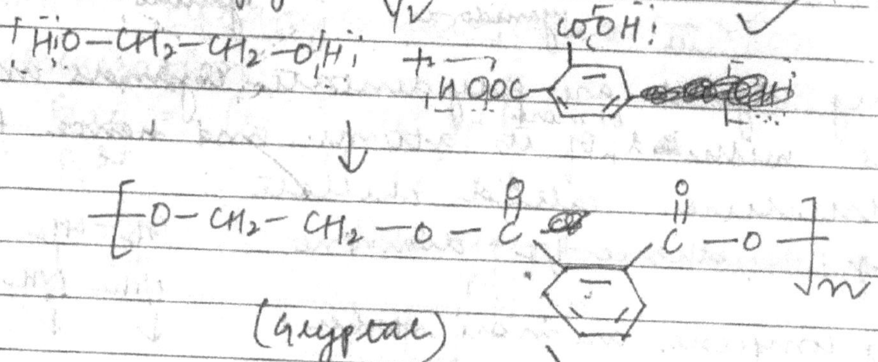

(Glyptal)

ii) Acrylonitrile : $H_2C=CH-CN$ — Ethenenitrile

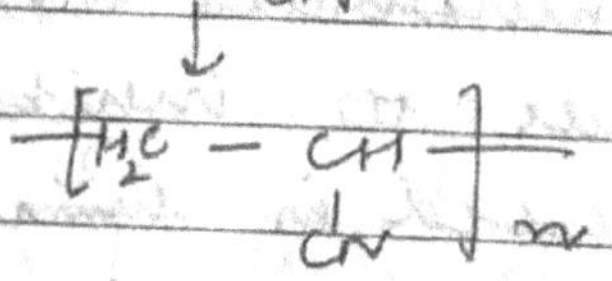

↓

$[H_2C-CH(CN)]_n$: Polyacrylonitrile (PAN) or Orlon

Ans27: i) $H_2S_2O_8$:

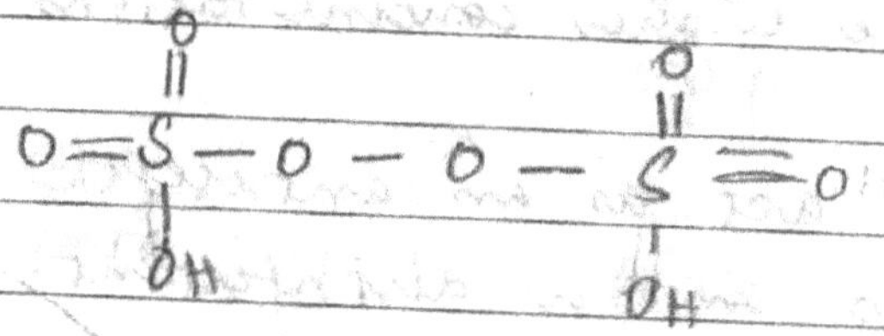

$O=\overset{O}{\overset{\|}{S}}(OH)-O-O-\overset{O}{\overset{\|}{S}}(OH)=O$

(ii) XeF_6 : distorted octahedral structure (due to 1 LP of Xe)

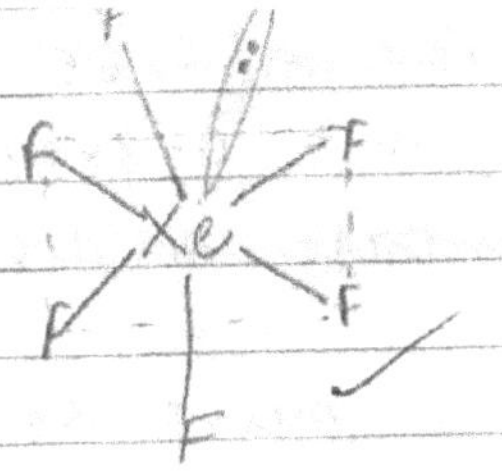

F, F, Xe, F, F, F

SECTION - C

Ans28: $\Delta T_f = 0.068$ $K_f = 1.86$ $m = 0.01$ $i = ?$

$\Delta T_f = i K_f m$ ½

$\Rightarrow 0.068 = i \times \frac{1.86 \times 0.01}{1.0}$ ½

$\Rightarrow i = \frac{680}{186} = 3.65$ ½

Now,

	$AlCl_3$	$\rightleftharpoons$ Al^{3+}	+ $3Cl^-$
t=0	1	0	0
t=t	1−α	α	3α

½

$i = \frac{1-\alpha+\alpha+3\alpha}{1} = 1+3\alpha = 3.65$

Rough

680 340
186 93

$93\overline{)340}$ 3.6
279
610
558
52

$186\overline{)680}$ 3.655
558
1220
1116
1040
930
1100

$\Rightarrow 3\alpha = 2.65$

$\Rightarrow \alpha = 0.8833$

percentage of dissociation = 88.33%

Ans 29: $i = 2A$ $m_{cu} = 2g$ $Cu^{2+} \rightarrow Cu + 2e$

According to faraday's 1st law: $n_{fac} = 2$

$m = Zit$ where $Z = \frac{eq\ wt}{96500} = \frac{mol.\ wt}{n_{fact} \times 96500}$

$\Rightarrow m_{cu} = Zit$

$\Rightarrow 2 = \frac{63.5 \times 2 \times t}{2 \times 96500}$

$\Rightarrow t = \frac{2 \times 96500}{63.5} = 3.0393 \times 10^3$ sec

$= 3040$ sec $= 3.04 \times 10^3$ sec

$= 0.84$ hrs.

NOW; $m_{Zn} = \frac{65}{2 \times 96500} \times 2 \times \frac{2 \times 96500}{63.5} \times 10$

$Zn^{2+} \rightarrow Zn + 2e$, $n = 2$

$= 2.0472$ gm.

Ans 30: (i) (a)

	Amylose	Amylopectin
1)	It ~~consist~~ compromises 15–20% of starch	1) It compsrises 80–85% of starch
2)	It is water soluble	2) It is water insoluble
3)	It consists of linear chain polymers of α-D glucose with C_1–C_4 linkage	3) It consists of branched chain polymers of αD glucose with C_1-C_4 linkage and C_1-C_6 linkage between the 2 linear chains

(b)(ii)

	Globular Protein	Fibrous protein
1)	In this the polypeptide chains are coiled together in a spherical shape	1) In this, 2 polypeptide chains run parallel to each other and are bonded to each other by disulphide bonds
2)	They are water soluble	2) They are water insoluble
3)	Eg: Insulin, albumin	3) Eg: Keratin, myosin
4)	It is 3° structure of protein	4) It is 3° structure of protein

(iii)

Nucleotide	Nucleoside
(Phosphorus – base – sugar)	(sugar / Base)
1) When the phosphorous compound are attached to 5' position of the sugar moiety which already has a base attached to its 1' positide	1) When the nitrogen base pairs are attached with the 1' position of sugar (Ribose sugar or β-D-2-deoxy ribose sugar)
2) It polymerises to form poly-nucleotides through phospho-diester linkages	2) It first attaches itself to phosphorous compounds at 5' and then form polynucleotides.

Ans 31

$CH_3-CH(CH_3)-CH_2-Br \xrightarrow{alc\ KOH} CH_3-C(CH_3)=CH_2$ (A) $\xrightarrow{HBr} CH_3-C(Br)(CH_3)-CH_3$ (B)

(B) $\xrightarrow{Na,\ dry\ ether} H_3C-C(CH_3)(CH_3)-C(CH_3)(CH_3)-CH_3$ (C)

$CH_3-CH(CH_3)-CH_2-Br \xrightarrow{Mg,\ ether} CH_3-CH(CH_3)-CH_2-MgBr$ (D) $\xrightarrow{H_2O} CH_3-CH(CH_3)-CH_3$ (E)

$CH_3-CH(CH_3)-CH_2-Br \xrightarrow{Na^+\ OC_2H_5^-} CH_3-CH(CH_3)-CH_2-O-C_2H_5$ (F)

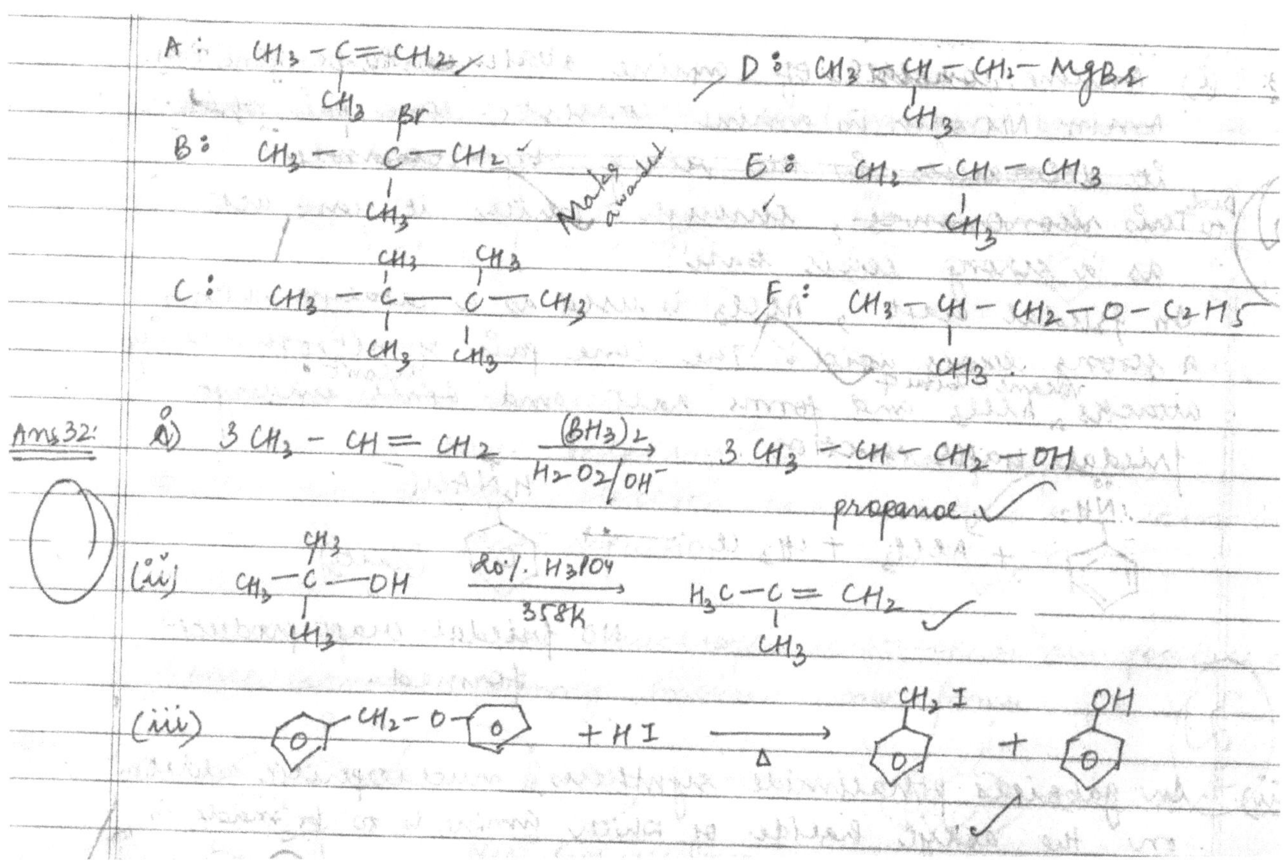

Ans 33: (i) Aniline consists of amine attached to benzene ring. ~~Amin~~ Nitrogen in amine consists lone pair ~~which it delocalises in the ring by resonance.~~ Due to this ~~resonance~~, through ~~which~~ it can act as a strong lewis base.
In friedal craft, $AlCl_3$ is used as a catalyst which is a strong lewis acid. The lone pair of nitrogen easily attacks vacant orbital of $AlCl_3$ and forms salt and ~~don't~~ doesn't undergo friedal crafts reaction.

$$C_6H_5\ddot{N}H_2 + AlCl_3 + CH_3Cl \longrightarrow C_6H_5\overset{+}{N}H_2AlCl_3^{-} \text{ (Salt)}$$

NO friedal craft product formed.

(ii) In gabriels pthalimide syntheses, nucleophilic addition on the alkyl halide of which amine is to be made is carried out.
In case of aromatic halides, nucleophilic substitution

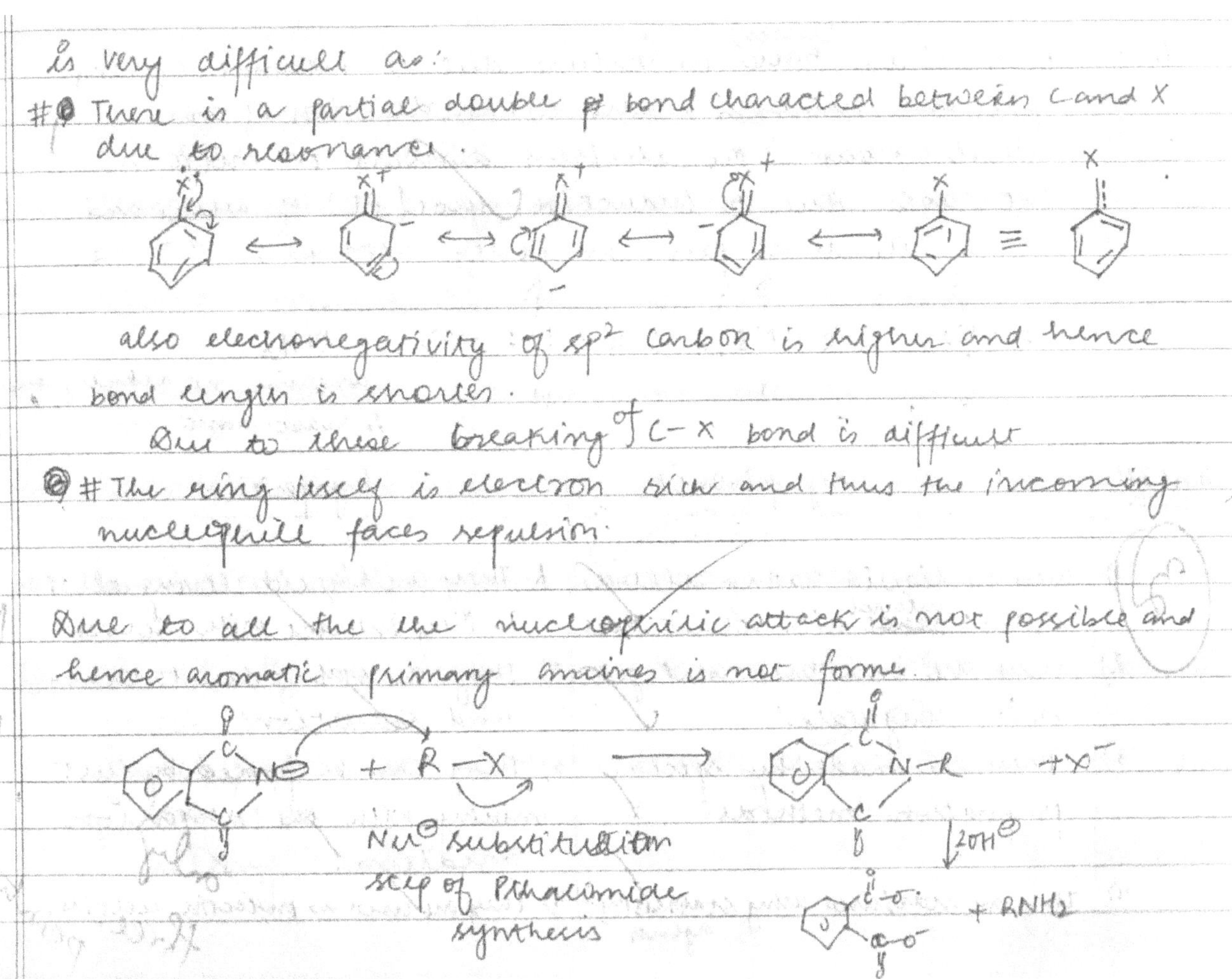

is very difficult as:

① There is a partial double bond character between C and X due to resonance.

also electronegativity of sp^2 carbon is higher and hence bond length is shorter.

Due to these breaking of C–X bond is difficult

② # The ring itself is electron rich and thus the incoming nucleophile faces repulsion.

Due to all the the nucleophilic attack is not possible and hence aromatic primary amines is not formed.

iii) Amines are (Lewis) basic in nature due to presence of lone pair on nitrogen. Due to introduction of an alkyl group, the electron density on nitrogen increases due to inductive effect (+I) of alkyl and hence its lone pair can easily attack.

$R_3N: > R_2NH > RNH_2 > NH_3$

NH_3 contains no alkyl group ∴ least basic.

Ans 34!

Lyophobic	Lyophilic
1) They are liquid hating colloids i.e. don't interact with solvent much	1) They are liquid loving colloids as they interact with solvent
2) They are unstable and gets easily coagulated	2) They are stable due to charge and solvation
3) They are made by special preparation methods	3) They can be formed by just mixing with the dispersion medium.
4) they are stabilised using stabilizing agents	4) They are used as protective colloids.

only three points

SECTION-D

Ans35: (a) (i) Transition metals have empty d-orbitals and can show variable oxidation state and hence shows catalytic properties. They have the capability to lower the activation energy of the reaction by providing an alternate path ~~for~~ to the reaction. They also provide large surface area for adsorption during heterogeneous catalysis.

Eg: $2SO_2 + O_2 \xrightarrow{V_2O_5} 2SO_3$ V_2O_5 : catalyst

(ii) Separation of a mixture of lanthanoids is difficult because they have similar atomic radii due to lanthanoid contraction and similar chemical properties.

(iii) Zn, Cd, Hg are non-transition metals i.e they have fully filled d-orbitals. They have no unpaired electrons and hence form weak metallic bonds. Due to this the enthalpy of atomisation is low and hence they have low melting point

(b) (i) (~~Sodium chromate~~) Na_2CrO_4 is converted to sodium dichromate $Na_2Cr_2O_7$ by placing it in an acidic medium like in dil ~~aq~~ H_2SO_4

$$2Na_2CrO_4 + 2H^+ \longrightarrow Na_2Cr_2O_7 + 2Na^+ + H_2O$$

(ii) Potassium manganate (K_2MnO_4) is prepared by pyrolusite ore (MnO_2) by fusing it with KOH followed ~~not by~~ with oxidation by atmospheric oxygen or HNO_3.

$$2MnO_2 + 4KOH + O_2 \longrightarrow 2K_2MnO_4 + 2H_2O$$

Ans 36: (A) (i) $C_6H_5CHO + CH_3CHO \xrightarrow{\text{dil NaOH}}$ (Aldol condensation Reaction) $C_6H_5-CH(OH)-CH_2-CHO$ (Aldol)

$\downarrow \Delta$

$C_6H_5-CH=CH-CHO$

(α-β unsaturated product)

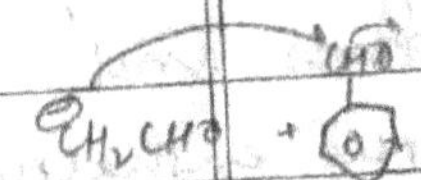

$CH_3CHO + C_6H_5CHO$

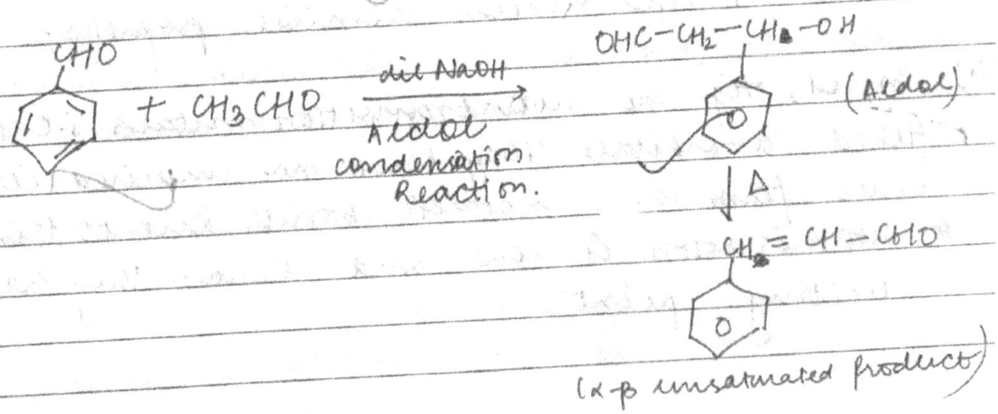

(ii) C_6H_5CHO (H–C=O on benzene ring) + $H_2N-NH-C_6H_5$ (Phenyl hydrazine) ⟶ $C_6H_5-CH=N-NH-C_6H_5$ (Hydrazone)

(iii) C_6H_5CHO + conc NaOH $\xrightarrow{\text{Cannizzaro Reaction}}$ $C_6H_5CH_2OH$ (benzyl alcohol) + $C_6H_5COO^{\ominus}Na^{+}$ (sodium benzoate).

(b) (i) The compounds can be distinguished by haloform (iodoform) reaction.

$CH_3-CH=CH-\overset{O}{\overset{\|}{C}}-CH_3$ (Methyl ketone) $\xrightarrow{I_2/NaOH}$ $CH_3-CH=CH-\overset{O}{\overset{\|}{C}}-O^-Na^+$ + $CHI_3\downarrow$ Yellow ppt (iodoform)

$CH_3-CH_2-\overset{O}{\overset{\|}{C}}-CH=CH_2$ $\xrightarrow{I_2/NaOH}$ X No yellow ppt

pent-3-en-2-one will give yellow precipitate of iodoform on reaction with sodium iodohacite as it contains methyl ketone group.

(ii) Benzaldehyde and benzoic acid can be distinguished by reaction with sodium carbonate. Benzoic acid will release CO_2 which turns lime water milky unlike benzaldehyde.

$C_6H_5COOH + Na_2CO_3 \longrightarrow C_6H_5COO^-Na^+ + CO_2\uparrow$

(CO_2) Turns lime water milky.

$C_6H_5CHO + Na_2CO_3 \longrightarrow \times$

Ans 37: (a) for 1st order reaction:

$$Kt = 2.303 \log\left(\frac{A_0}{A_t}\right)$$

$A_0 = A_0 \quad A_t = \frac{75}{100} A_0 = \frac{3}{4} A_0$

$$\Rightarrow K \times 40 = 2.303 \log\left(\frac{A_0}{3A_0} \times 4\right)$$

$\Rightarrow k = \frac{2.303}{40}(\log 4 - \log 3)$

$= \frac{2.303}{40} \times 0.1250$

$= 0.007196875 \text{ min}^{-1}$

$\approx 0.0072 \text{ min}^{-1}$

Now, 80% complete $A_t = \frac{20}{100} A_0$

$kt = 2.303 \log\left(\frac{A_0}{20A_0} \times 100\right)$

$t = \frac{2.303 \times 40 \times \log 5}{2.303 \times 0.125}$

$= \frac{40}{0.125} \times 0.6991 \times 1000$

$= 223.712$ minutes.

0.6021
0.4771
0.1250

2.303
.125
11515
46060
230300
.287875

4) 0.287875 (0.07196875

6991
32
13982
209730
223.712

(b) Order of the reaction is the sum of powers of the concentrations in molarity (or atm) of one reactants in the rate law expression.
They may not be equal to sum of ~~balanced~~ stoichiometric coefficients in balanced chemical reaction.

$R = K[A]^x[B]^y$: Rate law expression

Order $= x+y$

A biomolecular reaction can be made to follow first order kinetics if one of the reactant is taken in large excess, by which there will be no effect in the rate of reaction by changing the concentration of this excess reactant.
For eg: Hydrolysis of ester.

$CH_3COOCH_3 + H_2O \xrightarrow{H^+} CH_3COOH + CH_3-OH$

water is taken is huge amount and hence have no effect on rate of reaction.

$R = K[CH_3COOCH_3][H_2O]$ $[H_2O]$ is constant

$R = K'[CH_3COOCH_3]$ where $K' = K[H_2O]$

and hence it is converted to 1st order reaction.

These types of reactions are called Pseudo first order reaction.

Congratulations

1 Sample Paper

LATEST PATTERN

BLUE PRINT

S. No.	Chapter Name	Section-A		Section-B		Section-C		Section-D		Section-E		Total Marks
		(MCQs & A/R) 1 Mark		(VSA) 2 Marks		(SA) 3 Marks		(Case Study) 4 Marks		(LA) 5 Marks		
		Q. No.	Marks	Q. No.	Marks	Q. No.	Marks	Q. No.	Marks	Q. No.	Marks	
1	Solutions		0			28. a, b	3	32	4			**7**
2	Electrochemistry	5	1	23	2					33	5	**8**
3	Chemical Kinetics	4, 6, 12	3	19, 24	4							**7**
4	d -and f -Block Elements	3, 13, 17	3							35	5	**8**
5	Coordination Compounds	8	1	22	2	27. a, b, c	3					**6**
6	Haloalkanes and Haloarenes	2	1	21	2	26. b, 30. a, b	4					**7**
7	Alcohols, Phenols and Ethers	1, 9, 15	3	25	2	26. a	1					**6**
8	Aldehydes, Ketones and Carboxylic Acids	11, 14	2			26. b	1			34	5	**8**
9	Amines	7, 10, 18	3			29. a, b, c, d	3					**6**
10	Biomolecules	16	1	20	2			31	4			**7**
	Total Marks (Total Questions)	**18**	**18**	**7**	**14**	**5**	**15**	**2**	**8**	**3**	**15**	**70**

Time : 3 Hours **Max. Marks : 70**

General Instructions

Read the following instructions carefully

(a) *There are 35 questions in this question paper with internal choice.*
(b) *SECTION A consists of 18 multiple-choice questions carrying 1 mark each.*
(c) *SECTION B consists of 7 very short answer questions carrying 2 marks each.*
(d) *SECTION C consists of 5 short answer questions carrying 3 marks each.*
(e) *SECTION D consists of 2 case- based questions carrying 4 marks each.*
(f) *SECTION E consists of 3 long answer questions carrying 5 marks each.*
(g) ***All questions are compulsory.***
(h) ***Use of log tables and calculator are not allowed.***

SECTION-A

The following questions are multiple-choice questions with one correct answer. Each question carries 1 mark. There is no internal choice in this section.

1. An ether is more volatile than an alcohol having the same molecular formula. This is due to
(a) dipolar character of ethers (b) alcohols having resonance structures
(c) inter-molecular hydrogen bonding in ethers (d) inter-molecular hydrogen bonding in alcohols

2. When two halogen atoms are attached to same carbon atom then it is :
(a) *vic*-dihalide (b) *gem*-dihalide (c) α, ω-halide (d) α, β-halide

3. The transition element which shows the highest oxidation state is:
(a) Iron (b) Vanadium (c) Manganese (d) Chromium

4. Which option is valid for zero order reaction?
(a) $t_{1/2} = \frac{3}{2} t_{1/4}$ (b) $t_{1/2} = \frac{4}{3} t_{1/4}$ (c) $t_{1/2} = 2t_{1/4}$ (d) $t_{1/4} = (t_{1/4})^2$

5. Based on the cell notation for a spontaneous reaction, at the anode
$Ag(s) \mid AgCl(s) \mid Cl^-(aq) \parallel Br^-(aq) \mid Br_2(l) \mid C(s)$
(a) AgCl gets reduced (b) Ag gets oxidized (c) Br^- gets oxidized (d) Br_2 gets reduced

6. $3A \rightarrow 2B$, rate of reaction $\frac{d[B]}{dt}$ is equal to
(a) $-\frac{3}{2}\frac{d[A]}{dt}$ (b) $-\frac{2}{3}\frac{d[A]}{dt}$ (c) $-\frac{1}{3}\frac{d[A]}{dt}$ (d) $+2\frac{d[A]}{dt}$

7. Secondary amines could be prepared by:
(a) Reduction of nitriles (b) Hoffmann bromamide reaction
(c) Reduction of amides (d) Reduction of isonitriles

8. Which of the following does not have optical isomer?
(a) $[Co(NH_3)_3Cl_3]$ (b) $[Co(en)_3]Cl_3$ (c) $[Co(en)_2Cl_2]Cl$ (d) $[Co(en)(NH_3)_2Cl_2]Cl$

9. Isopropyl alcohol is obtained by reacting which of the following alkenes with concentrated H_2SO_4 followed by boiling with H_2O?
(a) Ethylene (b) Propylene (c) 2-Methylpropene (d) Isoprene

10. End product (A) of the following sequence of reactions is :

$$C_6H_5-NO_2 \xrightarrow[30\%HCl]{Fe} \xrightarrow{\text{Excess } CH_3Br} A$$

(a) $C_6H_5-NH_2$ (b) $C_6H_5-N(CH_3)_2$ (c) $C_6H_5-\overset{+}{N}H_3\overset{-}{Br}$ (d) $C_6H_4(NO_2)-OCH_3$ (o-nitroanisole)

11. Carbonyl compounds undergo nucleophilic addition because of
    (a) electronegativity difference of carbon and oxygen atoms.
    (b) electromeric effect.
    (c) more stable anion with negative charge on oxygen atom and less stable carbonium ion.
    (d) none of the above.

12. The rate constant for a first order reaction whose half life is 480 sec, is :
    (a) 1.44×10^{-3} sec^{-1} (b) 1.44 sec^{-1} (c) 0.72×10^{-3} sec^{-1} (d) 2.88×10^{-3} sec^{-1}

13. Chloro compound of vanadium has only spin magnetic moment of 1.73 BM. This vanadium chloride has the formula:
    (a) VCl_2 (b) VCl_4 (c) VCl_3 (d) VCl_5

14. A compound that gives a positive iodoform test is
    (a) 1-pentanol (b) 2-pentanone (c) 3-pentanone (d) pentanal

In the following questions (15-18) a statement of assertion followed by a statement of reason is given. Choose the correct answer out of the following choices.

(a) Both assertion and reason are correct statements, and reason is the correct explanation of the assertion.
(b) Both assertion and reason are correct statements, but reason is not the correct explanation of the assertion.
(c) Assertion is correct, but reason is wrong statement.
(d) Assertion is wrong, but reason is correct statement.

15. **Assertion:** *ter*-butyl methyl ether is not prepared by the reaction of *ter*-butyl bromide with sodium methoxide.
    Reason: Sodium methoxide is a strong nucleophile.

16. **Assertion :** Alpha (α)-amino acids exist as internal salt in solution as they have amino and carboxylic acid groups near vicinity.
    Reason : H^+ ion given by carboxylic group (–COOH) is captured by amino group ($-NH_2$) having lone pair of electrons.

17. **Assertion:** Cuprous ion (Cu^+) is colourless whereas cupric ion (Cu^{2+}) is blue in the aqueous solution.
    Reason: Cuprous ion (Cu^+) has unpaired electrons while cupric ion (Cu^{2+}) does not.

18. **Assertion:** Reduction of *m*-dinitrobenzene with ammonium sulphide gives *m*-nitroaniline.
    Reason: *m*-Nitroaniline formed gets precipitated and hence further reduction is prevented.

SECTION-B

This section contains 7 questions with internal choice in two questions. The following questions are very short answer type and carry 2 marks each.

19. The reaction, $SO_2Cl_2 \longrightarrow SO_2 + Cl_2$, is a first order gas reaction with $k = 2{\cdot}2 \times 10^{-5}$ sec^{-1} at 320 °C. What percentage of SO_2Cl_2 is decomposed on heating this gas for 90 minutes? (Antilog .05158 = 1.126)

20. Name the chemical components which constitute nucleotides. Write any two functions of nucleotides in a cell.

OR

Define the following terms:
(i) Glycosidic linkage (ii) Invert sugar

21. Complete the following reactions (giving major products):
    (a) $CH_3CH_2COOAg \xrightarrow{Br_2} ? \xrightarrow{Alc.KOH} ?$ (b) $CH_3CHBrCH_3 \xrightarrow{Alc.KOH} ? \xrightarrow[Peroxide]{HBr} ?$

22. A coordination compound having formula $CoCl_3.4NH_3$ does not liberate ammonia but precipitates chloride ion as AgCl. Give IUPAC name of the complex and write its structural formula.

OR

Why only transition metals are known to form π complexes?

23. Give reason :
    (a) Rusting of iron pipe can be prevented by joining it with a piece of magnesium.
    (b) Conductivity of an electrolyte solution decreases with the decrease in concentration.

24. The following values for the first order rate constant were obtained in a reaction :
    $T_1 = 298$ K, $k_1 = 3{\cdot}5 \times 10^{-5}$ s^{-1}, $T_2 = 308$ K, $k_2 = 14{\cdot}0 \times 10^{-5}$ s^{-1}. What is E_a of reaction?

25. Show how will you prepare
    (a) 1-phenylethanol from a suitable alkene.
    (b) cyclohexylmethanol using an alkyl halide by an S_N2 reaction.

SECTION-C

This section contains 5 questions with internal choice in two questions. The following questions are short answer type and carry 3 marks each.

26. (a) Give a chemical test to distinguish 1-propanol and 2-propanol.
(b) Why is $CHCl_3$ not used as an anaesthetic agent these days?
(c) Which of the stronger acid between α-Chloro propanoic acid and β-Chloro propanoic acid

27. $CoSO_4Cl.5NH_3$ exists in two isomeric forms 'A' and 'B'. Isomer 'A' reacts with $AgNO_3$ to give white precipitate, but does not react with $BaCl_2$. Isomer 'B' gives white precipitate with $BaCl_2$ but does not react with $AgNO_3$. Answer the following questions.
(a) Identify 'A' and 'B' and write their structural formulas.
(b) Name the type of isomerism involved.
(c) Give the IUPAC name of 'A' and 'B'.

28. In a cold climate, water gets frozen causing damage to the radiator of a car. Ethylene glycol is used as an antifreezing agent. Calculate the amount of ethylene glycol to be added to 4 kg of water to prevent it from freezing at –6°C.
(K_f for water = 1.85 K $mole^{-1}$ kg)

29. Write the missing product (s) in **any 3** of the following reactions.
(a) $C_6H_5N_2Cl + KI \longrightarrow$
(b) $C_6H_5NH_2 \xrightarrow{Br_2/H_2O}$
(c) $C_6H_5NH_2 \xrightarrow{(CH_3CO)_2O}$
(d) $C_6H_5NH_2 \xrightarrow{HCl}$

30. (a) What is the decreasing order of reactivity of the following in S_N2 reaction?
1-Bromo-2-methylbutane, 1-Bromo-2, 2-dimethylpropane, 1-Bromopentane.
(b) Arrange the compounds CH_3F, CH_3I, CH_3Br, CH_3Cl in order of increasing reactivity in bimolecular nucleophilic substitution (S_N2) reactions.

OR

Explain why:
(a) Allyl chloride is hydrolysed more readily than n-propyl chloride?
(b) Vinyl chloride is hydrolysed more slowly than ethyl chloride?
(c) Chloroform ($CHCl_3$) is a compound of chlorine but it does not give white precipitate with $AgNO_3$?

SECTION-D

The following questions are case-based questions. Each question has an internal choice and carries 4 (1+1+2) marks each. Read the passage carefully and answer the questions that follow.

31. Mild oxidizing agents, e.g. bromine water, Tollen's reagent, Fehling's solution etc., oxidize aldoses into aldonic acids. Both glucose and fructose can be oxidized by Tollen's reagent and Fehling's solution despite the presence of a keto group in fructose. Strong oxidizing agents like conc. HNO_3 oxidize glucose to a diabasic acid. Fructose under similar conditions is also oxidized. All carbohydrates are quantitatively oxidized by lead tetraacetate or periodic acid. This reaction is used to elucidate the structure of carbohydrates. Both glucose and fructose can be reduced by red P/HI, $LiAlH_4$, Clemmensen and Wolff-Kishner reduction.
Answer the following questions :
(a) What is number of moles of lead tetraacetate required to oxidize 100 mL of 0.1M fructose solution?
(b) What are the products of oxidation of fructose with conc. HNO_3?
(c) What is the basicity of acid produced by oxidation of glucose with conc. HNO_3?

OR

Name two reagents used for reduction of both glucose and fructose.

32. Vapour pressure of a liquid is the function of temperature. On increasing temperature, greater number of liquid molecules acquire kinetic energy sufficient to overcome the molecular attractions and pass into the vapour state. Hence vapour pressure increases, with increase in temperature, to a limiting value equal to the external pressure, usually 1 atmosphere in an open vessel. The corresponding temperature also attains a limiting value so long external pressure is fixed. However the vapour pressure of a liquid is altered on adding a foreign substance soluble in the former, it may be raised or lowered.
Vapour pressure-temperature plots for pure water, 0.5 m glucose and 0.5 m methanol are depicted in the figure as shown.

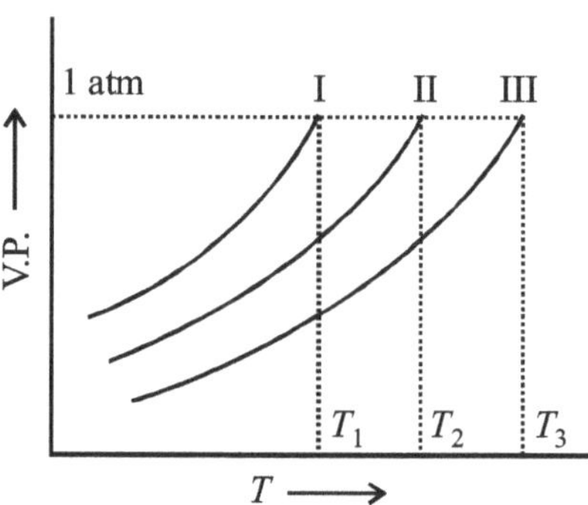

Answer the following questions :

(a) What will be the change in vapour pressure of a liquid by adding non-volatile solute?

(b) Which plot represents methanol and why?

(c) Boiling point of methanol is less than water. why?

OR

What is the elevation of boiling point of glucose solution in terms of T_1, T_2 and T_3?

SECTION-E

The following questions are long answer type and carry 5 marks each. Two questions have an internal choice.

33. (a) Consider a cell composed of the following two half-cells:

(i) $Mg(s)|Mg^{2+}(aq)$, and (ii) $Ag(s)|Ag^{+}(aq)$.

The emf of the cell is 2·96 V when $[Mg^{2+}] = 0{\cdot}130$ M and $[Ag^{+}] = 1{\cdot}0 \times 10^{-4}$ M. Calculate the standard emf of the cell. ($R = 8{\cdot}31\ JK^{-1}\ mol^{-1}$, $F = 96500\ C\ mol^{-1}$).

(b) Can we use a copper vessel to store 1 M $AgNO_3$ solution? $E_{Cu^{2+}/Cu} = +0\cdot34$ V, $E_{Ag^{+}/Ag} = 0\cdot80$

OR

(a) Explain why electrolysis of aqueous solution of NaCl gives H_2 at cathode and Cl_2 at anode. Write overall reaction.

$E^\circ_{Na^+/Na} = -2{\cdot}71V$, $E^\circ_{H_2O/H_2} = -0{\cdot}83V$, $E^\circ_{Cl_2/Cl^-} = +1{\cdot}36V$, $E^\circ_{O_2/H_2O} = +1{\cdot}23V$

(b) What happens when I_2 and F_2 are added to a solution containing 1M each of I^- and F^- ions.
Given: Reduction potentials of I_2 and F_2 are 0·54 volt and 2·87 volts respectively.

34. How will you convert

(a) Ethanal to lactic acid

(b) Ethanol to butan-2-one

(c) Acetone to *tert*-butyl alcohol

(d) Propene to propanone

(e) Benzaldehyde to benzophenone.

OR

(a) Complete the following reactions :

(i) $6HCHO + 4NH_3 \xrightarrow{Heat}$

(ii) $2CH_3-\underset{CH_3}{\overset{CH_3}{\overset{|}{\underset{|}{C}}}}-CHO + NaOH \longrightarrow$

(b) Give reasons for the following :

(i) Dialkyl cadmium is used to prepare ketones from acid chlorides and not from Grignard reagents.

(ii) Hydrazones of aldehydes and ketones are not prepared in strongly acidic medium.

35. (a) (i) Which of the following oxides in basic: V_2O_5 or CrO_3?

(ii) What is most stable oxidation state of Ti (Z = 22) is aqueous solution?

(iii) Why is copper sulphate pentahydrate coloured?

(b) Explain why

(i) E° for Mn^{3+}/Mn^{2+} couple is more positive than that for Fe^{3+}/Fe^{2+}.
[Atomic numbers of Mn = 25, Fe = 26]

(ii) Ce^{3+} can be easily oxidised to Ce^{4+}. [Atomic number of Ce = 58]

2 Sample Paper

LATEST PATTERN

BLUE PRINT

S. No.	Chapter Name	Section-A		Section-B		Section-C		Section-D		Section-E		Total Marks
		(MCQs & A/R) 1 Mark		(VSA) 2 Marks		(SA) 3 Marks		(Case Study) 4 Marks		(LA) 5 Marks		
		Q. No.	Marks	Q. No.	Marks	Q. No.	Marks	Q. No.	Marks	Q. No.	Marks	
1	Solutions	1, 6	2	22	2	26	3					**7**
2	Electrochemistry	7, 12	2	21	2			31	4			**8**
3	Chemical Kinetics	10, 13	2	20	2	27	3					**7**
4	d -and f -Block Elements	3, 11	2	19	2			32	4			**8**
5	Coordination Compounds	14	1							33	5	**6**
6	Haloalkanes and Haloarenes	5, 17	2							34	5	**7**
7	Alcohols, Phenols and Ethers	2, 18	2	23	2	28. a, b	2					**6**
8	Aldehydes, Ketones and Carboxylic Acids	4	1			28. c, 29. a	2			35	5	**8**
9	Amines	8, 15	2	24	2	29. b, c	2					**6**
10	Biomolecules	9, 16	2	25	2	30	3					**7**
	Total Marks (Total Questions)	**18**	**18**	**7**	**14**	**5**	**15**	**2**	**8**	**3**	**15**	**70**

Time : 3 Hours **Max. Marks : 70**

General Instructions

Read the following instructions carefully

(a) *There are 35 questions in this question paper with internal choice.*
(b) *SECTION A consists of 18 multiple-choice questions carrying 1 mark each.*
(c) *SECTION B consists of 7 very short answer questions carrying 2 marks each.*
(d) *SECTION C consists of 5 short answer questions carrying 3 marks each.*
(e) *SECTION D consists of 2 case- based questions carrying 4 marks each.*
(f) *SECTION E consists of 3 long answer questions carrying 5 marks each.*
(g) ***All questions are compulsory.***
(h) ***Use of log tables and calculator are not allowed.***

SECTION-A

The following questions are multiple-choice questions with one correct answer. Each question carries 1 mark. There is no internal choice in this section.

1. An ideal solution is formed when its components
(a) have no volume change on mixing (b) have no enthalpy change on mixing
(c) have both the above characteristics (d) have high solubility.

2. Which statement is not correct about alcohol?
(a) Molecular weight of alcohol is higher than water
(b) Alcohol of less no. of carbon atoms is less soluble in water than alcohol of more no. of carbon atoms
(c) Alcohol evaporates quickly
(d) All of the above

3. The correct order of atomic radii is :
(a) Ce > Lu > Ho (b) Ho > Lu > Ce (c) Lu > Ce < Ho (d) Ce > Ho > Lu

4. The catalyst used in Rosenmund's reduction is
(a) $HgSO_4$ (b) $Pd/BaSO_4$ (c) anhydrous $AlCl_3$ (d) anhydrous $ZnCl_2$

5. The halogen which is the most reactive in the halogenation of alkanes under sunlight is ....
(a) Fluorine (b) Chlorine (c) bromine (d) iodine

6. An aqueous solution of hydrochloric acid
(a) obeys Raoult's law (b) shows negative deviation from Raoult's law
(c) shows positive deviation from Raoult's law (d) obeys Henry's law at all compositions

7. Which of the following reaction is possible at anode?
(a) $2Cr^{3+} + 7H_2O \rightarrow Cr_2O_7^{2-} + 14H^+$ (b) $F_2 \rightarrow 2F^-$
(c) $(1/2)\,O_2 + 2H^+ \rightarrow H_2O$ (d) None of these.

8. Hinsberg's reagent is :
(a) $\begin{array}{l} COOC_2H_5 \\ | \\ COOC_2H_5 \end{array}$ (b) $C_6H_5SO_2Cl$ (c) $C_6H_5SO_2NH_2$ (d) $CH_3COCH_2COOC_2H_5$

9. α - D-(+)-glucose and β-D-(+)-glucose are
(a) conformers (b) epimers (c) anomers (d) enantiomers

10. Which of the following statement is true for the reaction, $H_2 + Br_2 \rightarrow 2HBr$. The rate law is $\frac{dx}{dt} = k[H_2][Br_2]^{1/2}$.
(a) order of reaction is 1.5.
(b) molecularity of the reaction is 2.
(c) by increasing the concentration of Br_2 four times the rate of reaction is doubled.
(d) all the above are correct.

11. The pair of metal ions that can give a spin only magnetic moment of 3.9 BM for the complex $[M(H_2O)_6]Cl_2$, is:
(a) V^{2+} and Co^{2+} (b) V^{2+} and Fe^{2+} (c) Co^{2+} and Fe^{2+} (d) Cr^{2+} and Mn^{2+}

12. What is the E°_{cell} for the reaction $Cu^{2+}(aq) + Sn^{2+}(aq) \rightleftharpoons Cu(s) + Sn^{4+}(aq)$ at 25 °C if the equilibrium constant for the reaction is 1×10^6?
(a) 0.5328 V (b) 0.3552 V (c) 0.1773 V (d) 0.7104 V

13. The plot of concentration of the reactant vs time for a reaction is a straight line with a negative slope. The reaction follows a rate equation
(a) zero order (b) first order (c) second order (d) third order

14. $[Pt(NH_3)_4Cl_2]Br_2$ complex can show :
(a) Hydrated as well as ionization isomerism. (b) Ionization as well as geometrical isomerism.
(c) Linkage as well as geometrical isomerism. (d) Ionization as well as optical isomerism.

In the following questions (15-18) a statement of assertion followed by a statement of reason is given. Choose the correct answer out of the following choices.
(a) Both assertion and reason are correct statements, and reason is the correct explanation of the assertion.
(b) Both assertion and reason are correct statements, but reason is not the correct explanation of the assertion.
(c) Assertion is correct, but reason is wrong statement.
(d) Assertion is wrong, but reason is correct statement.

15. **Assertion:** Anilinium chloride is more acidic than ammonium chloride.
Reason: Anilinium ion is resonance stabilized.

16. **Assertion :** Disruption of the natural structure of a protein is called denaturation.
Reason : The change in colour and appearance of egg during cooking is due to denaturation.

17. **Assertion :** S_N2 reactions always proceed with inversion of configuration.
Reason : S_N2 reaction of an optically active aryl halide with an aqueous solution of KOH always gives an alcohol with opposite sign of rotation.

18. **Assertion:** Phenol is a strong acid than ethanol.
Reason: Groups with +M effect decreases acidity at *p*-position.

SECTION-B

This section contains 7 questions with internal choice in two questions. The following questions are very short answer type and carry 2 marks each.

19. Why is ionic radius of Cu^{2+} less than that of Cr^{2+} whereas atomic number of Cu greater than that of Cr?

20. For the reaction : $aA + bB \rightarrow$ Products, the rate law is given by Rate = $k[A]^m[B]^n$. On making the concentration of A two fold and halving that of B, what will be the the ratio of the new rate to the earlier rate of the reaction?

OR

In a reaction with initially 0.12 M, the concentration of reactant is reduced to 0.06 M in 10 hour and to 0.03 M in 20 hour.
(i) What is order of reaction?
(ii) What is rate constant?

21. Calculate the λ^∞_m (NH_4OH) when corresponding values of NH_4Cl, NaOH and NaCl are 150, 248·1 and 126·4 S cm^2 mol^{-1} respectively.

22. If two substances A and B have $p_1^\circ : p_2^\circ = 1 : 2$ and contain mole fraction in solution as 1 : 2. Then, what will be the mole fraction of component 1 in vapour phase ?

23. Account for the following:
(a) Alcohols act as weak bases. (b) Ethanol has higher b.p. than methoxymethane.

OR

(a) Phenol is more acidic than ethanol.
(b) *m*-Aminophenol is a stronger acid than *o*-aminophenol.

24. Rearrange the following compounds as directed below:
(a) Increasing order of basic strength in their aqueous solutions.
NH_3, CH_3NH_2, $(CH_3)_2NH$, $(CH_3)_3N$
(b) Increasing order of basic strength in gas phase $C_2H_5NH_2$, $(C_2H_5)NH$, $(C_2H_5)_3N$ and CH_3NH_2

25. The tertiary structure of many proteins dissolved in water is disrupted by heating above 80 °C but primary structure is unaffected. Explain.

SECTION-C

This section contains 5 questions with internal choice in two questions. The following questions are short answer type and carry 3 marks each.

26. (a) State Raoult's law for solutions of volatile solutes.
(b) The vapour pressure of pure benzene at a certain temperature is 640 mm Hg. A non-volatile solid weighing 2.175g is added to 39.0g of benzene. The vapour pressure of the solution is 600 mm Hg. What is the molecular weight of the solid substance ?

OR

(a) Calculate the molality of 1 litre solution of 93% H_2SO_4 (weight/volume). The density of the solution is 1.84 g/mL.
(b) What is the effect of temperature on the solubility of a gas in a liquid?

27. (a) In some reactions, the energy possessed by colliding molecules is more than the threshold energy, yet the reaction is slow. Why?
(b) State one condition in which a bimolecular reaction may be kinetically of the first order.

28. Convert:
(a) Ethylalcohol to diethylether
(b) 1-Butanol to butanoic acid
(c) Give two chemical tests to distinguish aldehyde from ketones.

29. How will you convert (a) Butan-2-one to butan-2-ol.
(b) Acetone to isopropylamine
(c) Benzaldehyde to cyanobenzene

30. Differentiate between the following:
(a) Amylose and Amylopectin
(b) Peptide linkage and Glycosidic linkage
(c) Fibrous proteins and Globular proteins

OR

Write chemical reactions to show that open structure of D-glucose contains the following:
(a) Straight chain
(b) Five alcohol groups
(c) Aldehyde as carbonyl group

SECTION-D

The following questions are case-based questions. Each question has an internal choice and carries 4 (1+1+2) marks each. Read the passage carefully and answer the questions that follow.

31. Redox reactions play a pivotal role in chemistry and biology. The values of standard redox potential (E°) of two half-cell reactions decide which way the reaction is expected to proceed. A simple example is a Daniel cell in which zinc goes into solution and copper gets deposited. Given below are a set of half-cell reactions (acidic medium) along with their E° (V with respect to normal hydrogen electrode) values. Using this data obtain the correct explanations to questions given.

$I_2 + 2e^- \rightarrow 2I^-$ $E° = 0.54$
$Cl_2 + 2e^- \rightarrow 2Cl^-$ $E° = 1.36$
$Mn^{3+} + e^- \rightarrow Mn^{2+}$ $E° = 1.50$
$Fe^{3+} + e^- \rightarrow Fe^{2+}$ $E° = 0.77$
$O_2 + 4H^+ + 4e^- \rightarrow 2H_2O$ $E° = 1.23$

Answer the following questions:
(a) Explain how iodine ion is oxidised by chlorine.

(b) Sodium fusion extract, obtained from aniline, on treatment with iron (II) sulphate and H_2SO_4 in presence of air gives a Prussian blue precipitate. The blue colour is due to the formation of which complex ?

(c) Explain in why oxygen cannot oxidise chloride ion.

OR

Mn^{2+} is not able to undergo oxidation in presence of O_2, explain.

32. A water insoluble solid "*A*" turns yellow on heating and becomes white again on cooling. When "*A*" is treated with HCl (aq) it forms a clear solution "*B*". "*A*" when treated with NaOH (aq) also gives a clear solution "*C*". When H_2S (g) is bubbled through clear solution "*B*" no change is observed but when H_2S is bubbled through clear solution "*C*", a white precipitate of compound "*D*" is observed.

Answer the following questions :

(a) Identify compound "A"

(b) What is compound "*B*"?

(c) What will be the nature of compound "A"?

OR

The compound obtained during the reaction of "*C*" with H_2S.

SECTION-E

The following questions are long answer type and carry 5 marks each. Two questions have an internal choice.

33. (a) Draw the structures of optical isomers of

(i) $[Cr(C_2O_4)_3]^3$ (ii) $[PtCl_2(en)_2]^{2+}$ (iii) $[Cr(NH_3)_2Cl_2(en)]^+$

(b) Write the IUPAC nomenclature of the given complex along with its hybridisation and structure.

$K_2[Cr(NO)(NH_3)(CN)_4]$, $\mu = 1.73$ BM

OR

(a) Write the IUPAC names of the following coordination compounds:

(i) $[Pt(NH_3)_2Cl(NO_2)]$ (ii) $K_3[Cr(C_2O_4)_3]$

(b) $[NiCl_4]^{2-}$ is paramagnetic while $[Ni(CO)_4]$ is diamagnetic though both are tetrahedral. Why?

(c) Explain the following cases giving appropriate reasons.

(i) Nickel does not form low spin octahedral complexes.

(ii) The π-complexes are known for the transition metals only.

(iii) Co^{2+} is easily oxidised to Co^{3+} in the presence of a strong ligand.

34. (a) What will be the IUPAC name of the following?

(i) $H_3C(H)C{=}C(H)CH_2Br$ (H₃C and H on one carbon, H and CH_2Br on the other) (ii) $ClCH_2C \equiv CCH_2Br$

(b) Account for the following:

(i) Reaction of alkyl chlorides with aqueous KOH leads to alcohols while with alcoholic KOH, alkenes are major products.

(ii) $(CH_3)_3C$–Cl reacts faster than $CH_3CH_2CH(Cl)CH_2CH_3$ towards S_N1 reaction.

OR

(a) Account for the following:

(i) Order of reactivity of haloalkanes is RI > RBr > RCl.

(ii) Neopentyl chloride, $(CH_3)_3CCH_2Cl$ does not follow S_N2 mechanism.

(b) Write the missing product(s) of the following reaction(s)?

(i) $CH_3CH_2CH{=}CH_2 + HBr$ (ii) $CH_2{=}CH_2 + Br_2$

35. Write chemical reactions to carry out the following conversions :

(a) Butan-1-ol to butanoic acid

(b) Benzyl alcohol to phenylethanoic acid

(c) 3-Nitrobromobenzene to 3-Nitrobenzoic acid

(d) 4-Methylacetophenone to benzene-1, 4-dicarboxylic acid

(e) Butanal to butanoic acid.

3 Sample Paper

LATEST PATTERN

BLUE PRINT

S. No.	Chapter Name	Section-A		Section-B		Section-C		Section-D		Section-E		Total Marks
		(MCQs & A/R) 1 Mark		(VSA) 2 Marks		(SA) 3 Marks		(Case Study) 4 Marks		(LA) 5 Marks		
		Q. No.	Marks	Q. No.	Marks	Q. No.	Marks	Q. No.	Marks	Q. No.	Marks	
1	Solutions	4, 14	2	25	2	26	3					**7**
2	Electrochemistry	9, 18	2	23	2			32	4			**8**
3	Chemical Kinetics	5, 16	2	21	2	30. a, b, c	3					**7**
4	d -and f -Block Elements	10, 17	2	20	2			31	4			**8**
5	Coordination Compounds	2	1							33	5	**6**
6	Haloalkanes and Haloarenes	1, 11	2							34	5	**7**
7	Alcohols, Phenols and Ethers	6	1	22	2	29. a, b, c	3					**6**
8	Aldehydes, Ketones and Carboxylic Acids	7, 12	2	19, 24	4	27. a, b	2					**8**
9	Amines	3, 13	2			27. c, 28	4					**6**
10	Biomolecules	8, 15	2							35	5	**7**
	Total Marks (Total Questions)	**18**	**18**	**7**	**14**	**5**	**15**	**2**	**8**	**3**	**15**	**70**

Time : 3 Hours **Max. Marks : 70**

General Instructions

Read the following instructions carefully

(a) *There are 35 questions in this question paper with internal choice.*

(b) *SECTION A consists of 18 multiple-choice questions carrying 1 mark each.*

(c) *SECTION B consists of 7 very short answer questions carrying 2 marks each.*

(d) *SECTION C consists of 5 short answer questions carrying 3 marks each.*

(e) *SECTION D consists of 2 case- based questions carrying 4 marks each.*

(f) *SECTION E consists of 3 long answer questions carrying 5 marks each.*

(g) ***All questions are compulsory.***

(h) ***Use of log tables and calculator are not allowed***

SECTION-A

The following questions are multiple-choice questions with one correct answer. Each question carries 1 mark. There is no internal choice in this section.

1. The process of converting alkyl halides into alcohols involves ....
(a) addition reaction (b) substitution reaction (c) dehydrohalogenation (d) rearrangement reaction

2. The type of isomerism present in pentamminenitrochromium (III) chloride is
(a) optical (b) linkage (c) ionisation (d) polymerisation

3. Which of the following amines will not give N_2 gas on treatment with nitrous acid ($NaNO_2 + HCl$) ?
(a) $C_2H_5NH_2$ (b) CH_3NH_2 (c) $(CH_3)_2CHNH_2$ (d) All will give N_2

4. Which solution has the highest vapour pressure?
(a) 0.02 M NaCl at 50 °C (b) 0.03 M sucrose at 15 °C
(c) 0.005 M $CaCl_2$ at 50 °C (d) 0.005 M $CaCl_2$ at 25 °C

5. The rate constant for a first order reaction whose half life is 480 sec, is :
(a) 1.44×10^{-3} sec^{-1} (b) 1.44 sec^{-1} (c) 0.72×10^{-3} sec^{-1} (d) 2.88×10^{-3} sec^{-1}

6. Which of the following cannot be made by using Williamson's synthesis?
(a) Methoxybenzene (b) Benzyl *p*-nitrophenyl ether
(c) Methyl tertiary butyl ether (d) Di-tert-butyl ether

7. Among the following the strongest acid is
(a) CH_3COOH (b) C_6H_5COOH (c) *m*-$CH_3OC_6H_4COOH$ (d) *p*-$CH_3OC_6H_4COOH$

8. Insulin production and its action in human body are responsible for the level of diabetes. This compound belongs to which of the following categories?
(a) A carbohydrate (b) A hormone (c) A co-enzyme (d) An antibiotic

9. What will be the reduction potential for the following half-cell reaction at 298 K?
(Given : $[Ag^+] = 0.1$ M and $E^\circ_{cell} = +0.80$ V)
(a) 0.741 V (b) 0.80 V (c) −0.80 V (d) −0.741 V

10. For *d*-block elements the first ionization potential is of the order
(a) Zn > Fe > Cu > Cr (b) Sc = Ti < V = Cr (c) Zn < Cu < Ni < Co (d) V > Cr > Mn > Fe

11. Which of the following is a primary halide?
(a) Isopropyl iodide (b) Secondary butyl iodide (c) Tertiary butyl bromide (d) Neohexyl chloride

12. The cyanohydrin of a compound on hydrolysis gives an optically active α-hydroxy acid. The compound is?
(a) Diethyl ketone (b) Formaldehyde (c) Acetaldehyde (d) Acetone

13. Which one of the following on reduction with lithium aluminium hydride yields a secondary amine?
(a) Methyl isocyanide (b) Acetamide (c) Methyl cyanide (d) Nitroethane.

14. Value of Henry's constant K_H _______.
(a) increases with increase in temperature. (b) decreases with increase in temperature.
(c) remains constant. (d) first increases then decreases.

In the following questions (15-18) a statement of assertion followed by a statement of reason is given. Choose the correct answer out of the following choices.

(a) Both assertion and reason are correct statements, and reason is the correct explanation of the assertion.
(b) Both assertion and reason are correct statements, but reason is not the correct explanation of the assertion.
(c) Assertion is correct, but reason is wrong statement.
(d) Assertion is wrong, but reason is correct statement.

15. **Assertion :** Alpha (α)-amino acids exist as internal salt in solution as they have amino and carboxylic acid groups in near vicinity.
Reason : H^+ ion given by carboxylic group (–COOH) is captured by amino group ($-NH_2$) having lone pair of electrons.

16. **Assertion :** Inversion of cane sugar is a pseudo first order reaction.
Reason : Water is present in excesss during hydrolysis.

17. **Assertion:** Transition metals are good catalysts.
Reason: V_2O_5 or Pt is used in the preparation of H_2SO_4 by contact process.

18. **Assertion:** On increasing dilution, the specific conductance keep on increasing.
Reason: On increasing dilution, degree of ionisation of weak electrolyte increases and molality of ions also increases.

SECTION-B

This section contains 7 questions with internal choice in two questions. The following questions are very short answer type and carry 2 marks each.

19. How will you convert the following?
(a) Ethanol to propanone (acetone).
(b) Benzene to acetophenone.

OR

(a) Toluene to benzaldehyde.
(b) Isopropyl iodide to 2,3-dimethylbutane

20. Name an important alloy which contains some of the lanthanoid metals. Mention its two uses.

21. What is meant by the rate constant, 'k' of a reaction? If the concentration is expressed in mol L^{-1} and time in seconds, what will be the units of rate constant k for (i) zero order reaction (ii) first order reaction?

OR

Calculate the rate of reaction from the rate law: $-\frac{d[A]}{dt} = k[A][B]^2$, when the concentration of A and B are $0 \cdot 01$ M and $0 \cdot 02$ M respectively and $k = 5 \cdot 1 \times 10^{-3}\ L^2\ mol^{-2}\ s^{-1}$.

22. Out of cyclohexanol or phenol, which one is more acidic and why?

23. The resistance of a 0.01 N solution of an electrolyte was found to be 210 ohm at 298 K using a conductivity cell with a cell constant of 0.88 cm^{-1}. Calculate specific conductance and equivalent conductance of solution.

24. (a) Why the oxidation of toluene to benzaldehyde with CrO_3 is carried out in presence of acetic anhydride?
(b) Tertiary-butyl benzene does not give benzoic acid when oxidized with $KMnO_4$. Why?

25. Define the following:
(a) Molality of solution
(b) Osmotic pressure

SECTION-C

This section contains 5 questions with internal choice in two questions. The following questions are short answer type and carry 3 marks each.

26. In a cold climate, water gets frozen causing damage to the radiator of a car. Ethylene glycol is used as an antifreezing agent. Calculate the amount of ethylene glycol to be added to 4 kg of water to prevent it from freezing at –6°C.
(K_f for water = 1.85 K $mole^{-1}$ kg)

27. How will you convert
(a) a primary alcohol to an aldehyde.
(b) 3–Hydroxy pentan-2-one shows positive Tollen's test.
(c) Phenol to N-phenylethanamide.

28. Give the structures of A and B in the following sequence of reactions:

(a) $CH_3COOH \xrightarrow[\Delta]{NH_3} A \xrightarrow{NaOBr} B$

(b) $C_6H_5NO_2 \xrightarrow{Fe/HCl} A \xrightarrow[0°-5°C]{NaNO_2+HCl} B$

(c) $C_6H_5N_2^+Cl^- \xrightarrow[\Delta]{CuCN} A \xrightarrow{H_2O/H^+} B$

OR

(a) How will you distinguish between the following pairs of compounds:
(i) Aniline and Ethanamine
(ii) Aniline and N-Methylaniline
(b) Arrange the following compounds in decreasing order of their boiling points:
Butanol, Butanamine, Butane

29. (a) Anhydrous $CaCl_2$ is not recommended as a drying agent for alcohols and amines.
(b) Why are Grignard reagents soluble in ether but not in benzene?
(c) Explain why the cleavage of aryl ethers with hydrogen halides always yield phenol and a molecule of halide and not aryl halide and alcohol.

OR

Draw the structure and name the product formed if the following alcohols are oxidised. Assume that an excess of oxidising agent is used.
(a) $CH_3CH_2CH_2CH_2OH$ (b) 2-butanol (c) 2-methyl-1-propanol

30. The decomposition of H_2O_2 in presence of iodide ion is found to be first order with rate constant $1{\cdot}01 \times 10^{-2}$ min^{-1} by following graphical method. Calculate the rate of reaction when,
(a) Conc. of H_2O_2 is 0·4 mol L^{-1}
(b) Conc. of H_2O_2 is 0·15 mol L^{-1}
(c) What conc. of H_2O_2 would give rate of $1{\cdot}12 \times 10^{-2}$ mol L^{-1} min^{-1}?

SECTION-D

The following questions are case-based questions. Each question has an internal choice and carries 4 (1+1+2) marks each. Read the passage carefully and answer the questions that follow.

31. On the basis of the figure given below, answer the following questions:

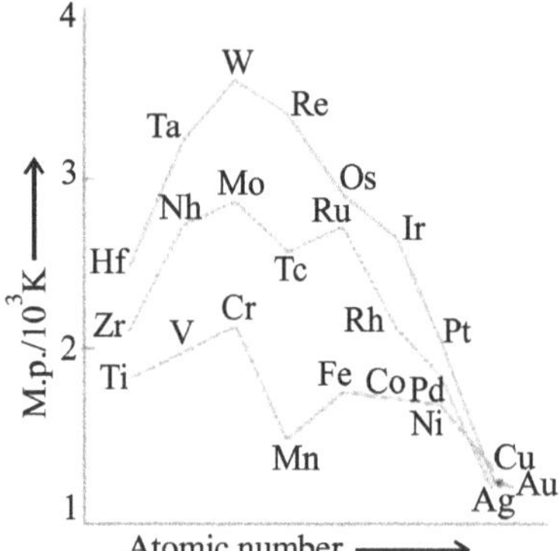

Answer the following questions :
(a) Why Manganese has lower melting point than Chromium?
(b) In the third transition series, identify and name the metal with the highest melting point.
(c) Why do transition metals of 3*d* series have lower melting points as compared to 4*d* series?

OR

Zn, Cd, Hg have low m.p. and are comparatively softer than other transition metals–Justify.

32. Both conductivity and molar conductivity change with the concentration of the electrolyte. Conductivity always decreases with decrease in concentration both, for weak and strong electrolytes. This can be explained by the fact that the number of ions per unit volume that carry the current in a solution decreases on dilution. The conductivity of a solution at any given concentration is the conductance of one unit volume of solution kept between two platinum electrodes with unit area of cross section and at a distance of unit length. Molar conductivity of a solution at a given concentration is the conductance of the volume V of solution containing one mole of electrolyte kept between two electrodes with area of cross section A and distance of unit length.

Answer the following questions :

(a) Conductivity decreases with dilution whereas Molar conductivity increases. Why?
(b) Conductivity of solutions of different electrolytes in the same solvent and at a given temperature is different. Why?
(c) Conductivity of metals decreases with increase of temperature whereas that of electrolytic solution increases. Why?

OR

For strong electrolytes, molar conductivity increases slowly with dilution. Why?

SECTION-E

The following questions are long answer type and carry 5 marks each. Two questions have an internal choice.

33. (a) Designate the coordination entities and counter ions in the coordination compounds: $[Cr(NH_3)_6]Cl_3$; $K_4[Fe(CN)_6]$, $K_2[PtCl_4]$; $[Ni(CO)_4]$; $K_2[Ni(CN)_4]$.

(b) By considering the complex $K_3[Fe(C_2O_4)_3]$ indicate the following:
(i) Central atom
(ii) Coordination sphere
(iii) Ionisation sphere
(iv) Coordination number
(v) Oxidation number of central atom

OR

(a) What is meant by crystal field splitting energy? On the basis of crystal field theory, write the electronic configuration of d^4 in terms of t_{2g} and e_g in an octahedral field when
(i) $\Delta_0 > P$
(ii) $\Delta_0 < P$

(b) In which case will be splitting larger – 3d-orbitals or 4d-orbitals?
(c) Why does NH_2–NH_2 act as monodentate ligand, not bidentate ligand?

34. (a) (i) Write the structure of the product when chlorobenzene is treated with methyl chloride in the presence of sodium metal and dry ether.
(ii) Write the structure of the alkene formed by dehydrohalogenation of 1-bromo-1 methylcyclohexane with alcoholic KOH.

(b) Following compounds are given to you :
2-Bromopentane, 2-Bromo-2-methylbutane, 1-Bromopentane
(i) Write the compound which is most reactive towards S_N2 reaction.
(ii) Write the compound which is optically active.
(iii) Write the compound which is most reactive towards β-elimination reaction.

35. (a) Define the following terms with a suitable example in each:
(a) Polysaccharides
(b) Denatured protein

(b) (i) What is the difference between native protein and denatured protein?
(ii) Which one of the following is a disaccharide :
Glucose, Lactose, Amylose, Fructose
(iii) Write the name of the vitamin responsible for the coagulation of blood.

OR

(a) Write the product when D-glucose react with conc. HNO_3.
(b) Amino acids show amphoteric behaviour. Why?
(c) Write one difference between α-helix and β-pleated structures of proteins.
(d) Define the following with an example of each:
(i) Fibrous protein
(ii) Essential amino acids

4 Sample Paper

LATEST PATTERN

BLUE PRINT

S. No.	Chapter Name	Section-A (MCQs & A/R) 1 Mark		Section-B (VSA) 2 Marks		Section-C (SA) 3 Marks		Section-D (Case Study) 4 Marks		Section-E (LA) 5 Marks		Total Marks
		Q. No.	Marks	Q. No.	Marks	Q. No.	Marks	Q. No.	Marks	Q. No.	Marks	
1	Solutions	3, 16	2	23	2	27	3					**7**
2	Electrochemistry	4, 15, 18	3	25	2	29	3					**8**
3	Chemical Kinetics	9, 12	2							33	5	**7**
4	d -and f -Block Elements	5	1	22	2					35	5	**8**
5	Coordination Compounds	2	1	20	2	30	3					**6**
6	Haloalkanes and Haloarenes	6	1	19	2			32	4			**7**
7	Alcohols, Phenols and Ethers	7, 13	2	21	2	26. a, b	2					**6**
8	Aldehydes, Ketones and Carboxylic Acids	1, 11	2			26. c	1			34	5	**8**
9	Amines	8, 14	2					31	4			**6**
10	Biomolecules	10, 17	2	24	2	28	3					**7**
	Total Marks (Total Questions)	**18**	**18**	**7**	**14**	**5**	**15**	**2**	**8**	**3**	**15**	**70**

Time : 3 Hours **Max. Marks : 70**

General Instructions

Read the following instructions carefully

(a) *There are 35 questions in this question paper with internal choice.*

(b) *SECTION A consists of 18 multiple-choice questions carrying 1 mark each.*

(c) *SECTION B consists of 7 very short answer questions carrying 2 marks each.*

(d) *SECTION C consists of 5 short answer questions carrying 3 marks each.*

(e) *SECTION D consists of 2 case- based questions carrying 4 marks each.*

(f) *SECTION E consists of 3 long answer questions carrying 5 marks each.*

(g) ***All questions are compulsory.***

(h) ***Use of log tables and calculator are not allowed.***

SECTION-A

The following questions are multiple-choice questions with one correct answer. Each question carries 1 mark. There is no internal choice in this section.

1. Which produces ketone on treatment with Grignard reagent?
(a) methyl cyanide (b) acetaldehyde (c) methyl alcohol (d) acetic acid

2. For an octahedral complex, which of the following *d*-electron configuration will give maximum CFSE?
(a) High spin with d^6 configuration (b) Low spin with d^4 configuration
(c) Low spin with d^5 configuration (d) High spin with d^7 configuration

3. The decrease in the vapour pressure of solvent depends on the
(a) quantity of non-volatile solute present in the solution
(b) nature of non-volatile solute present in the solution
(c) molar mass of non-volatile solute present in the solution
(d) physical state of non-volatile solute present in the solution

4. On the basis of the following E° values, the strongest oxidizing agent is :
$[Fe(CN)_6]^{4-} \rightarrow [Fe(CN)_6]^{3-} + e^-$; $E° = -0.35$ V
$Fe^{2+} \rightarrow Fe^{3+} + e^-$; $E° = -0.77$ V
(a) $[Fe(CN)_6]^{4-}$ (b) Fe^{2+} (c) Fe^{3+} (d) $[Fe(CN)_6]^{3-}$

5. Which one of the following statements concerning lanthanide elements is false?
(a) Lanthanides are separated from one another by ion exchange method.
(b) The ionic radii of trivalent lanthanides steadily increase with increase in atomic number.
(c) All lanthanides are highly dense metals.
(d) Most characteristic oxidation state of lanthanides is +3.

6. Among the following which one can have a *meso* form?
(a) $CH_3CH(OH)CH(Cl)C_2H_5$ (b) $CH_3CH(OH)CH(OH)CH_3$
(c) $C_2H_5CH(OH)CH(OH)CH_3$ (d) $HOCH_2CH(Cl)CH_3$

7. What is the correct order of reactivity of alcohols in the following reaction? $R-OH + HCl \xrightarrow{ZnCl_2} R-Cl + H_2O$
(a) $1° > 2° > 3°$ (b) $1° < 2° < 3°$ (c) $3° > 2° > 1°$ (d) $3° > 1° > 2°$

8. In an acidic medium, ... behaves as the strongest base
(a) nitrobenzene (b) aniline (c) phenol (d) cresol

9. The order of a reaction with rate equal to $k[A]^{3/2}[B]^{-1/2}$ is :
(a) 1 (b) $-\frac{1}{2}$ (c) $-\frac{3}{2}$ (d) 2

10. The function of DNA in an organism is
(a) to assist in the synthesis of RNA molecule
(b) to store information of heredity characteristics
(c) to assist in the synthesis of proteins and polypeptides
(d) all of these.

11. Reduction of benzoyl chloride with Pd and $BaSO_4$ gives :
(a) benzyl chloride (b) benzaldehyde
(c) benzoic acid (d) benzene sulphonyl chloride

12. In a chemical reaction $X \rightarrow Y$, it is found that the rate of reaction doubles when the concentration of X is increased four times. The order of the reaction with respect to X is
(a) 1 (b) 0 (c) 2 (d) $\frac{1}{2}$

13. Which of the following is the correct order of the acidity of the three compounds ?

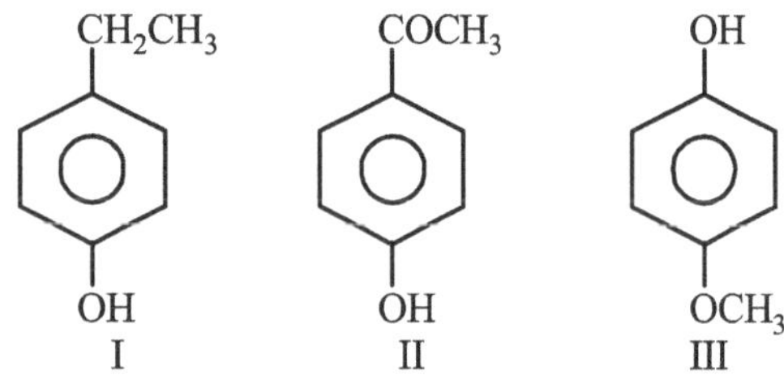

(a) II > III > I (b) III > II > I (c) II > I > III (d) III > I > II

14. Out of the following, the strongest base in aqueous solution is
(a) Methylamine (b) Dimethylamine
(c) Trimethylamine (d) Aniline

In the following questions (15-18) a statement of assertion followed by a statement of reason is given. Choose the correct answer out of the following choices.
(a) Both assertion and reason are correct statements, and reason is the correct explanation of the assertion.
(b) Both assertion and reason are correct statements, but reason is not the correct explanation of the assertion.
(c) Assertion is correct, but reason is wrong statement.
(d) Assertion is wrong, but reason is correct statement.

15. **Assertion:** If $\overset{\circ}{\lambda}_{Na^+}$ and $\overset{\circ}{\lambda}_{Cl^-}$ are molar limiting conductivity of sodium and chloride ions respectively, then the limiting molar conductivity for sodium chloride is given by the equation :

$$\overset{\circ}{\Lambda}_{NaCl} = \overset{\circ}{\lambda}_{Na^+} + \overset{\circ}{\lambda}_{Cl^-}$$

Reason: This is according to Kohlrausch law of independent migration of ions.

16. **Assertion :** The vapour pressure of a liquid decreases if some non-volatile solute is dissolved in it.
Reason : The relative lowering of vapour pressure of a solution containing a non-volatile solute is equal to the mole fraction of the solute in the solution.

17. **Assertion :** Disruption of the natural structure of a protein is called denaturation.
Reason : During denaturation secondary and tertiary structures are destroyed but primary structure remains intact.

18. **Assertion:** When 1M $CuSO_4$ (aq) solution is electrolysed using copper electrodes, copper is dissolved at anode and copper gets deposited at cathode.
Reason: The standard oxidation potential of copper is less than the standard oxidation potential of water and standard reduction potential of copper is greater than the standard reduction potential of water.

SECTION-B

This section contains 7 questions with internal choice in two questions. The following questions are very short answer type and carry 2 marks each.

19. What precautions are taken in preservation of chloroform?

20. Some complexes of Ni (II) are diamagnetic while some of others are paramagnetic. Justify.

21. How will you convert :
(a) Ethyl alcohol to n-propyl amine, (b) Phenol to benzoic acid, and

OR

Write the equation for the reaction of HI with the following:
(a) 1-Propoxypropane (b) Methoxybenzene

22. What happens when:
(a) $S_2O_3^{2-}$ is oxidised by MnO_4^- in neutral aqueous medium.
(b) Fe^{2+} is oxidised by $Cr_2O_7^{2-}$ in acidic medium.

23. (a) Why vapour pressure of a liquid is constant at constant temperature?
(b) 2 g each of the solutes A and B (mol. mass of A > B) are dissolved separately in 20 g each of the same solvent C. Which will show greater lowering of vapour pressure and why?

24. What are nucleotides? Name two classes of nitrogen containing bases found in nucleotide.

25. The conductivity of 0.02 M $AgNO_3$ at 25 °C is $2.428 \times 10^{-3}\ \Omega^{-1}\,cm^{-1}$. What is its molar conductivity?

OR

Conductivity of a solution is $6.23 \times 10^{-5}\ \Omega^{-1}\ cm^{-1}$ and its resistance is 13710 Ω. If the electrodes are 0.7 cm apart, calculate the cross-sectional area of the electrode.

SECTION-C

This section contains 5 questions with internal choice in two questions. The following questions are short answer type and carry 3 marks each.

26. Account for the following:
(a) Alcohols act as weak bases. (b) Ethanol has higher b.p. than methoxymethane.
(c) Explain why *o*-hydroxy benzaldehyde is a liquid at room temperature while *p*-hydroxy benzaldehyde is a high melting solid.

27. The density of 10% by mass of KCl solution is 1.06 g cm^{-3}. Calculate the molarity of the solution.

OR

If 2g each of solutes A and B (Molecular mass of A > B) are dissolved separately in 20 g each of the same solvent C. Which will show greater lowering of vapour pressure and why ?

28. (a) Give the appropriate term to describe the following:
(i) A molecule with a full positive charge and a full negative charge on different parts of the same molecule.
(ii) A compound formed by condensing together a number of amino acid molecules.
(iii) The change which occurs when a solution of a protein is heated.
(iv) The class of proteins to which keratin belongs.
(b) What does the letter 'D' before the name of a monosaccharide indicate?

29. Consider a cell composed of two half-cells:
(i) Cu(s), Cu^{2+} (aq), and (ii) Ag(s) / Ag^+ (aq).
Calculate
(a) the standard cell potential, and
(b) the cell potential when concentration of Cu^{2+} is 2M and concentration of Ag^+ is 0·05 M, at 298 K.

(Given: $E^\circ_{Cu^{2+}/Cu} = +0.34V$, $E^\circ_{Ag^+/Ag} = 0{\cdot}80\,V$, $R = 8{\cdot}314\ JK^{-1}\,mol^{-1}$, $F = 96500\ C\,mol^{-1}$)

30. A metal complex having composition $Cr(NH_3)_4Cl_2Br$ has been isolated in two forms **'A'** and **'B'**. The form **'A'** reacts with $AgNO_3$ to give a white precipitate readily soluble in dilute aqueous ammonia, whereas **'B'** gives a pale yellow precipitate soluble in concentrated ammonia. Write the formula of **'A'** and **'B'** and state the hybridization of chromium in each. Calculate their magnetic moments (spin only value).

OR

The oxidation state of Fe in both $[Fe(H_2O)_6]^{2+}$ and $[Fe(CN)_6]^{4-}$ is +2 and they are expected to exhibit same magnetic character. However the former has been found to be paramagnetic while the later has been found to be diamagnetic. Why?

SECTION-D

The following questions are case-based questions. Each question has an internal choice and carries 4 (1+1+2) marks each. Read the passage carefully and answer the questions that follow.

31. The conversion of an amide to an amine with one carbon atom less by the action of alkaline hypohalite is known as Hoffmann degradation.

$$RCONH_2 + Br_2 + 4KOH \longrightarrow RNH_2$$

The most important feature of the reaction is the rearrangement of N-bromamide anion to isocyanate :

$$R-\overset{O}{\overset{\|}{C}}-NH_2 \xrightarrow{Br_2} R-\overset{O}{\overset{\|}{C}}-NHBr \xrightarrow{OH^-} \underset{I}{R-\overset{O}{\overset{\|}{C}}-\ddot{\underset{\cdot\cdot}{N}}-Br} \longrightarrow \underset{II}{R-\overset{O}{\overset{\|}{C}}-N} \longrightarrow \underset{\text{Isocyanate, III}}{\overset{O}{\overset{\|}{C}}=N-R}$$

$$\xrightarrow{H_2O} H_2N-R + CO_2$$

Hoffmann reaction is accelerated if the migrating group is more electron-releasing.

Answer the following questions :

(a) What is the change in carbon chain during Hoffman reaction?

(b) Which type of amine is produced by Hoffman reaction?

(c) Mention the gas evolved along with amine in Hoffman reaction.

OR

Name one migrating group which will not accelerate Hoffman reaction.

32. Isopropyl bromide was treated separately with sodium tert-butoxide and sodium ethoxide under two different conditions.
Reaction I : Treatment of isopropyl bromide with sodium tert-butoxide at 40°C gave almost exclusively compound A.
Reaction - II : Treatement of isopropyl bromide with sodium ethoxide at 30°C yielded compound A along with small amount of an ether B ($C_5H_{12}O$).
Compound A was readily oxidized by a neutral solution of cold dilute potassium permangnate to give a brown precipitate.

Answer the following questions :

(a) Which type of reaction can be used to explain the formation of A.

(b) Compound A is

(c) What happened when product A is treated with cold and alkaline $KMnO_4$.

OR

What is the IUPAC name of the compound B.

SECTION-E

The following questions are long answer type and carry 5 marks each. Two questions have an internal choice.

33. (a) Consider the following data for the reaction :

$$A + B \longrightarrow \text{Products}$$

S.No	Initial concentration [A]	Initial concentration [B]	Initial rate (mol $L^{-1}s^{-1}$)
1	0.10 M	1.0 M	2.1×10^{-3}
2	0.20 M	1.0 M	8.4×10^{-3}
3	0.20 M	2.0 M	8.4×10^{-3}

Determine the order of reaction with respect to A and with respect to B and the overall order of the reaction.

(b) What is the rate of reaction and the order of reaction, if the mechanism is

$2NO + H_2 \longrightarrow N_2 + H_2O_2$ (Slow) $H_2O_2 + H_2 \longrightarrow 2H_2O$ (Fast)

OR

(a) A first order reaction is 20% complete in 20 minutes. Calculate the time it will take the reaction to complete 80%.

(b) What are pseudo unimolecular reactions? Give two examples.

34. (a) Explain Why?

(i) During the preparation of ammonia derivatives from aldehydes or ketones, pH of the reaction is carefully controlled.

(ii) Carboxylic acids do not form oximes.

(b) Write chemical equations to illustrate each of the following reactions:

(i) Gatterman – Koch reaction

(ii) Cannizzaro reaction

OR

(a) Formic acid reduces Tollen's reagent while other carboxylic acids do not. Justify.

(b) Why are boiling points of aldehydes and ketones lower than those of the corresponding acids?

(c) Why is benzoic acid a stronger acid than acetic acid?

(d) Give IUPAC names of the following:

(i) 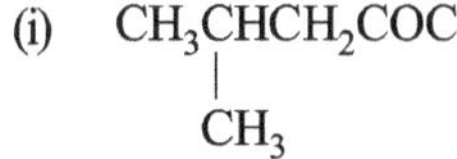

(ii) 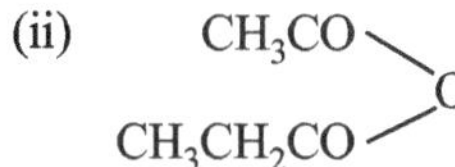

35. (a) Complete the following :

(i) Why do *d*-block elements have greater tendency to form complexes that *f*-block elements?

(ii) Name the element which finds use in X-ray tube.

(b) Explain why?

(i) *d*-Block elements have greater tendency to form complexes than *f*-block elements.

(ii) As compared to other transition elements Zn, Cd and Hg have very low melting point.

5 Sample Paper

LATEST PATTERN

BLUE PRINT

S. No.	Chapter Name	Section-A (MCQs & A/R) 1 Mark		Section-B (VSA) 2 Marks		Section-C (SA) 3 Marks		Section-D (Case Study) 4 Marks		Section-E (LA) 5 Marks		Total Marks
		Q. No.	Marks	Q. No.	Marks	Q. No.	Marks	Q. No.	Marks	Q. No.	Marks	
1	Solutions	3, 9	2	20	2	28	3					**7**
2	Electrochemistry	1, 7, 15	3	22	2	29	3					**8**
3	Chemical Kinetics	10	1	23	2			31	4			**7**
4	d -and f -Block Elements	4, 14	2			26. a	1			34	5	**8**
5	Coordination Compounds	5, 17	2	21	2	26. b, c	2					**6**
6	Haloalkanes and Haloarenes	6, 18	2			27. a	1	32	4			**7**
7	Alcohols, Phenols and Ethers	12	1							33	5	**6**
8	Aldehydes, Ketones and Carboxylic Acids	13	1			27. b, c	2			35	5	**8**
9	Amines	16	1	24	2	30	3					**6**
10	Biomolecules	2, 8, 11	3	19, 25	4							**7**
	Total Marks (Total Questions)	**18**	**18**	**7**	**14**	**5**	**15**	**2**	**8**	**3**	**15**	**70**

Time : 3 Hours **Max. Marks : 70**

General Instructions

Read the following instructions carefully

(a) *There are 35 questions in this question paper with internal choice.*

(b) *SECTION A consists of 18 multiple-choice questions carrying 1 mark each.*

(c) *SECTION B consists of 7 very short answer questions carrying 2 marks each.*

(d) *SECTION C consists of 5 short answer questions carrying 3 marks each.*

(e) *SECTION D consists of 2 case- based questions carrying 4 marks each.*

(f) *SECTION E consists of 3 long answer questions carrying 5 marks each.*

(g) ***All questions are compulsory.***

(h) ***Use of log tables and calculator are not allowed.***

SECTION-A

The following questions are multiple-choice questions with one correct answer. Each question carries 1 mark. There is no internal choice in this section.

1. Effect of dilution on conductivity of solution:

(a) Increases (b) Decreases (c) Unchanged (d) None of these

2. Primary structure of a protein is

(a) sequence in which α-amino acids are linked to one another

(b) sequence in which amino acids of one polypeptide chain are joined to other chain

(c) the folding patterns of polypeptide chains

(d) the pattern in which the polypeptide chains are arranged

3. A solution of sucrose (molar mass = 342 g mol^{-1}) has been prepared by dissolving 68.5 g of sucrose in 1000 g of water. The freezing point of the solution obtained will be

(K_f for water = 1.86 K kg mol^{-1}).

(a) – 0.372°C (b) – 0.520°C (d) + 0.372°C (d) – 0.570°C

4. Out of the following transition elements, the maximum number of oxidation states are shown by

(a) Sc(Z = 21) (b) Cr(Z = 24) (c) Mn(Z = 25) (d) Fe(Z = 26)

5. Which of the following will give a white precipitate upon reacting with $AgNO_3$?

(a) $K_2[Pt(en)_2Cl_2]$ (b) $[Co[Pt(NH_3)Cl_3]$ (c) $[Cr[Pt(H_2OH)_6]Cl_3$ (d) $[Fe(H_2O_3)Cl_3]$

6. Aryl halides can not be prepared by the reaction of aryl alcohols with PCl_3, PCl_5 or $SOCl_2$ because

(a) phenols are highly stable compounds.

(b) carbon-oxygen bond in phenols has a partial double bond character.

(c) carbon-oxygen bond is highly polar

(d) all of these

7. Kohlrausch gave the following relation for strong electrolytes:

$$\wedge = \wedge_0 - A\sqrt{C}$$

Which of the following equality holds?

(a) $\wedge = \wedge_0$ as $C \to \sqrt{A}$ (b) $\wedge = \wedge_0$ as $C \to \infty$ (c) $\wedge = \wedge_0$ as $C \to 0$ (d) $\wedge = \wedge_0$ as $C \to 1$

8. Three cyclic structures of monosaccharides are given below which of these are anomers.

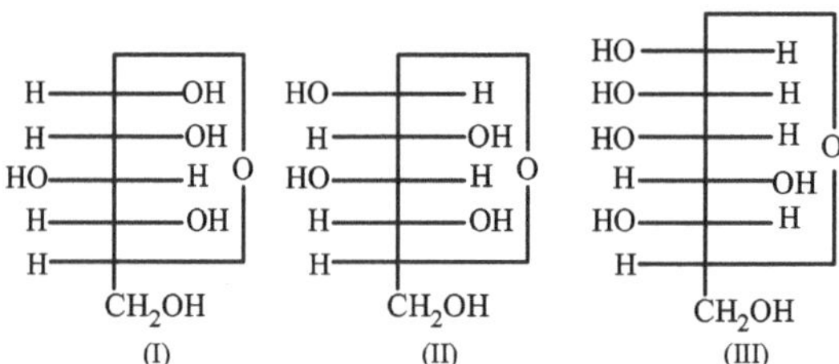

(a) I and II (b) II and III (c) I and III (d) III is anomer of I and II

***FOR VISUALLY CHALLANGED LEARNERS**

*8. The two forms of D–glucopyranose obtained from the solution of D-glucose are better called

(a) isomers (b) anomers (c) epimers (d) enantiomers

9. Molarity of H_2SO_4 is 18 M. Its density is 1.8 g/mL. Hence molality is

(a) 36 (b) 200 (c) 500 (d) 18

10. In a zero-order reaction for every 10° rise of temperature, the rate is doubled. If the temperature is increased from 10°C to 100°C, the rate of the reaction will become :

(a) 256 times (b) 512 times (c) 64 times (d) 128 times

11. DNA and RNA contain four bases each. Which of the following bases is not present in RNA?

(a) Adenine (b) Uracil (c) Thymine (d) Cytosine

12. An aromatic ether is not cleaved by HI even at 525 K. The compound is

(a) $C_6H_5OCH_3$ (b) $C_6H_5OC_6H_5$ (c) $C_6H_5OC_3H_7$ (d) Tetrahydrofuran

13. 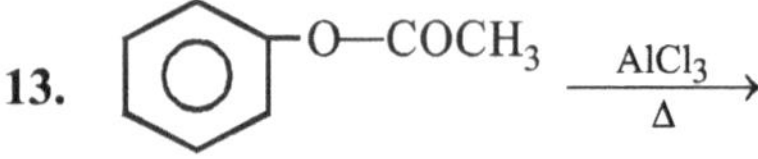

The product obtained is/are

(a) *o*-product (b) *m*-product (c) *o*- and *p*-products (d) *o*-, *m*- and *p*-products

***FOR VISUALLY CHALLANGED LEARNERS.**

*13. Benzoic acid is treated with lithium aluminium hydride. The compound obtained is

(a) benzaldehyde (b) benzyl alcohol (c) toluene (d) benzene

14. Which of the following ions has the maximum magnetic moment?

(a) Mn^{2+} (b) Fe^{2+} (c) Ti^{2+} (d) Cr^{2+}

In the following questions (15-18) a statement of assertion followed by a statement of reason is given. Choose the correct answer out of the following choices.

(a) Both assertion and reason are correct statements, and reason is the correct explanation of the assertion.

(b) Both assertion and reason are correct statements, but reason is not the correct explanation of the assertion.

(c) Assertion is correct, but reason is wrong statement.

(d) Assertion is wrong, but reason is correct statement.

15. **Assertion :** Conductivity of an electrolyte increases with decrease in concentration.

Reason : Number of ions per unit volume decreases on dilution.

16. **Assertion:** Aniline is better nucleophile than anilium ion.

Reason: Anilium ion have positive charge.

17. **Assertion:** The $[Ni(en)_3]Cl_2$ (en = ethylenediamine) has lower stability than $[Ni(NH_3)_6]Cl_2$.

Reason: In $[Ni(en)_3]Cl_2$, the geometry of Ni is trigonal bipyramidal.

18. **Assertion:** Aryl halides undergo nucleophilic substitution with ease.

Reason: Carbon-halogen bond in aryl halides have partial double bond character.

SECTION-B

This section contains 7 questions with internal choice in two questions. The following questions are very short answer type and carry 2 marks each.

19. Write down the structures and names of the products obtained when D–glucose is treated with

(i) acetic anhydride (ii) hydrocyanic acid

20. An aqueous solution freezes at 272.07 K while pure water freezes at 273 K. Determine the molality and boiling point of the solution. Given $K_f = 1.86$ K/m; $K_b = 0.512$ K/m.

OR

What is molarity of the resulting solution obtained by mixing 2.5 L of 0.5 M urea solution and 500 mL of 2M urea solution ?

21. Square planar complexes with coordination number of four exhibit geometrical isomerism whereas tetrahedral complexes do not why?

OR

Arrange the following complexes in order of increasing electrical conductivity:

$[Co(NH_3)_3Cl_3]$, $[Co(NH_3)_5Cl]Cl_2$, $[Co(NH_3)_6]Cl_3$, $[Co(NH_3)_4Cl_2]Cl$.

22. Why is there a steep rise in the molar conductivity of a weak electrolyte when its concentration becomes very low?

23. Following reaction takes place in one step :

$$2NO(g) + O_2(g) \rightleftharpoons 2NO_2(g)$$

How will be the rate of the above reaction change if the volume of the reaction vessel is diminished to one-third of its original volume? Will there be any change in the order of the reaction with reduced volume?

24. Describe the following giving the relevant chemical equation in each case.

(i) Carbylamine reaction

(ii) Hoffmann's bromamide reaction

25. Why does glucose reacts with Fehling's solution and phenyl hydrazine, but not with $NaHSO_3$?

SECTION-C

This section contains 5 questions with internal choice in two questions. The following questions are short answer type and carry 3 marks each.

26. (a) For some of first row transition elements, the E° values are for (M^{2+}/M)

V	Cr	Mn	Fe	Co	Ni	Cu
−1·18 V	−0·91V	−1·18V	0·44V	−0·28V	−0·25V	+0·34V

Give suitable explanation for the irregular trend in these values.

Give suitable reasons for following statements:

(b) Two complexes of nickel $[Ni(CN)_4]^{2-}$ and $[Ni(CO)_4]$ have different structures but do not differ in magnetic behaviour.

(c) Square planar complexes of MX_2L_2 type with co-ordination number of 4 exhibit geometrical isomerism while tetrahedral complexes with similar composition do not.

27. (a) Which compound in the following pair will react fast with regard to S_N2 reaction and why?

Cl (2-chlorobutane skeletal structure) or (1-chlorobutane skeletal structure) Cl

You are provided with four reagents:

Fehling solution$_4$, I_2/NaOH, $NaHSO_3$ and Schiff's reagent. Write which two reagents can be used to distinguish between the compounds in each of the following pairs:

(b) CH_3CHO and C_6H_5CHO

(c) $C_6H_5COCH_3$ and $C_6H_5COC_6H_5$

28. A 0.01 m aqueous solution of $AlCl_3$ freezes at –0.068 °C. Calculate the percentage of dissociation.
[Given: K_f for water = 1.86 K kg mol^{-1}]

29. (a) Calculate the *e.m.f.* of the cell in which the reaction is ;

$$Mg(s) + 2Ag^+(aq) \longrightarrow Mg^{2+}(aq) + 2Ag(s)$$

when $[Mg^{2+}] = 0.130$ M and $[Ag^+] = 1.0 \times 10^{-4}$ M. Given $E^\circ_{Mg^{2+}/Mg} = -2.37$ V and $E^\circ_{Ag^+/Ag} = +0.80$ V

(b) Calculate cell potential at 25°C.
[Given: $E^\circ_{Zn^{2+}|Zn} = -0.76$ V; $E^\circ_{Cu^{2+}|Cu} = +0.34$ V]

OR

For the cell: $Zn(s) | Zn^{2+}(2\,M) || Cu^{2+}(0.5\,M) | Cu(s)$
(a) Write equation for each half-reaction
(b) Calculate cell potential at 25°C.
[Given: $E^\circ_{Zn^{2+}|Zn} = -0.76$ V; $E^\circ_{Cu^{2+}|Cu} = +0.34$ V]

30. Give reasons: **(Any 3)**:
(a) Aniline does not undergo Friedal-Craft's reaction.
(b) Aromatic primary amines cannot be prepared by Gabriel phthalimide synthesis.
(c) Aliphatic amines are stronger bases than ammonia.
(d) Aqueous solution of diazonium salts are good conductors.

SECTION-D

The following questions are case-based questions. Each question has an internal choice and carries 4 (1+1+2) marks each. Read the passage carefully and answer the questions that follow.

31. Several techniques have been developed to determine the order of reaction. The rate of a reaction cannot be predicted on the basis of the overall equation, but it can be predicted on the basis of the rate-determining step. For instance, the following reaction can be broken down into three steps.

$$A + D \xrightarrow{k} F + G \qquad \text{(Reaction - 1)}$$

Step - 1 : $A \xrightarrow{k_1} B + C$ (slow)

Step - 2 : $B + D \xrightarrow{k_2} E + F$ (fast)

Step - 3 : $E + C \xrightarrow{k_3} G$ (fast)

In this case, the first step in the reaction pathway is the rate-determining step. Therefore, the overall rate of the reaction must be equal to the rate of the first step, $k_1[A]$ where k's are the rate constants of different steps.

In some cases, it is desirable to measure the rate of a reaction in relation to only one species. In a second-order reaction involving two reacting substances for instance, a large excess of one substance is included in the reaction vessel. Since a relatively small amount of this large concentration is reacted, we assume that the concentration or this substance essentially remains unchanged. Such a reaction is called a pseudo first-order reaction. A new rate constant, K', is established, equal to the product of the rate constant of the original reaction, k, and the concentration of the species in excess.

Answer the following questions :
(a) What is the molecularity of the Reaction - 1?
(b) What is the differential rate law of reaction -1?
(c) Which is the rate determining step of the reaction-1?
(d) What is the molecularity of a pseudo first order reaction?

OR

For the reaction, $2N_2O_5 \longrightarrow 4NO_2 + O_2$ What is the differential rate laws with respect to all the species imvohed in the reaction?

32. The substitution reaction of alkyl halide mainly occurs by S_N1 or S_N2 mechanism. Whatever mechanism alkyl halides follow for the substitution reaction to occur, the polarity of the carbon halogen bond is responsible for these substitution reactions. The rate of S_N1 reactions are governed by the stability of carbocation whereas for S_N2 reactions steric factor is the deciding factor. If the starting material is a chiral compound, we may end up with an inverted product or racemic mixture depending upon the type of mechanism followed by alkyl halide. Cleavage of ethers with HI is also governed by steric factor and stability of carbocation, which indicates that in organic chemistry, these two major factors help us in deciding the kind of product formed.

Answer the following questions :

(a) Predict the stereochemistry of the product formed if an optically active alkyl halide undergoes substitution reaction by S_N1 mechanism.

(b) Name the instrument used for measuring the angle by which the plane polarised light is rotated.

(c) Give one use of CHI_3.

(d) Predict the major product formed when 2-bromopentane reacts with alcoholic KOH.

OR

Write the structures of the products formed when anisole is treated with HI.

SECTION-E

The following questions are long answer type and carry 5 marks each. Two questions have an internal choice.

33. (a) How do you convert the following:

(i) Phenol to Anisole

(ii) Ethanol to Propan-2-ol

(b) Write mechanism of the following reaction:

$$C_2H_5OH \xrightarrow[443K]{H_2SO_4} CH_2=CH_2+H_2O$$

(c) Why phenol undergoes electrophilic substitution more easily than benzene?

OR

(a) Account for the following:

(i) o-nitrophenol is more steam volatile than p-nitrophenol.

(ii) t-butyl chloride on heating with sodium methoxide gives 2-methylpropene instead of t-butylmethylether.

(b) Write the reaction involved in the following:

(i) Reimer-Tiemann reaction

(ii) Friedal-Crafts Alkylation of Phenol

(c) Give simple chemical test to distinguish between Ethanol and Phenol.

34. Explain the following:

(a) Why are Zn, Cd and Hg not considered transition metals?

(b) Why are the compounds of transition metals generally coloured?

(c) Why do Zr and Hf exhibit almost similar properties?

(d) What is the basic difference in electronic configuration of lanthanides and those of actinides?

(e) The first ionisation energies of elements of first transition series do not vary much with increasing atomic number.

OR

(a) Ce (III) can be easily oxidised to Ce (IV). Explain, why.

(b) What is meant by lanthanoid contraction? What effect does it have on the chemistry of the elements which follow lanthanoids?

35. How will you prepare :

(a) Propiophenone from propanenitrile

(b) 4-Chlorobenzaldehyde from 4-chlorotoluene

(c) Cyclohexanecarbaldehyde from cyclohexylmethanol

(d) 4-Methoxyacetophenone from anisole

(e) 4-Methylbenzaldehyde from toluene

6 Sample Paper

LATEST PATTERN

BLUE PRINT

S. No.	Chapter Name	Section-A		Section-B		Section-C		Section-D		Section-E		Total Marks
		(MCQs & A/R) 1 Mark		(VSA) 2 Marks		(SA) 3 Marks		(Case Study) 4 Marks		(LA) 5 Marks		
		Q. No.	Marks	Q. No.	Marks	Q. No.	Marks	Q. No.	Marks	Q. No.	Marks	
1	Solutions	1, 15	2	25	2	27	3					**7**
2	Electrochemistry	5	1	21	2					35	5	**8**
3	Chemical Kinetics	10, 16	2	22	2	28	3					**7**
4	d -and f -Block Elements	6	1	23	2					34	5	**8**
5	Coordination Compounds	2, 17	2					32	4			**6**
6	Haloalkanes and Haloarenes	7, 11	2	19	2	26	3					**7**
7	Alcohols, Phenols and Ethers	3, 12	2	20	2	29. a, b	2					**6**
8	Aldehydes, Ketones and Carboxylic Acids	4, 14, 18	3	24	2	30	3					**8**
9	Amines	8	1							33	5	**6**
10	Biomolecules	9, 13	2			29. c, d	1	31	4			**7**
	Total Marks (Total Questions)	**18**	**18**	**7**	**14**	**5**	**15**	**2**	**8**	**3**	**15**	**70**

Time : 3 Hours **Max. Marks : 70**

General Instructions

Read the following instructions carefully

(a) *There are 35 questions in this question paper with internal choice.*

(b) *SECTION A consists of 18 multiple-choice questions carrying 1 mark each.*

(c) *SECTION B consists of 7 very short answer questions carrying 2 marks each.*

(d) *SECTION C consists of 5 short answer questions carrying 3 marks each.*

(e) *SECTION D consists of 2 case- based questions carrying 4 marks each.*

(f) *SECTION E consists of 3 long answer questions carrying 5 marks each.*

(g) ***All questions are compulsory.***

(h) ***Use of log tables and calculator are not allowed.***

SECTION-A

The following questions are multiple-choice questions with one correct answer. Each question carries 1 mark. There is no internal choice in this section.

1. Which of the following factor do not affect solubility of solid solute in liquid?

(a) Temperature (b) Pressure (c) Nature of solute (d) All of these

2. In which of the following pairs both the complexes show optical isomerism?

(a) *cis*-$[Cr(C_2O_4)_2Cl_2]^{3-}$, *cis*- $[Co(NH_3)_4Cl_2]$ (b) $[Co(en)_3]Cl_3$, *cis*-$[Co(en)_2Cl_2]Cl$

(c) $[PtCl(dien)]Cl$, $[NiCl_2Br_2]^{2-}$ (d) $[Co(NO_3)_3(NH_3)_3]$, *cis*-$[Pt(en)_2Cl_2]$

3. Mark the correct order of decreasing acid strength of the following compounds.

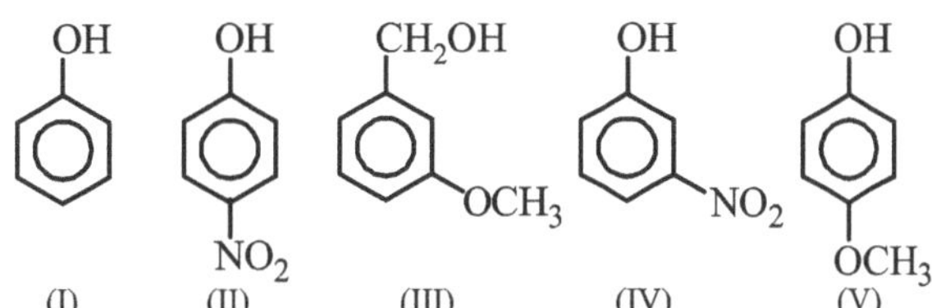

(a) V > IV > II > I > III (b) II > IV > I > III > V (c) IV > V > III > II > I (d) V > IV > III > II > I

4. CH_3COCH_3 can be converted to $CH_3CH_2CH_3$ by the action of

(a) HIO_3 (b) HNO_3 (c) HI (d) H_3PO_3

5. Standard electrode potential of three metals *X*, *Y* and *Z* are – 1.2 V, + 0.5 V and – 3.0 V, respectively. The reducing power of these metals will be :

(a) $Y > Z > X$ (b) $X > Y > Z$ (c) $Z > X > Y$ (d) $X > Y > Z$

6. The electronic configuration of Pt (atomic number 78) is:

(a) $[Xe]\,4f^{14}\,5d^9\,6s^1$ (b) $[Kr]\,4f^{14}\,5d^{10}$ (c) $[Xe]\,4f^{14}\,5d^{10}$ (d) $[Xe]\,4f^{14}\,5d^8\,6s^2$

7. Which one of the following is not an allylic halide?

(a) 4-Bromopent-2-ene (b) 3-Bromo-2-methylbut-1-ene

(c) 1-Bromobut-2-ene (d) 4-Bromobut-1-ene

8. Arrange the following compounds in order of increasing basic strength. (weakest → strongest)

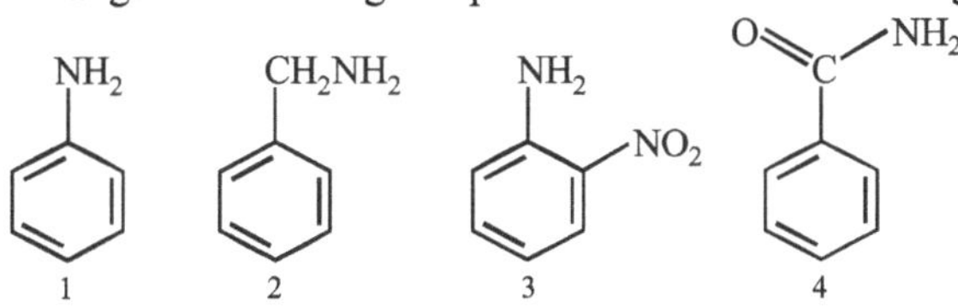

(a) 4 < 2 < 1 < 3 (b) 4 < 3 < 1 < 2 (c) 4 < 1 < 3 < 2 (d) 2 < 1 < 3 < 4

9. Which is the least stable form of glucose ?
(a) α-D-Glucose (b) β-D-Glucose (c) Open chain structure (d) All are equally stable

10. The rate of the reaction $2N_2O_5 \rightarrow 4NO_2 + O_2$ can be written in three ways :
$$\frac{-d[N_2O_5]}{dt} = k[N_2O_5]; \frac{d[NO_2]}{dt} = k'[N_2O_5]$$
$$\frac{d[O_2]}{dt} = k''[N_2O_5]$$
The relationship between k and k' and between k and k'' are:
(a) $k' = 2k ; k' = k$ (b) $k' = 2k ; k'' = k/2$ (c) $k' = 2k ; k'' = 2k$ (d) $k' = k ; k'' = k$

11. The total number of acyclic isomers including the stereoisomers with the molecular formula C_4H_7Cl
(a) 11 (b) 12 (c) 9 (d) 10

12. Consider the reactions :
(i) $(CH_3)_2CH-CH_2Br \xrightarrow{C_2H_5OH} (CH_3)_2CH-CH_2OC_2H_5 + HBr$
(ii) $(CH_3)_2CH-CH_2Br \xrightarrow{C_2H_5O^-} (CH_3)_2CH-CH_2OC_2H_5 + Br^-$
The mechanisms of reactions (i) and (ii) are respectively:
(a) S_N1 and S_N2 (b) S_N1 and S_N1 (c) S_N2 and S_N2 (d) S_N2 and S_N1

13. α-Amino acids are
(a) acidic due to –COOH group and basic due to $-NH_2$ group
(b) acidic due to $-NH_3^+$ group and basic due to $-COO^-$ group.
(c) neither acidic nor basic.
(d) none is true.

14. The intermediate formed in aldol condensation is
(a) aldol (b) carbanion (c) alcohol (d) α-hydrogen ester

In the following questions (15-18) a statement of assertion followed by a statement of reason is given. Choose the correct answer out of the following choices.
(a) Both assertion and reason are correct statements, and reason is the correct explanation of the assertion.
(b) Both assertion and reason are correct statements, but reason is not the correct explanation of the assertion.
(c) Assertion is correct, but reason is wrong statement.
(d) Assertion is wrong, but reason is correct statement.

15. **Assertion :** A non volatile solute is added in liquid solvent then freezing point of mixture decreases.
Reason : Vapour pressure decreases by addition of non volatile solute, so equilibrium point where V.P. of solid and V.P. of liquid are equal can reach at lower temperature.

16. **Assertion :** The kinetics of the reaction $mA + nB + pC \longrightarrow m'X + n'Y + p'Z$
obey the rate expression as $\frac{dX}{dt} = k[A]^m[B]^n$.
Reason : The rate of the reaction does not depend upon the concentration of *C*.

17. **Assertion :** $[Ni(CO)_4]$ has square planar geometry while $[Ni(CN)_4]^{2-}$ has tetrahedral geometry.
Reason : Geometry of any complex does not depend upon the nature of ligands attached.

18. **Assertion:** 2, 2-dimethylpropanal undergoes Cannizzaro reaction with conc. NaOH.
Reason: Cannizzaro reaction is a disproportionation reaction.

SECTION-B

This section contains 7 questions with internal choice in two questions. The following questions are very short answer type and carry 2 marks each.

19. Which compound in the following pair will react fast with regard to S_N2 reaction and why?
(cyclohexyl)$-CH_2Cl$ or (cyclohexyl)$-Cl$

20. Account for the following:
(a) Phenol is more acidic than ethanol.
(b) *m*-Aminophenol is a stronger acid than *o*-aminophenol.

21. The conductivity of 0.001M acetic acid is 7.8×10^{-5} S cm^{-1}. Calculate its degree of dissociation of $\Lambda°m$ for acetic acid is 390 S cm^2 mol^{-1}.

22. (a) A reaction, $P + Q \longrightarrow$ products, has rate law equation, rate = $k\,[P]^{1/3}\,[Q]^3$. Suggest the suitable changes in initial concentration of P and Q so as to make the initial rate 16 times.
(b) Write the rate equation for the reaction $2A + B \longrightarrow C$, if the order of the reaction is zero.

23. Explain the following giving reasons :
(a) It is difficult to separate lanthanoid elements in pure state.
(b) The transition elements form interstitial compounds.

OR

Explain, why?
(a) Ce^{4+} is used as an oxidising agent in volumetric analysis.
(b) Zn^{2+} salts are white while Cu^{2+} salts are blue.

24. Name the reagents A, B and C in the following sequence of reactions:

$$CH_3CHO \xrightarrow{A} CH_3COOH \xrightarrow{B} CH_3COCl \xrightarrow{C} \begin{matrix} CH_3CO \\ \quad\quad\; O \\ CH_3CO \end{matrix}$$

25. Why is the vapour pressure of an aqueous solution of glucose lower than that of water?

OR

At 100°C the vapour pressure of a solution of 6.5g of a solute in 100 g water is 732 mm. If $K_b = 0.52$, what will be the boiling point of this solution?

SECTION-C

This section contains 5 questions with internal choice in two questions. The following questions are short answer type and carry 3 marks each.

26. A chloro derivative (A) on treatment with zinc copper couple gives a hydrocarbon with five carbon atoms. When A is dissolved in ether and treated with sodium 2, 2, 5, 5-tetramethyl hexane is formed. What is the formula of the compound A?

27. Calculate the mass of ascorbic acid (Molar mass = 176 g mol^{-1}) to be dissolved in 75 g of acetic acid, to lower its freezing point by 1.5°C. (k_f = 3.9 K kg mol^{-1})

28. The following rate data were obtained at 300 K for the reaction :
$2A + B \longrightarrow C + D$

Exp. No.	[A] (mol/L)	[B] (mol/L)	Rate of formation of D (mol / L / min)
1	0.1	0.1	6×10^{-3}
2	0.3	0.2	7.2×10^{-2}
3	0.3	0.4	2.88×10^{-1}
4	0.4	0.1	2.40×10^{-2}

Determine the rate law, order and rate constant for reaction.

29. Give explanation for **any 3** of the following:
(a) Arrange the following compound in decreasing order of boiling point and account for the order:
Pentan-1-ol, 2-methylbutan-2-ol, 3-methylbutane-2-ol
(b) Arrange the following compounds in increasing order of reactivity with Lucas Reagent at room temperature:
Butan-1-ol, Butan-2-ol, 2-Methyl-2-propanol.
(c) What is mutarotation?
(d) What is meant by inversion of sugar?

30. An organic compound (A), which has a characteristic odour, on treatment with NaOH gives two compound (B) and (C). Compound (A) has molecular formula C_7H_8O which on oxidation gives back compound (C). Compound (C) is the sodium salt of an acid. Compound (C) when heated with soda lime yields an aromatic hydrocarbon (D). Deduce the structures of (A), (B), (C) and (D).

OR

A compound A of molecular formula, C_4H_9Br, yields a compound B of molecular formula $C_4H_{10}O$ when treated with aqueous NaOH. On oxidation, the compound B yields a ketone C. Vigorous oxidation of the ketone yields a mixture of ethanoic and propanoic acids. Deduce the structures of A, B and C.

SECTION-D

The following questions are case-based questions. Each question has an internal choice and carries 4 (1+1+2) marks each. Read the passage carefully and answer the questions that follow.

31. Amino acids contain an $-NH_2$ (basic) as well as a $-COOH$ (acidic) group. They exist as zwitter ions

$$H_2N-\underset{\displaystyle R}{\overset{|}{C}}H-COOH \qquad H_3\overset{+}{N}-\underset{\displaystyle R}{\overset{|}{C}}H-COO^-$$

(General Structure) (Zwitter ion)

which explain their several characteristic properties, like decomposition on heating, solubility in water and large dipole moment.

Thus in solution, amino acids may exist as dipolar (neutral pH), cation (in strongly acidic solution), or anion (in strongly basic solution).

Amino acids undergo usual reactions of the $-COOH$ group as well as $-NH_2$ group.

Answer the following questions:

(a) Which basic group is present in amino acid?

(b) What is the existing form of amino acid in strongly basic medium?

(c) What is zwitter ion?

(d) Explain the polar nature of amino acids.

OR

Write the name and structure of the simplest amino acid.

32. The ions or molecules bound to the central atom in the coordination entity are called ligands. These may be simple ions, small molecules or may be large molecules. Ligands can be classified into catagories such as unidentate, bidentate, polydentate ligand which depends upon the number of donor atoms of the ligand. i.e., when a ligand is bound to a metal ion through a single donor atom as with NH_3, the ligand is said to be unidentate. Similarly oxalate is a bidentate ligand since it can bind through two donor atoms, when several donor atoms are present in a single ligand as in $N(CH_2CH_2NH_2)_3$, the ligand is said to be polydentate. when a di or polydentate ligand used its two or more donor atom simultaneously to bind a single metal ion, it is said to be chelate ligand.

Answer the following questions :

(a) What are the donor atoms of oxalate ion, ethylene diamine, thiocyanate ion, nitrate ion? Describe with structures

(b) Categorise the ligands: Oxalate, Ethylene diamine, thiocyanate and nitrate ion.

OR

What is the d-electron configuration of an octahedral complex in low spin and high spin cases for d^6 system?

SECTION-E

The following questions are long answer type and carry 5 marks each. Two questions have an internal choice.

33. (a) Synthesise benzylamine by

(i) Hofmann degradation; (ii) Alkyl halideamination; (iii) Gabriel method

(b) Account for the fact that before nitration, aniline is converted to acetanilide.

(c) Account for the fact that it is difficult to prepare pure amines by ammonolysis of alkyl halides.

34. (a) For M^{2+}/M and M^{3+}/M^{2+} systems, the E° values of some metals are given :

$Cr^{2+}/Cr = +0.9\,V$; $Cr^{3+}/Cr^{2+} = -0.4\,V$

$Mn^{2+}/Mn = +1.2\,V$; $Mn^{3+}/Mn^{2+} = +1.5\,V$

$Fe^{2+}/Fe = +0.4\,V$; $Fe^{3+}/Fe^{2+} = +0.8\,V$.

Use this data to comment upon :

(i) The stability of Fe^{3+} in acid solution as compared to that of Cr^{3+} or Mn^{3+}.

(ii) The ease with which iron can be oxidised to its divalent state as compared to the similar process for either chromium or manganese metal.

(b) (i) Of the ions, Ag^{1+}, Co^{2+} and Ti^{4+} which one will be coloured in aqueous solutions? (Ag (Z = 47), Co (Z = 27, Ti (Z = 22))

(ii) If each one of the above ionic species is in turn placed in a magnetic field, then how will it respond and why?

OR

On the basis of Lanthanoid contraction, explain the following:

(a) Nature of bonding in La_2O_3 and Lu_2O_3.

(b) Trends in the stability of oxo salts of lanthanoids from La to Lu.

(c) Stability of the complexes of lanthanoids.

(d) Radii of 4*d* and 5*d* block elements.

(e) Trends in acidic character of lanthanoid oxides.

35. (a) Calculate $\Delta G°$ for the reaction

$Zn(s) + Cu^{2+}(aq)\ Zn^{2+}(aq) + Cu(s)$

Given: E° for $Zn^{2+}/Zn = -0.76$ V and E° for $Cu^{2+}/Cu = +0.34$ V

$R = 8.314\ JK^{-1}\ mol^{-1}$; $F = 96500\ C\ mol^{-1}$

(b) Give two advantages of fuel cells.

OR

(a) Out of the following pairs, predict with reason which pair will allow greater conduction of electricity:

(i) Silver wire at 30°C or silver wire at 60°C.

(ii) 0.1 M CH_3COOH solution or 1 M CH_3COOH solution.

(iii) KCl solution at 20°C or KCl solution at 50°C.

(b) Give two points of differences between electro chemical and electrolytic cells.

7 Sample Paper

LATEST PATTERN

BLUE PRINT

S. No.	Chapter Name	Section-A		Section-B		Section-C		Section-D		Section-E		Total Marks
		(MCQs & A/R) 1 Mark		(VSA) 2 Marks		(SA) 3 Marks		(Case Study) 4 Marks		(LA) 5 Marks		
		Q. No.	Marks	Q. No.	Marks	Q. No.	Marks	Q. No.	Marks	Q. No.	Marks	
1	Solutions	5, 8	2							33	5	**7**
2	Electrochemistry	2, 13, 16	3	20	2	27	3					**8**
3	Chemical Kinetics	6, 17	2	24	2	30	3					**7**
4	d -and f -Block Elements	10	1	19	2					35	5	**8**
5	Coordination Compounds			25	2			32	4			**6**
6	Haloalkanes and Haloarenes	3, 9	2			26. a	1	31	4			**7**
7	Alcohols, Phenols and Ethers	4, 11	2	21	2	26. b, c	2					**6**
8	Aldehydes, Ketones and Carboxylic Acids	1, 15, 18	3							34	5	**8**
9	Amines	14	1	22	2	28	3					**6**
10	Biomolecules	7, 12	2	23	2	29	3					**7**
	Total Marks (Total Questions)	**18**	**18**	**7**	**14**	**5**	**15**	**2**	**8**	**3**	**15**	**70**

Time : 3 Hours **Max. Marks : 70**

General Instructions

Read the following instructions carefully

(a) *There are 35 questions in this question paper with internal choice.*

(b) *SECTION A consists of 18 multiple-choice questions carrying 1 mark each.*

(c) *SECTION B consists of 7 very short answer questions carrying 2 marks each.*

(d) *SECTION C consists of 5 short answer questions carrying 3 marks each.*

(e) *SECTION D consists of 2 case- based questions carrying 4 marks each.*

(f) *SECTION E consists of 3 long answer questions carrying 5 marks each.*

(g) ***All questions are compulsory.***

(h) ***Use of log tables and calculator are not allowed.***

SECTION-A

The following questions are multiple-choice questions with one correct answer. Each question carries 1 mark. There is no internal choice in this section.

1. Acetaldehyde does not respond to

(a) Tollen's test (b) Benedict's test (c) Lucas test (d) Iodoform test

2. The chemical reaction,

$2AgCl(s) + H_2(g) \longrightarrow 2HCl(aq) + 2Ag(s)$

taking place in a galvanic cell is represented by the notation

(a) $Pt(s) | H_2(g), 1\ bar | 1M\,KCl(aq) | AgCl(s) | Ag(s)$

(b) $Pt(s) | H_2(g), 1\ bar | 1M\,HCl(aq) | 1M\,Ag^+(aq) | Ag(s)$

(c) $Pt(s) | H_2(g), 1\ bar | 1M\,HCl(aq) | AgCl(s) | Ag(s)$

(d) $Pt(s) | H_2(g), 1\ bar | 1M\,HCl(aq) | Ag(s) | AgCl(s)$

3. The structure of the major product formed in the following reaction

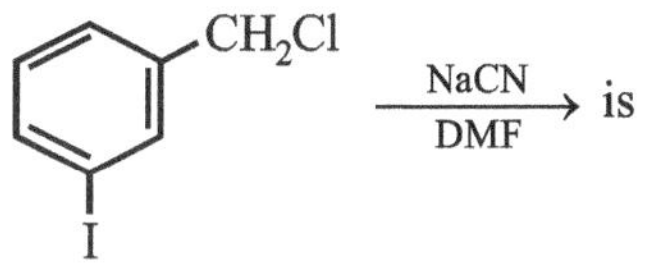

(benzene ring with CH_2Cl and I) $\xrightarrow[DMF]{NaCN}$ is

(a) 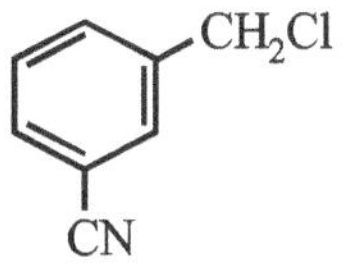 (benzene ring with CH_2Cl and CN)

(b) 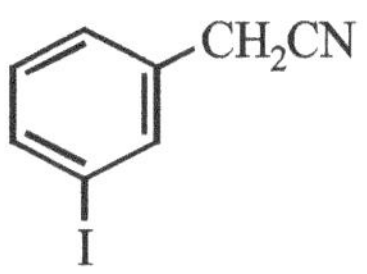 (benzene ring with CH_2CN and I)

(c) 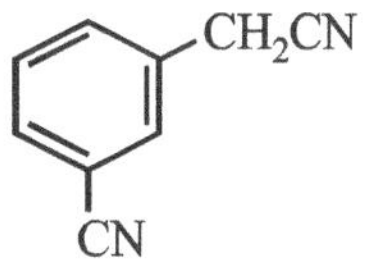 (benzene ring with CH_2CN and CN)

(d) 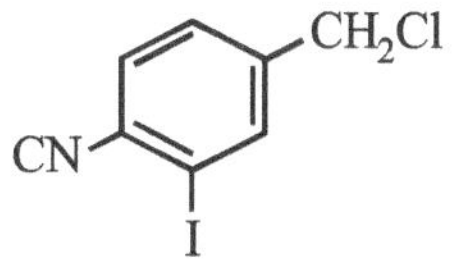 (benzene ring with CH_2Cl, CN and I)

4. When phenol is reacted with $CHCl_3$ and NaOH followed by acidification, salicyladehyde is obtained. Which of the following species are involved in the above mentioned reaction as intermediate?

(a) 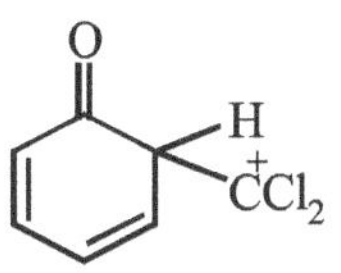 (cyclohexadienone with H and $\overset{+}{C}Cl_2$)

(b) (phenol with $CHCl_2$)

(c) (cyclohexadienone with H and CHCl–OH)

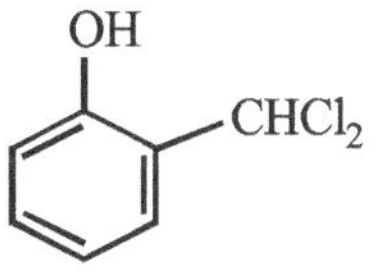

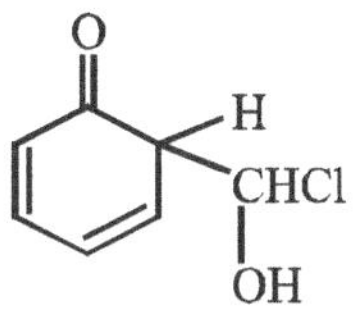

(d) 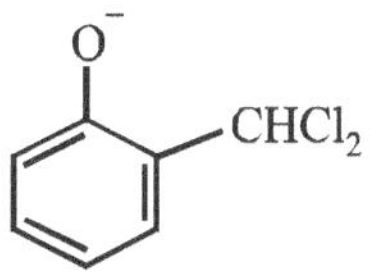 (phenoxide O^- with $CHCl_2$)

5. On the basis of information given below mark the correct option.

Information

(i) In bromoethane and chloroethane mixture intermolecular interactions of A — A and B — B type are nearly same as A — B type interactions.

(ii) In ethanol and acetone mixture A — A or B — B type intermolecular interactions are stronger than A — B type interactions.

(iii) In chloroform and acetone mixture A — A or B — B type intermolecular interactions are weaker than A — B type interactions.
(a) Solution (ii) and (iii) will follow Raoult's law
(b) Solution (i) will follow Raoult's law
(c) Solution (ii) will show negative deviation from Raoult's law
(d) Solution (iii) will show positive deviation from Raoult's law

6. The plot of concentration of the reactant vs time for a reaction is a straight line with a negative slope. The reaction follows a rate equation
(a) zero order (b) first order (c) second order (d) third order

7. Which of the following statements is incorrect?
(a) In α-helix structure a polypeptide chain forms all possible hydrogen bonds by twisting into a right handed screw.
(b) In β-structure of proteins all peptide chains are stretched out to nearly maximum extension.
(c) During denaturation 1° and 2° structures are destroyed but 3° structure remains intact.
(d) All the above statements are incorrect.

8. The solubility of N_2 in water at 300 K and 500 torr partial pressure is 0.01 g L^{-1}. The solubility (in g L^{-1}) at 750 torr partial pressure is :
(a) 0.0075 (b) 0.005 (c) 0.02 (d) 0.015

9. Which one is the most reactive towards S_N1 reaction?
(a) $C_6H_5CH(C_6H_5)Br$ (b) $C_6H_5CH(CH_3)Br$ (c) $C_6H_5C(CH_3)(C_6H_5)Br$ (d) $C_6H_5CH_2Br$

10. Which of the following pairs has the same size?
(a) Fe^{2+}, Ni^{2+} (b) Zr^{4+}, Ti^{4+} (c) Zr^{4+}, Hf^{4+} (d) Zn^{2+}, Hf^{4+}

11. Which of the following reactions will not result in the formation of anisole?
(a) Phenol + dimethyl sulphate in presence of a base (b) Sodium phenoxide is treated with methyl iodide
(c) Reaction of diazomethane with phenol (d) Reaction of methylmagnesium iodide with phenol

12. Which L-sugar on oxidation gives an optically active dibasic acid (2COOH groups)?

(a) 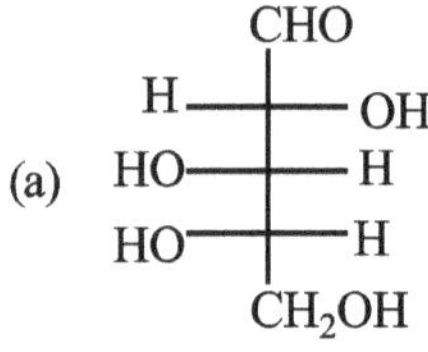

(b) 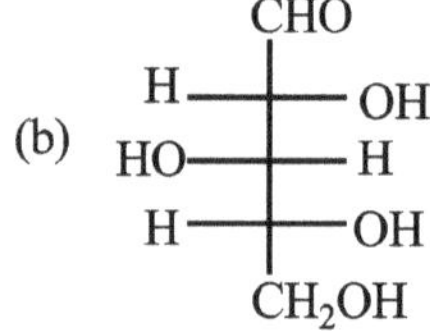

(c) 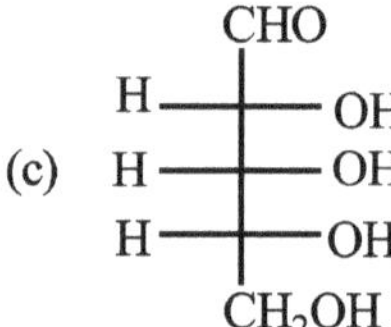

(d) 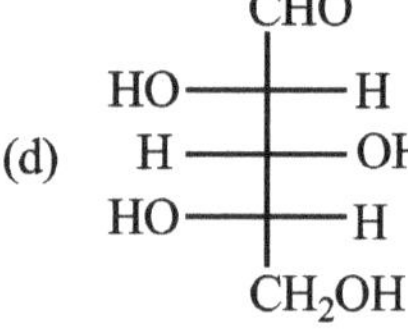

OR

***FOR VISUALLY CHALLENGED LEARNER**

*12. Rapid interconversion of α-D-glucose and β-D-glucose to solution is known as:
(a) racemization (b) asymmetric induction
(c) fluxional isomerization (d) mutarotation

13. The unit of specific conductivity is
(a) ohm cm^{-1} (b) ohm cm^{-2} (c) ohm^{-1} cm (d) ohm^{-1} cm^{-1}

14. Which of the following reactions will not give a primary amine?
(a) $CH_3CONH_2 \xrightarrow{Br_2/KOH}$ (b) $CH_3CN \xrightarrow{LiAlH_4}$
(c) $CH_3NC \xrightarrow{LiAlH_4}$ (d) $CH_3CONH_2 \xrightarrow{LiAlH_4}$

In the following questions (15-18) a statement of assertion followed by a statement of reason is given. Choose the correct answer out of the following choices.

(a) Both assertion and reason are correct statements, and reason is the correct explanation of the assertion.
(b) Both assertion and reason are correct statements, but reason is not the correct explanation of the assertion.
(c) Assertion is correct, but reason is wrong statement.
(d) Assertion is wrong, but reason is correct statement.

15. **Assertion:** Nitration of benzoic acid gives *m*-nitrobenzoic acid.
Reason : Carboxyl group increases the electron-density at *meta*-position.

16. **Assertion :** Specific conductance decreases with dilution whereas equivalent conductance increases.
Reason : On dilution, number of ions per millilitre decreases but total number of ions increases considerably.

17. **Assertion :** The order of a reaction can have fractional value.
Reason : The order of a reaction cannot be written from balanced equation of a reaction.

18. **Assertion :** Acetaldehyde on treatment with alkali gives aldol.
Reason : Acetaldehyde molecule contains α-hydrogen atom.

SECTION-B

This section contains 7 questions with internal choice in two questions. The following questions are very short answer type and carry 2 marks each.

19. Use the data to answer the following and also justify giving reason:

	Cr	Mn	Fe	Co
$E^0_{M^{2+}/M}$	−0.91	−1.18	−0.44	−0.28
$E^0_{M^{3+}/M^{2+}}$	−0.41	+1.57	+0.77	+1.97

(a) Which is a stronger reducing agent in aqueous medium, Cr^{2+} or Fe^{2+} and why?
(b) Which is the most stable ion in +2 oxidation state and why?

20. Write the name of the cell which is generally used in transistors. Write the reactions taking place at the anode and the cathode of this cell.

21. (a) Arrange the following compounds in the increasing order of their acid strength:
p-cresol, *p*-nitrophenol, phenol
(b) Write the mechanism (using curved arrow notation) of the following reaction:

$$CH_2=CH_2 \xrightarrow{H_3O^+} CH_3-\overset{+}{C}H_2 + H_2O$$

OR

Write the structures of the products when Butan–2 – ol reacts with the following
(a) CrO_3 (b) $SOCl_2$

22. Arrange the following in increasing order of their basic strength.
(i) $C_6H_5-NH_2, C_6H_5-CH_2-NH_2, C_6H_5-NH-CH_3$
(ii) [aniline (NH_2 on benzene ring)], [p-nitroaniline (NH_2 and NO_2 para on benzene ring)], [p-toluidine (NH_2 and CH_3 para on benzene ring)]

23. Why on electrolysis in acidic solution amino acids migrate towards cathode while in alkaline solution these migrate towards anode?

24. In the reaction $A + 2B \longrightarrow 3C + 2D$, the rate of disappearance of B is 1×10^{-2} mol L^{-1} s^{-1}. What will be the rate of the reaction and rate of disappearance of A and appearance of C?

25. Write IUPAC name of the complex $[Pt(en)_2Cl_2]$. Draw structures of geometrical isomers for this complex.

OR

Using IUPAC norms write the formulae for the following:
(i) Hexaamminecobalt(III) sulphate
(ii) Potassium trioxalatochromate(III)

SECTION-C

This section contains 5 questions with internal choice in two questions. The following questions are short answer type and carry 3 marks each.

26. (a) Why haloarenes undergo electrophilic substitution reaction?
Write the chemical equations involved in the below reactions.
(b) Phenol reacts with conc. HNO_3 ?
(c) Ethyl chloride reacts with $NaOC_2H_5$?

27. Calculate Δ_rG^0 and log K_c for the following reaction:

$$Cd^{2+}(aq) + Zn(s) \longrightarrow Zn^{2+}(aq) + Cd(s)$$

Given: $E^0_{Cd^{2+}/Cd} = -0.403$ V; $E^0_{Zn^{2+}/Zn} = -0.763$ V

OR

Chromium metal is electroplated using an acidic solution containing CrO_3 according to the following equation:

$$CrO_3(aq) + 6H^+ + 6e^- \longrightarrow Cr(s) + 3H_2O$$

Calculate how many grams of chromium will be electroplated by 24,000 coulombs. How long will it take to electroplate 1.5 g chromium using 12.5 A current?
[Atomic mass of Cr = 52 g mol^{-1}, 1 F = 96500 C mol^{-1}]

28. An aromatic compound 'A' on heating with Br_2 and KOH forms a compound 'B' of molecular formula C_6H_7N which on reacting with $CHCl_3$ and alcoholic KOH produces a foul smelling compound 'C'. Write the structures and IUPAC names of compounds A, B and C.

29. Why does glucose reacts with Fehling's solution and phenyl hydrazine, but not with $NaHSO_3$?

30. Following data are obtained for the reaction :
$N_2O_5 \rightarrow 2NO_2 + \frac{1}{2}O_2$

t/s	0	300	600
$[N_2O_5]$/ mol L^{-1}	1.6×10^{-2}	0.8×10^{-2}	0.4×10^{-2}

(a) Show that it follows first order reaction.
(b) Calculate the half-life.
(Given log 2 = 0.3010 log 4 = 0.6021)

OR

For the first order thermal decomposition reaction, the following data were obtained :
$C_2H_5Cl(g) \longrightarrow C_2H_4(g) + HCl(g)$

Time/sec	Total pressure/atm
0	0.30
300	0.50

Calculate the rate constant.
(Given : log 2 = 0.301, log 3 = 0.4771, log 4 = 0.6021)

SECTION-D

The following questions are case-based questions. Each question has an internal choice and carries 4 (1+1+2) marks each. Read the passage carefully and answer the questions that follow.

31. The reactions of haloalkanes may be divided into the following categories: (i) Nucleophilic substitution (ii) Elimination reactions (iii) Reaction with metals. (i) Nucleophilic substitution reactions in this type of reaction, a nucleophile reacts with haloalkane (the substrate) having a partial positive charge on the carbon atom bonded to halogen. A substitution reaction takes place and halogen atom, called leaving group departs as halide ion. Since the substitution reaction is initiated by a nucleophile, it is called nucleophilic substitution reaction. It is one of the most useful classes of organic reactions of alkyl halides in which halogen is bonded to sp^3 hybridised carbon. This reaction has been found to proceed by two different mechanims substitution nucleophilic bimolecular (S_N2) The reaction between CH_3Cl and hydroxide ion to yield methanol and chloride ion follows a second order kinetics, i.e., the rate depends upon the concentration of both the reactants. Substitution nucleophilic unimolecular (S_N1) S_N1 reactions are generally carried out in polar protic solvents (like water, alcohol, acetic acid, etc.). The reaction between *tert*-butyl bromide and hydroxide ion yields *tert*-butyl alcohol and follows the first order kinetics.

Answer the following questions :

(a) Write reaction of 1-Chlorobutane on heating with alcoholic KOH.

(b) Write treatment of 1, 3-dichloropropane on reaction with alc. KOH.

(c) Why Alkyl halides give elimination reaction with alcoholic KOH, but nucleophilic substitution with aqueous KOH?

OR

Why S_N2 reactions always proceed with inversion of configuration?

32. Werner was the first to describe the bonding features in coordination compounds. But his theory could not answer basic questions on magnetic and optical properties of coordination compounds. Many approaches have been put forth to explain the nature of bonding in coordination compounds.. It is usually possible to predict the geometry of a complex from the knowledge of its magnetic behaviour on the basis of the valence bond theory. The crystal field theory (CFT) is an electrostatic model which considers the metal-ligand bond to be ionic arising purely from electrostatic interactions between the metal ion and the ligand. According to the theory, the degeneracy of the *d* orbitals has been removed due to ligand electron-metal electron repulsions in the octahedral complex to yield three orbitals of lower energy, t_{2g} set and two orbitals of higher energy, e_g set. This splitting of the degenerate levels due to the presence of ligands in a definite geometry is termed as crystal field splitting.

Answer the following questions :

(a) Why NF_3 is a weaker ligand than $N(CH_3)_3$?

(b) $[FeF_6]^{3-}$ is a low spin complex, Justify.

(c) Potassium ferrocyanide is diamagnetic, whereas potassium ferricyanide is paramagnetic, Explain.

OR

$[Cr(H_2O)_6]^{2+} \rightarrow [Cr(H_2O)_6]^{3+}$ while converting, colour continuously changes, why?

SECTION-E

The following questions are long answer type and carry 5 marks each. Two questions have an internal choice.

33. (a) The vapour pressures of pure liquids A and B are 70 mm and 90mm Hg respectively at 25 °C. The mole fraction of 'A' in a solution of two is 0.3. Assuming that A and B form an ideal solution, calculate the partial pressure of each component is equilibrium with the solution.

(b) (i) Two liquids A and B oil at 145 °C and 190 °C respectively. Which of them has a higher vapour pressure at 80 °C?

(ii) Why is the vapour pressure of a solution of glucose in water lower than that of water?

OR

(a) Vapour pressure of pure water at 35°C is 31.82 mm Hg. When 27.0 g of solute is dissolved in 100 g of water (at the same temperature) vapour pressure of the solution, thus formed is 30.95 mm Hg. Calculate the molecular mass of solute.

(b) (i) What are non-ideal solutions ?

(ii) What role does the molecular interaction play in deciding the vapour pressure of following solutions?

(1) Alcohol and acetone (2) Chloroform and acetone

34. An organic compound [A] with molecular formula $C_9H_{10}O$ forms an orange-red precipitate [B] with 2, 4 – DNP reagent. Compound [A] gives yellow precipitate [C] on heating with iodine in the presence of sodium hydroxide along with a colourless compound [D]. The compound [A] does not reduce Tollen's reagent or Fehling's solution nor does it decolourise bromine water or Baeyer's reagent. On drastic oxidation with chromic acid, compound [A] gives a carboxylic acid [E] having molecular formula $C_7H_6O_2$. Deduce the structure of the organic compounds [A] to [E].

OR

(a) You are provided with four reagents:
Fehling's solution, I_2/NaOH, $NaHSO_3$ and Schiff's reagent. Which reagents can be used to distinguish between the compounds in each of the following pairs:
(i) CH_3CHO and CH_3COCH_3 (ii) CH_3CHO and C_6H_5CHO
(iii) $C_6H_5COCH_3$ and $C_6H_5COC_6H_5$

(b) How will you convert :
(i) Formaldehyde to acetaldehyde (ii) Acetaldehyde to methyl alcohol.

35. (a) Size of trivalent lanthanoid cations decreases with increase in the atomic number.
(b) Transition metal fluorides are ionic in nature, whereas, bromides and chlorides are usually covalent in nature.
(c) Which oxidation state of Mn is most stable and why?
(d) Which transition element show highest oxidation state and in which compound?
(e) Which is the densest transition element?

8 Sample Paper

LATEST PATTERN

BLUE PRINT

S. No.	Chapter Name	Section-A (MCQs & A/R) 1 Mark		Section-B (VSA) 2 Marks		Section-C (SA) 3 Marks		Section-D (Case Study) 4 Marks		Section-E (LA) 5 Marks		Total Marks
		Q. No.	Marks	Q. No.	Marks	Q. No.	Marks	Q. No.	Marks	Q. No.	Marks	
1	Solutions	3, 15	2	19	2	30	3					**7**
2	Electrochemistry	7	1	20	2					34	5	**8**
3	Chemical Kinetics	9, 16	2							33	5	**7**
4	d -and f -Block Elements	2, 14	2	22	2	27, 28. a	4					**8**
5	Coordination Compounds	4, 13	2	25	2	28. b, c	2					**6**
6	Haloalkanes and Haloarenes	5, 12	2	24	2	26	3					**7**
7	Alcohols, Phenols and Ethers	8	1							35	5	**6**
8	Aldehydes, Ketones and Carboxylic Acids	10, 17	2	23	2			31	4			**8**
9	Amines	1, 11, 18	3			29	3					**6**
10	Biomolecules	6	1	21	2			32	4			**7**
	Total Marks (Total Questions)	**18**	**18**	**7**	**14**	**5**	**15**	**2**	**8**	**3**	**15**	**70**

Time : 3 Hours **Max. Marks : 70**

General Instructions

Read the following instructions carefully

(a) *There are 35 questions in this question paper with internal choice.*

(b) *SECTION A consists of 18 multiple-choice questions carrying 1 mark each.*

(c) *SECTION B consists of 7 very short answer questions carrying 2 marks each.*

(d) *SECTION C consists of 5 short answer questions carrying 3 marks each.*

(e) *SECTION D consists of 2 case- based questions carrying 4 marks each.*

(f) *SECTION E consists of 3 long answer questions carrying 5 marks each.*

(g) ***All questions are compulsory.***

(h) ***Use of log tables and calculator are not allowed.***

SECTION-A

The following questions are multiple-choice questions with one correct answer. Each question carries 1 mark. There is no internal choice in this section.

1. Which of the following compounds can be prepared in good yield by Gabriel phthalimide synthesis?

(a) 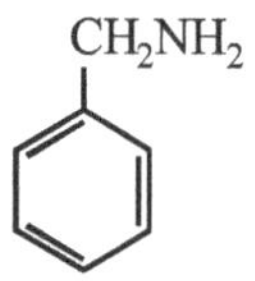 $C_6H_5-CH_2NH_2$ (benzene ring bearing CH_2NH_2)

(b) $CH_3-CH_2-NHCH_3$

(c) 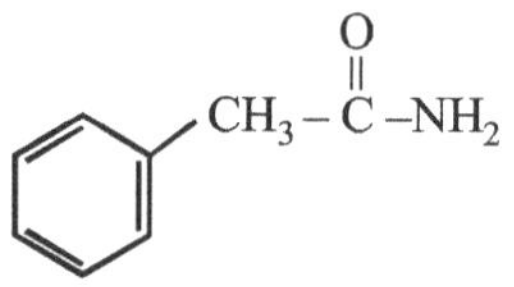 benzene ring bearing $CH_3-\overset{\overset{O}{||}}{C}-NH_2$

(d) 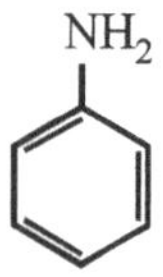 $C_6H_5-NH_2$ (benzene ring bearing NH_2)

2. In which of the following pairs both the ions are coloured in aqueous solutions?

(a) Sc^{3+}, Ti^{3+} (b) Sc^{3+}, Co^{2+} (c) Ni^{2+}, Cu^{+} (d) Ni^{2+}, Ti^{3+}

(At. no. : Sc = 21, Ti = 22, Ni = 28, Cu = 29, Co = 27)

3. How much ethyl alcohol must be added to 1 litre of water so that the solution will freeze at –14°C? (K_f for water = 1.86°C/mol)

(a) 7.5 mol (b) 8.5 mol (c) 9.5 mol (d) 10.5 mol

4. The hypothetical complex chloro-diaquatriamminecobalt (III) chloride can be represented as

(a) $[CoCl(NH_3)_3(H_2O)_2]Cl_2$ (b) $[Co(NH_3)_3(H_2O)Cl_3]$

(c) $[Co(NH_3)_3(H_2O)_2Cl]$ (d) $[Co(NH_3)_3(H_2O)_3]Cl_3$

5. 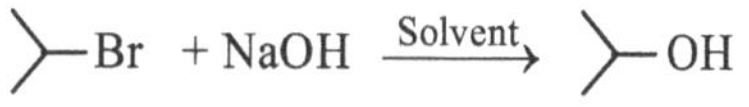 $(CH_3)_2CH-Br + NaOH \xrightarrow{\text{Solvent}} (CH_3)_2CH-OH$

For which solvent rate of S_N2 will be maximum?

(a) Benzene (b) 100% H_2O

(c) 100% acetone (d) 75% H_2O + 25% acetone

6. Denaturation of proteins leads to loss of its biological activity by

(a) Formation of amino acids (b) Loss of primary structure

(c) Loss of both primary and secondary structures (d) Loss of both secondary and tertiary structures

7. In a hydrogen-oxygen fuel cell, combustion of hydrogen occurs to
(a) produce high purity water
(b) create potential difference between two electrodes
(c) generate heat
(d) remove adsorbed oxygen from elctrode surfaces

8. 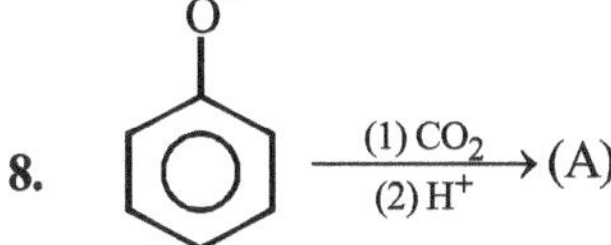

Which of the following is true statement about the reaction?
(a) Ortho isomer is major if PhONa is used
(b) Para isomer is major if PhOK is used
(c) Product formed is further used for preparation of drug aspirin
(d) All of these

9. Diazonium salt decomposes as

$C_6H_5N_2^+Cl^- \rightarrow C_6H_5Cl + N_2$

At 0°C, the evolution of N_2 becomes two times faster when the initial concentration of the salt is doubled. Therefore, it is
(a) a first order reaction
(b) a second order reaction
(c) independent of the initial concentration of the salt
(d) a zero order reaction

10. Aldehydes and ketones can be distinguished by :
(a) Ammonia (b) H_2SO_4 (c) Alkaline $KMnO_4$ (d) Fehling solution

11. The correct order of basicity of the following compounds

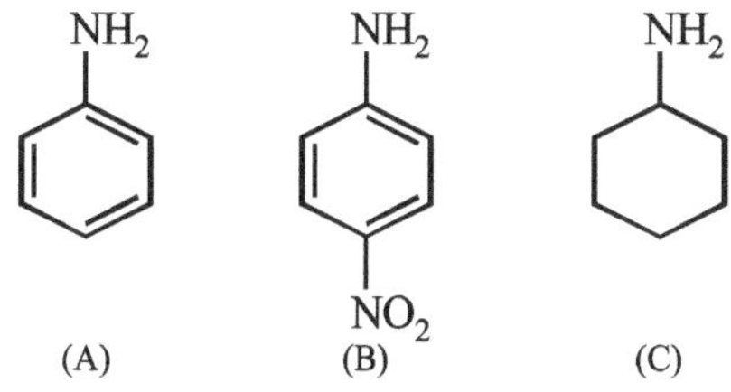

(a) B>A>C (b) A>B>C (c) C>A>B (d) C>B>A

12. A set of compounds in which the reactivity of halogen atom in the ascending order is
(a) chlorobenzene, vinyl chloride, chloroethane
(b) chloroethane, chlorobenzene, vinyl chloride
(c) vinyl chloride, chlorobenzene, chloroethane
(d) vinyl chloride, chloroethane, chlorobenzene

13. Which of the following is paramagnetic?

(a) $\left[Fe(CN)_6\right]^{4-}$ (b) $\left[Ni(CO)_4\right]$ (c) $\left[Ni(CO)_4\right]^{2-}$ (d) $[CoF_6]^{3-}$

14. The starting material for the manufacture of $KMnO_4$ is
(a) pyrolusite (b) manganite (c) magnatite (d) haematite

In the following questions (15-18) a statement of assertion followed by a statement of reason is given. Choose the correct answer out of the following choices.

(a) Both assertion and reason are correct statements, and reason is the correct explanation of the assertion.
(b) Both assertion and reason are correct statements, but reason is not the correct explanation of the assertion.
(c) Assertion is correct, but reason is wrong statement.
(d) Assertion is wrong, but reason is correct statement.

15. **Assertion :** If one component of a solution obeys Raoult's law over a certain range of composition, the other component will not obey Henry's law in that range.

16. **Assertion :** The rate of the reaction is the rate of change of concentration of a reactant or a product.
Reason : Rate of reaction remains constant during the course of reaction.

17. **Assertion :** Isobutanal does not give iodoform test.
Reason : It does not have α-hydrogen.

18. **Assertion:** N, N-Diethylethanamine is more basic than N, N-Dimethylethanamine.
Reason: + I effect of ethyl is more than methyl.

SECTION-B

This section contains 7 questions with internal choice in two questions. The following questions are very short answer type and carry 2 marks each.

19. Arrange the following solutions in increasing order of osmotic pressure:
(i) 34.2 g L^{-1} of sucrose (ii) 60 g L^{-1} of urea (iii) 90 g L^{-1} of glucose

20. Using the E^0 values of X and Y, predict which is better for coating the surface of iron to prevent rust and why?

Given: [$E^0_{(Fe^{2+}/Fe)} = -0.44$ V

$E^0_{(X^{2+}/X)} = -2.36$ V

$E^0_{(Y^{2+}/Y)} = -0.14$ V]

21. (a) Write the Zwitter ion structure of glycine.
(b) What type of substance is phenyl alanine hydroxylase? What is its importance for us?

22. Give reasons for the following:
(a) Cr^{3+} exhibits paramagnetism. (b) Mn exhibits more number of oxidation states than V.

23. How do you convert the following?
(a) Ethanal to Propanone
(b) Toluene to Benzoic acid

OR

Account for the following :
(a) Aromatic carboxylic acids do not undergo Friedel Crafts reaction.
(b) pK_a value of 4-nitrobenzoic acid is lower than that of benzoic acid.

24. Complete the following reactions:

(a) $(CH_3)_2C{=}CH-CH(CH_3)Br$ ... as printed: $\begin{matrix} CH_3 \\ CH_3 \end{matrix}\!\!>C-CH\!\!<\begin{matrix} CH_3 \\ Br \end{matrix} \xrightarrow{CH_3OH}$ Major product?

(b) Ethylbenzene $\xrightarrow[\text{(iii) alc.KOH}]{\text{(i) } Br_2, Fe \quad \text{(ii) } Cl_2, \Delta}$ Major product?

25. What are chelates and the chelating agents?

OR

$[Fe(CN)_6]^{3-}$ ion has magnetic moment of 1.73 B.M. while $[Fe(H_2O)_6]^{3+}$ has a magnetic moment of 5.92 B.M. Explain.

SECTION-C

This section contains 5 questions with internal choice in two questions. The following questions are short answer type and carry 3 marks each.

26. Give reasons for the following :

(a) The presence of – NO_2 group at ortho or para position increases the reactivity of haloarenes towards nucleophilic substitution reactions.

(b) *p*-Dichlorobenzene has higher melting point than that of ortho or meta isomer.

(c) Thionyl chloride method is preferred for preparing alkyl chloride from alcohols.

OR

(a) Write equation for preparation of l-iodobutane from l-chlorobutane.

(b) Out of 2-bromopentane, 2-bromo-2-methylbutane and 1-bromopentane, which compound is most reactive towards elimination reaction and why?

(c) Give IUPAC name of

$$CH_3-CH=CH-\overset{\overset{\displaystyle CH_3}{|}}{\underset{\underset{\displaystyle Br}{|}}{C}}-CH_3$$

27. What are paramagnetic substances? Account for the paramagnetic character of transition metal compounds. How does the paramagnetic character of the bivalent ions of first transition metal series vary from Ti (Z = 22) to copper (Z = 29)?

28. Answer **any 3** of the followings:

(a) Scandium the first member of first transition series does not exhibit variable oxidation state. Explain.

(b) Write the chemical formula for pentaamminechloroplatinum (IV) chloride.

(c) Write IUPAC name for linkage isomer of $[Co(NH_3)_5ONO]Cl_2$.

(d) Name the type of isomerism exhibited by the following isomers:
$[Pt(NH_3)_4][PtCl_6]$ and $[Pt(NH_3)_4Cl_2][PtCl_4]$

29. Give the structures of A, B and C in the following reaction :

(a) $C_6H_5N_2^+Cl^- \xrightarrow{CuCN} A \xrightarrow{H_2O/H^+} B \xrightarrow[\Delta]{NH_3} C$

(b) $C_6H_5NO_2 \xrightarrow{Sn+HCl} A \xrightarrow[273K]{NaNO_2+HCl} B \xrightarrow[\Delta]{H_2O/H^+} C$

30. Given reasons for the following :

(a) Measurement of osmotic pressure method is preferred for the determination of molar masses of macromolecules such as proteins and polymers.

(b) Aquatic animals are more comfortable in cold water than in warm water.

(c) Elevation of boiling point of 1 M KCl solution is nearly double than of 1 M sugar solution.

SECTION-D

The following questions are case-based questions. Each question has an internal choice and carries 4 (1+1+2) marks each. Read the passage carefully and answer the questions that follow.

31. The carbonyl carbon atom is sp^2-hybridised and forms three sigma bonds. The fourth valence electron of carbon remains in its *p*-orbital and forms a π-bond with oxygen by overlap with *p*-orbital of an oxygen. In addition, the oxygen atom also has two non bonding electron pairs. Thus, the carbonyl carbon and the three atoms attached to it lie in the same plane and the π-electron cloud is above and below this plane. The bond angles are approximately 120° as expected of a trigonal coplanar structure. Aldehydes and ketones are generally prepared by oxidation of primary and secondary alcohols. The aldehydes and ketones undergo a number of reactions due to the acidic nature of α-hydrogen. The acidity of α-hydrogen atoms of carbonyl compounds is due to the strong electron withdrawing effect of the carbonyl group and resonance stabilisation of the conjugate base.

Answer the following questions :

(a) Why does acetaldehyde on treatment with alkali give aldol?
(b) Hydroxyketones are not directly used in Grignard reaction—Justify.
(c) What is the expected product when RCOCl, $(RCO)_2O$ and RCOOR all react with Grignard reagents?

OR

Formaldehyde is a planar molecule—Explain.

32. Proteins are the most abundant molecules of the living system and form the fundamental basis of structure and functions of life. The word protein is derived from Greek word, "proteios" which means primary or of prime importance. All proteins are polymers of α-aminoacids. Amino acids contain amino group and carboxyl functional groups and classified as acidic, basic or neutral depending upon the relative number of amino and carboxyl groups in the molecule. proteins are the polymers of α-amino acids and they are connected to each other by peptide bond. Peptide likage is an amide formed between —COOH gp and —NH_2 group. Proteins are classified into two types on the basis of molecular shape. Fibrous protein in which polypeptide chains run parallel and held together by H-bonds and disulphide bond. Another type is globular protein in which chains of polypetide coil around to give spherical shape.
Answer the following questions :

(a) What is denaturation?
(b) Give one example of denaturation?
(c) What happens when denaturation occurs. How does the peptide bond form in protein?

OR

What is isoelectric point? Does the isoelectric point migrate under the influence of electric field?

SECTION-E

The following questions are long answer type and carry 5 marks each. Two questions have an internal choice.

33. (a) The decomposition of a compound is found to follow the first order rate law. If it takes 15 minutes for 20 percent of the original material to react, calculate
(i) the specific rate constant.
(ii) the time in which 10 percent of the original material remains unreacted.
(iii) the time it takes for the next 20 percent of the reactant left to react.
(b) Why does liquid bromine react slowly as compared to vapours of bromine?
(c) Why does the rate of a reaction not remain constant throughout the reaction?

OR

For the chemical reaction, $A + 2B \longrightarrow 2C + D$, the experimentally determined information has been tabulated below :

Experiment	$[A]_0$	$[B]_0$	Initial rate of reaction
1	0.30	0.30	0.096
2	0.60	0.30	0.384
3	0.30	0.60	0.192
4	0.60	0.60	0.768

For the above reaction,
(a) Calculate the order of reaction w.r.t. both the reactants A and B.
(b) Write the expression for rate law.
(c) Calculate the value of the rate constant.
(d) Write the expression for the rate of reaction in terms of A and C.

34. (a) The value of Λ^{∞} for NH_4Cl, NaOH and NaCl are 129.8, 248.1 and 126.4 ohm^{-1} cm^2 mol^{-1} respectively. Calculate Λ^{∞} for NH_4OH solution.

(b) The equivalent conductivities of acetic acid at 298 K at the concentrations of 0.1 M and 0.001M are 5.20 and 49.2 S cm^2 eq^{-1} respectively. Calculate the degree of dissociation of acetic acid at these concentrations.

Given that : $\Lambda^{\infty}(H^+)$ and $\Lambda^{\infty}(CH_3COO^-)$

are 349.8 and 40.9 ohm^{-1} cm^2 eq^{-1} respectively.

OR

(a) Calculate $\Delta G°$ for the reaction :

$Cu^{2+}(aq) + Fe(s) \rightleftharpoons Fe^{2+}(aq) + Cu(s)$

Given that : $E^0_{Cu^{2+}/Cu} = +0.34$ V, $E^0_{Fe^{2+}/Fe} = -0.44$ V

(b) A solution of copper (II) sulphate is electrolysed between copper electrodes by a current of 10.0 amperes passing for one hour. What changes occur at the electrodes and in the solution ?

35. (a) Out of t-butyl alcohol and n-butanol, which one will undergo acid catalyzed dehydration faster and why?

(b) Carry out the following conversions:

(i) Phenol to salicylaldehyde

(ii) *t*-Butylchloride to *t*-butyl ethyl ether

(iii) Propene to propanol

9 Sample Paper

LATEST PATTERN

BLUE PRINT

S. No.	Chapter Name	Section-A (MCQs & A/R) 1 Mark		Section-B (VSA) 2 Marks		Section-C (SA) 3 Marks		Section-D (Case Study) 4 Marks		Section-E (LA) 5 Marks		Total Marks
		Q. No.	Marks	Q. No.	Marks	Q. No.	Marks	Q. No.	Marks	Q. No.	Marks	
1	Solutions	1, 7, 15	3					31	4			**7**
2	Electrochemistry	11	1	19	2					33	5	**8**
3	Chemical Kinetics	5, 14	2	22	2	27	3					**7**
4	d -and f -Block Elements	12	1	25	2					35	5	**8**
5	Coordination Compounds	8	1	20	2	28	3					**6**
6	Haloalkanes and Haloarenes	6, 9	2	21	2	30	3					**7**
7	Alcohols, Phenols and Ethers	2, 10, 18	3			26	3					**6**
8	Aldehydes, Ketones and Carboxylic Acids	13	1	24	2					34	5	**8**
9	Amines	3, 16	2					32	4			**6**
10	Biomolecules	4, 17	2	23	2	29	3					**7**
	Total Marks (Total Questions)	**18**	**18**	**7**	**14**	**5**	**15**	**2**	**8**	**3**	**15**	**70**

Time : 3 Hours **Max. Marks : 70**

General Instructions

Read the following instructions carefully

(a) *There are 35 questions in this question paper with internal choice.*
(b) *SECTION A consists of 18 multiple-choice questions carrying 1 mark each.*
(c) *SECTION B consists of 7 very short answer questions carrying 2 marks each.*
(d) *SECTION C consists of 5 short answer questions carrying 3 marks each.*
(e) *SECTION D consists of 2 case- based questions carrying 4 marks each.*
(f) *SECTION E consists of 3 long answer questions carrying 5 marks each.*
(g) ***All questions are compulsory.***
(h) ***Use of log tables and calculator are not allowed.***

SECTION-A

The following questions are multiple-choice questions with one correct answer. Each question carries 1 mark. There is no internal choice in this section.

1. For a binary ideal liquid solution, the total vapour pressure of the solution is given as:
(a) $P_{total} = P_A^\circ + (P_A^\circ - P_B^\circ)x_B$
(b) $P_{total} = P_B^\circ + (P_A^\circ - P_B^\circ)x_A$
(c) $P_{total} = P_B^\circ + (P_B^\circ - P_A^\circ)x_A$
(d) $P_{total} = P_B^\circ + (P_B^\circ - P_A^\circ)x_B$

2. The compound which reacts fastest with Lucas reagent at room temperature is
(a) butan-1-ol (b) butan-2-ol (c) 2-methylpropan-1-ol (d) 2-methylpropan-2-ol

3. 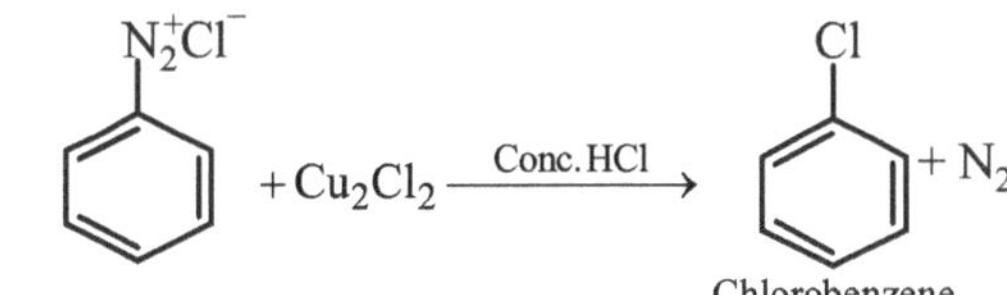

Above reaction is known as:
(a) Strecker's reaction (b) Sandmeyer's reaction (c) Wohl-Ziegler reaction (d) Stephen's reaction

4. Optical rotations of some compounds alongwith their structures are given below which of them have D configuration.

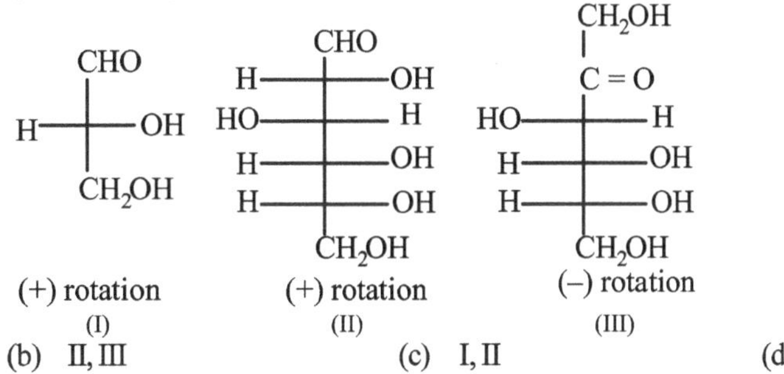

(a) I, II, III (b) II, III (c) I, II (d) III

*** FOR VISUALLY CHALLENGED LEARNERS**

*4. Glycosidic linkage is actually an :
(a) Carbonyl bond (b) Ether bond (c) Ester bond (d) Amide bond

5. The rate of the reaction $2NO + Cl_2 \longrightarrow 2NOCl$ is given by the rate equation, rate = $k\,[NO]^2\,[Cl_2]$
The value of the rate constant can be increased by:
(a) increasing the concentration of NO.
(b) increasing the temperature.
(c) increasing the concentration of the Cl_2
(d) doing all of the above

6. Chlorobenzene is formed by reaction of chlorine with benzene in the presence of $AlCl_3$. Which of the following species attacks the benzene ring in this reaction?
(a) Cl^- (b) Cl^+ (c) $AlCl_3$ (d) $[AlCl_4]^-$

7. A solution is prepared by dissolving 10 g NaOH in 1250 mL of a solvent of density 0.8 g/mL. The molality of the solution in mol kg^{-1} is
(a) 0.25 (b) 0.2 (c) 0.008 (d) 0.0064

8. The complex that can show *fac*- and *mer*- isomers is:
(a) $[Co(NH_3)_4Cl_2]^+$ (b) $[Pt(NH_3)_2Cl_2]$ (c) $[CoCl_2(en)_2]$ (d) $[Co(NH_3)_3(NO_2)_3]$

9. Which of the statement(s) is/are true, regarding following reaction?

$$RR'R''CBr \xrightarrow{Nu^-} RR'R''CNu + Br^-$$

(i) The reaction involves the formation of transition state.
(ii) Higher the nucleophilic character of the nucleophile, faster will be the reaction.
(iii) The product is always optically inactive.
(a) (ii) only (b) (ii) and (iii) (c) All the three (d) None of the three

10. *tert*-Butyl ethyl ether can't be prepared by which reaction?
(a) $tert-\text{Butanol} + \text{ethanol} \xrightarrow{H^+}$
(b) *tert*-Butyl bromide + sodium ethoxide →
(c) Sodium *tert*-butoxide + ethyl bromide →
(d) $\text{Isobutene} + \text{ethanol} \xrightarrow{H^+}$

11. Standard reduction potentials of the half reactions are given below :
$F_2(g) + 2e^- \rightarrow 2F^-(aq)$; $E° = +2.85$ V
$Cl_2(g) + 2e^- \rightarrow 2Cl^-(aq)$; $E° = +1.36$ V
$Br_2(l) + 2e^- \rightarrow 2Br^-(aq)$; $E° = +1.06$ V
$I_2(s) + 2e^- \rightarrow 2I^-(aq)$; $E° = +0.53$ V
The strongest oxidising and reducing agents respectively are
(a) F_2 and I^- (b) Br_2 and Cl^- (c) Cl_2 and Br^- (d) Cl_2 and I_2

12. Which of the following transition element shows the highest oxidation state?
(a) Mn (b) Fe (c) V (d) Cr

13. A compound does not react with 2, 4 dinitrophenyl-hydrazine, the compound is :
(a) Acetone (b) Acetaldehdye (c) CH_3OH (d) $CH_3CH_2COCH_3$

14. The chemical reaction $2O_3 \longrightarrow 3O_2$ proceeds as follows:
$O_3 \xrightarrow{\text{Fast}} O_2 + O$; $O + O_3 \xrightarrow{\text{Slow}} 2O_2$ the rate law expression should be
(a) $r = k[O_3]^2$ (b) $r = k[O_3]^2[O_2]^{-1}$ (c) $r = k^3[O_3][O_2]^2$ (d) $r = [O_3][O_2]^2$

In the following questions (15-18) a statement of assertion followed by a statement of reason is given. Choose the correct answer out of the following choices.
(a) Both assertion and reason are correct statements, and reason is the correct explanation of the assertion.
(b) Both assertion and reason are correct statements, but reason is not the correct explanation of the assertion.
(c) Assertion is correct, but reason is wrong statement.
(d) Assertion is wrong, but reason is correct statement.

15. **Assertion :** The molecular weight of acetic acid determined by depression in freezing point method in benzene and water was found to be different.
Reason : Water is polar and benzene is non-polar.

16. **Assertion:** Reduction of *m*-dinitrobenzene with ammonium sulphide gives *m*-nitroaniline.
Reason: *m*-Nitroaniline formed gets precipitated and hence further reduction is prevented.

17. **Assertion :** Oxidation of glucose by Br_2 water gives saccharic acid.
Reason : Br_2 water oxidizes –CHO but not alcohol.

18. **Assertion:** The major products formed by heating $C_6H_5CH_2OCH_3$ with HI are $C_6H_5CH_2I$ and CH_3OH.
Reason: Benzyl cation is more stable than methyl cation.

SECTION-B

This section contains 7 questions with internal choice in two questions. The following questions are very short answer type and carry 2 marks each.

19. Calculate the degree of dissociation (α) of acetic acid if its molar conductivity (Λ_m) is 39.05 S $cm^2 mol^{-1}$.
Given $\lambda^\circ(H^+) = 349.6$ S cm^2 mol^{-1} and $\lambda^\circ(CH_3COO^-) = 40.9$ S cm^2 mol^{-1}

20. $[Co(NH_3)_6]^{3+}$ is an inner orbital complex whereas $[Ni(NH_3)_6]^{2+}$ is an outer orbital complex. Explain why.

OR

State reason for each of the following
(i) CO is stronger complexing reagent than NH_3.
(ii) The molecular shape of $Ni(CO)_4$ is not the same as that of $[Ni(CN)_4]^{2-}$.

21. Identify X, Y and Z in the following sequence of reactions?

$$CH_3CH_2CH_2Br \xrightarrow{\text{Alk. KOH}} (X) \xrightarrow{H_2O/H^+} (Y) \xrightarrow{PCl_5} (Z)$$

22. Analyse the given graph, drawn between concentration of reactant vs. time.

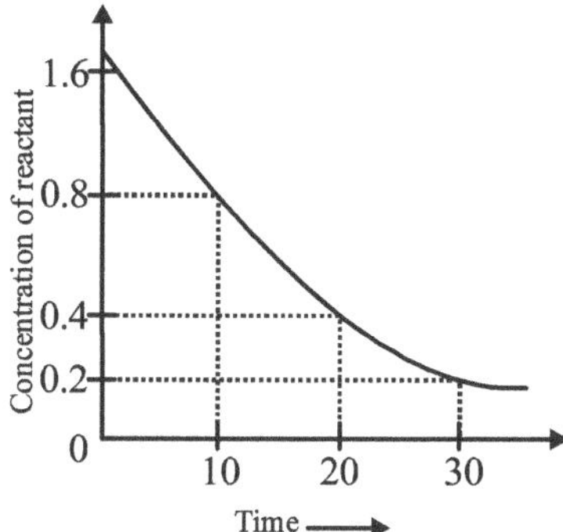

(a) Predict the order of reaction.
(b) Theoretically, can the concentration of the reactant reduce to zero after infinite time? Explain

OR

For a reaction

$$2H_2O_2 \xrightarrow[\text{alkaline medium}]{I^-} 2H_2O + O_2$$

the proposed mechanism is as given below:
(1) $H_2O_2 + I^- \rightarrow H_2O + IO^-$ (slow)
(2) $H_2O_2 + IO^- \rightarrow H_2O + I^- + O_2$ (fast)
  (a) Write rate law for the reaction.
  (b) Write the overall order of reaction.
  (c) Out of steps (1) and (2), which one is rate determining step?

23. (a) Mention the name of the bases produced on hydrolysis of DNA.
(b) What is an invert sugar?

24. (a) What is the composition of Fehling's reagent?
(b) Draw structure of the semicarbazone of Ethanal.

25. (a) Which metal in the first transition series (3*d* series) exhibits +1 oxidation state most frequently and why?
(b) Which of the following cations are coloured in aqueous solutions and why?
Sc^{3+}, V^{3+}, Ti^{4+}, Mn^{2+}
(At. nos. Sc = 21, V = 23, Ti = 22, Mn = 25)

SECTION-C

This section contains 5 questions with internal choice in two questions. The following questions are short answer type and carry 3 marks each.

26. (a) Anhydrous $CaCl_2$ is not recommended as a drying agent for alcohols and amines.
(b) Why are Grignard reagents soluble in ether but not in benzene?
(c) Explain why the cleavage of aryl ethers with hydrogen halides always yield phenol and a molecule of halide and not aryl halide and alcohol.

OR

Draw the structure and name the product formed if the following alcohols are oxidised. Assume that an excess of oxidising agent is used.
(a) $CH_3CH_2CH_2CH_2OH$ (b) 2-butanol (c) 2-methyl-1-propanol

27. The following rate data were obtained at 300 K for the reaction :
$2A + B \longrightarrow C + D$

Exp. No.	[A] (mol/L)	[B] (mol/L)	Rate of formation of D (mol / L / min)
1	0.1	0.1	6×10^{-3}
2	0.3	0.2	7.2×10^{-2}
3	0.3	0.4	2.88×10^{-1}
4	0.4	0.1	2.40×10^{-2}

Determine the rate law, order and rate constant for reaction.

28. Among $Ag(NH_3)_2Cl$, $[Ni(CN)_4]^{2-}$ and $[CuCl_4]^{2-}$, which
(a) has square planar geometry?
(b) remains colourless in aqueous solution and why?
[Ag (Z = 47), Ni (Z = 28), Cu (Z = 29)].

29. Give the plausible explanation for the following (any 3):
(a) Glucose doesn't give 2,4-DNP test.
(b) The two strands in DNA are not identical but are complementary.
(c) Starch and cellulose both contain glucose unit as monomer, yet they are structurally different.
(d) Coagulation of protein is known as denaturing.

30. (a) Out of $(CH_3)_3C - Br$ and $(CH_3)_3C–I$, which one is more reactive towards S_N1 and why?
(b) Write the product formed when p-nitrochlorobenzene is heated with aqueous NaOH at 443 K followed by acidification.
(c) The major product obtained in the following reaction is :

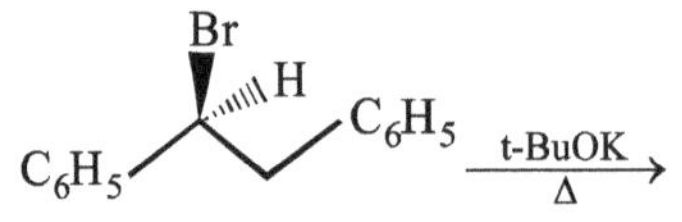

Br, H, C_6H_5, C_6H_5 $\xrightarrow[\Delta]{\text{t-BuOK}}$

SECTION-D

The following questions are case-based questions. Each question has an internal choice and carries 4 (1+1+2) marks each. Read the passage carefully and answer the questions that follow.

31. The word "colligative" has been adapted or taken from the Latin word "colligatus" which translates to "bound together". A colligative property is a property of a solution that is dependent on the ratio between the total number of solute particles (in the solution) to the total number of solvent particles. Colligative properties are not dependent on the chemical nature of the solution's components. Dilute solution containing non-volatile solute exhibit some properties which depend only on the number of solute particles present and not on the type of solute present. These properties are called colligative properties. These properties are mostly seen in dilute solutions. There are different types of colligative properties of a solution. These include, vapour pressure lowering, boiling point elevation, freezing point depression and osmotic pressure.

Answer the following questions :
(a) Name the colligative property which is used for determining the molecular weight of macromolecules. Why?
(b) What will happen to colligative properties if the solute is an electrolyte?
(c) Why colligative properties do not depend on the chemical nature of solution's components?

OR

Someone has added a non electrolyte solid to the pure liquid but forgot that among which of the two beakers he has added that solid. How can this problem be solved?

32. The conversion of an amide to an amine with one carbon atom less by the action of alkaline hydrohalite is known as Hoffmann bromamide degradation.

(i) → (ii) → (iii) → (iv) → (v) → (vi)

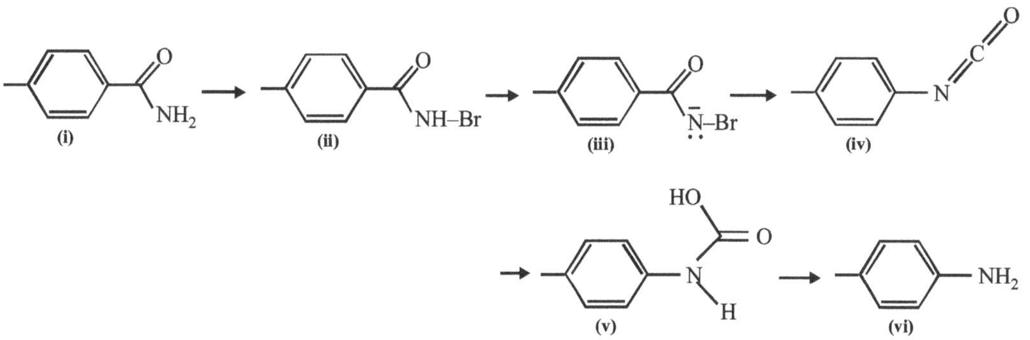

In this reaction, RCONHBr is formed from which the reaction has derived its name. Hoffmann reaction is accelerated if the migrating group is more electron-releasing. Hoffmann degradation reaction is an intramolecular reaction.

Answer the following questions :

(a) Which is the rate determining step in Hofmann bromamide degradation?

(b) Which amide can give propanamine by Hoffmann bromamide reaction?

(c) What are the constituent amines formed when the mixture of (i) and (ii) undergoes Hofmann bromamide degradation?

$CONH_2$ (i) and $C^{15}ONH_2$ (ii)

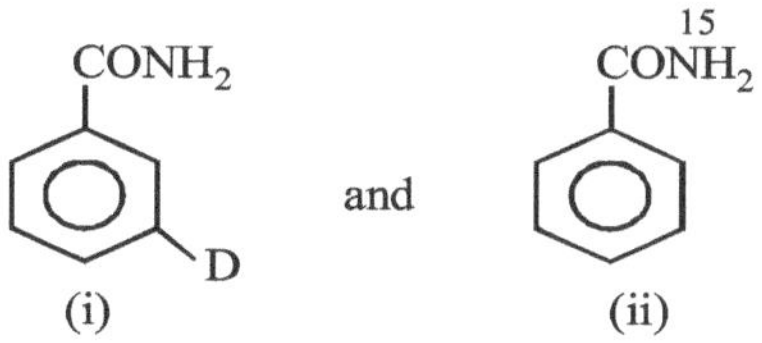

OR

Which one is more basic among structure (i), (vi), (ii)?

SECTION-E

The following questions are long answer type and carry 5 marks each. Two questions have an internal choice.

33. (a) Which of the following solutions has larger molar conductance?

(i) 0.10 M solution which has resistivity equal to 58 Ω cm.

(ii) 0.08 M solution having conductivity equal to $2.0 \times 10^{-2}\ \Omega^{-1}\ cm^{-1}$.

(b) Knowing that :

$Cu^{2+}(aq) + 2e^- \longrightarrow Cu(s);\ E^\circ = +0.34\ V$

$2Ag^+(aq) + 2e^- \longrightarrow 2Ag(s);\ E^\circ = +0.80\ V$

reason out whether, 1M silver nitrate solution can be stored in copper vessel or 1M copper sulphate solution in silver vessel.

(c) How does molar conductivity of KCl vary with concentration?

OR

The following chemical reaction is occurring in an electrochemical cell.

$Mg(s) + 2Ag^+(0.0001\ M) \longrightarrow Mg^{2+}(0.10\ M) + 2Ag(s)$

The E° electrode values are:

$Mg^+/Mg = -2.36\ V;\ Ag^+/Ag = 0.81\ V$

For this cell,

(a) (i) Calculate E° value for the $2\ Ag^+/2\ Ag$.

(ii) Calculate standard cell potential E°_{cell}.

(b) Calculate cell potential E_{cell}.

(c) (i) Give symbolic representation of the above cell.
(ii) Will the above cell reaction be spontaneous?

34. (a) An alkene 'A' (Mol. formula C_5H_{10}) on ozonolysis gives a mixture of two compounds 'B' and 'C'. Compound 'B' gives positive Fehling's test and also forms iodoform on treatment with I_2 and NaOH. Compound 'C' does not give Fehling's test but forms iodoform. Identify the compounds A, B and C. Write the reaction for ozonolysis and formation of iodoform from B and C.

(b) Suggest a reason for the large difference in the boiling points of butanol and butanal, although they have the same solubility in water.

(c) There are two – NH_2 group in semicarbazide. However, only one is involved in the formation of semi carbazones. Give reason.

OR

(a) A compound (A), molecular formula $C_5H_{10}O$ gives a positive 2, 4-DNP test but a negative Tollen's test. It can be oxidised to carboxylic acid (B), of molecular formula $C_3H_6O_2$, when treated with alkaline $KMnO_4$ under vigorous conditions. The salt of B gives a hydrocarbon C on Kolbe's electrolytic decarboxylation. Identify A, B and C and write chemical equations of the reactions.

(b) Complete the following reactions by identifying A, B and C.

(i) $A + H_2(g) \xrightarrow{Pd/BaSO_4} (CH_3)_2CHCHO$ (ii) $CH_3-\underset{CH_3}{\overset{CH_3}{\underset{|}{\overset{|}{C}}}}-\underset{O}{\underset{||}{C}}-CH_3 + NaOI \longrightarrow B + C$

35. (a) Which one is more basic $La(OH)_2$ or $La(OH)_3$, and why?

(b) Explain why,
(i) As we move from V to Zn in 3*d*- series we find that there is no regular variation of reduction potentials $E^\circ(M^{2+}/M)$.
(ii) Zn, Cd, Hg have low m.pt and b.pt compared to other members of transition elements.
(iii) The element chromium is very hard but mercury is a liquid.
(iv) $HgCl_2$ and $SnCl_2$ cannot exist together. Explain why.

10 Sample Paper

LATEST PATTERN

BLUE PRINT

S. No.	Chapter Name	Section-A		Section-B		Section-C		Section-D		Section-E		Total Marks
		(MCQs & A/R) 1 Mark		(VSA) 2 Marks		(SA) 3 Marks		(Case Study) 4 Marks		(LA) 5 Marks		
		Q. No.	Marks	Q. No.	Marks	Q. No.	Marks	Q. No.	Marks	Q. No.	Marks	
1	Solutions	7	1	21	2			32	4			**7**
2	Electrochemistry	3, 12	2	24	2	26, 27. a	4					**8**
3	Chemical Kinetics	4, 13	2							34	5	**7**
4	d -and f -Block Elements	16	1			27. b, c, d	2			35	5	**8**
5	Coordination Compounds	17	1	19	2	29	3					**6**
6	Haloalkanes and Haloarenes	5, 8	2	20	2	30	3					**7**
7	Alcohols, Phenols and Ethers	6, 9	2					31	4			**6**
8	Aldehydes, Ketones and Carboxylic Acids	18	1	22	2					33	5	**8**
9	Amines	1, 10, 14	3	23	2	28 a	1					**6**
10	Biomolecules	2, 11, 15	3	25	2	28 b, c	2					**7**
	Total Marks (Total Questions)	**18**	**18**	**7**	**14**	**5**	**15**	**2**	**8**	**3**	**15**	**70**

Time : 3 Hours **Max. Marks : 70**

General Instructions

Read the following instructions carefully

(a) *There are 35 questions in this question paper with internal choice.*

(b) *SECTION A consists of 18 multiple-choice questions carrying 1 mark each.*

(c) *SECTION B consists of 7 very short answer questions carrying 2 marks each.*

(d) *SECTION C consists of 5 short answer questions carrying 3 marks each.*

(e) *SECTION D consists of 2 case- based questions carrying 4 marks each.*

(f) *SECTION E consists of 3 long answer questions carrying 5 marks each.*

(g) ***All questions are compulsory.***

(h) ***Use of log tables and calculator are not allowed.***

SECTION-A

The following questions are multiple-choice questions with one correct answer. Each question carries 1 mark. There is no internal choice in this section.

1. Which of the following is not a property of diazonium salts?
(a) Diazonium salts are colourless crystalline solids.
(b) Being ionic in nature they are soluble in water.
(c) Most of these salts decomposes when dried.
(d) The aqueous solutions of these salts are poor conductors of electricity

2. In fibrous proteins, polypeptide chains are held together by
(a) van der waals forces (b) electrostatic forces of attraction
(c) hydrogen bonds (d) covalent bonds

3. For the galvanic cell $Zn \mid Zn^{2+}(0.1M) \parallel Cu^{2+}(1.0M) \mid Cu$ the cell potential increase if:
(a) $[Zn^{2+}]$ is increased (b) $[Cu^{2+}]$ is increased
(c) $[Cu^{2+}]$ is decreased (d) surface area of anode is increased

4. The given plots represents the variation of the concentration of a reactant R with time for two different reactions (i) and (ii). The respective orders of the reactions are:

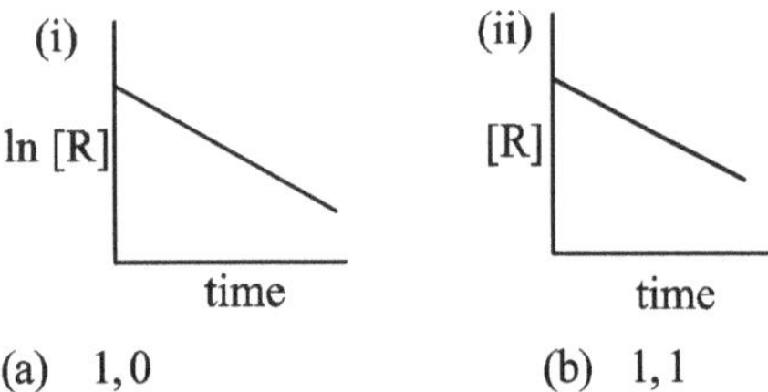

(a) 1, 0 (b) 1, 1 (c) 0, 1 (d) 0, 2

OR

The following results were obtained during kinetic studies of the reaction;
$2A + B \rightarrow$ Products

Experiment	[A] (in mol L^{-1})	[B] (in mol L^{-1})	Initial Rate of reaction (in mol L^{-1} min^{-1})
I	0.10	0.20	6.93×10^{-3}
II	0.10	0.25	6.93×10^{-3}
III	0.20	0.30	1.386×10^{-2}

The time (in minutes) required to consume half of A is:
(a) 5 (b) 10 (c) 1 (d) 100

5. Arrange the following compounds in the increasing order of their densities.

(i) 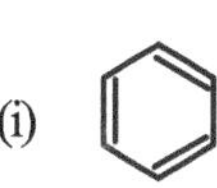 (ii) 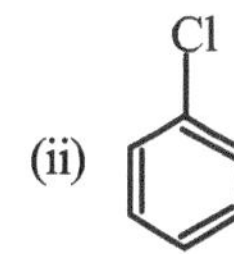

(iii) 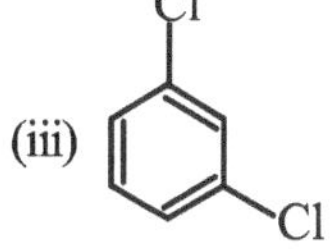

(iv) 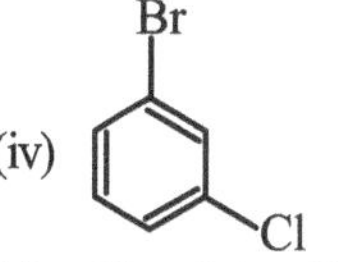

(a) (i) < (ii) < (iii) < (iv) (b) (i) < (iii) < (iv) < (ii) (c) (iv) < (iii) < (ii) < (i) (d) (ii) < (iv) < (iii) < (i)

6. The major reason that phenol is a better Bronsted acid than cyclohexanol is that:
(a) it is a beter proton donor.
(b) the cyclohexyl group is an electron donating group by induction, which destabilizes the anion formed in the reaction by resonance.
(c) phenol is able to stabilize the anion formed in the reaction.
(d) the phenyl group is an electron withdrawing group by induction, which stabilizes the anion formed in the reaction.

7. For a dilute solution, Raoult's law states that:
(a) the lowering of vapour pressure is equal to the mole fraction of solute
(b) the relative lowering of vapour pressure is equal to the mole fraction of solute
(c) the relative lowering of vapour pressure is proportional to the amount of solute in solution
(d) the vapour pressure of the solution is equal to the mole fraction of solvent

8. Reaction of $C_6H_5CH_2Br$ with aqueous sodium hydroxide follows ....
(a) S_N1 mechanism
(b) S_N2 mechanism
(c) Any of the above two depending upon the temperature of reaction
(d) Saytzeff rule

9. How many alcohols with molecular formula $C_4H_{10}O$ are chiral in nature?
(a) 1 (b) 2 (c) 3 (d) 4

10. Which of the following is not a primary amine?
(a) *tert*-Butylamine (b) *sec*-Butylamine (c) *iso*-Butylamine (d) Dimethylamine

11. In both DNA and RNA, heterocylic base and phosphate ester linkages are at –
(a) C_5' and C_1' respectively of the sugar molecule (b) C_1' and C_5' respectively of the sugar molecule
(c) C_2' and C_5' respectively of the sugar molecule (d) C_5' and C_2' respectively of the sugar molecule

12. Which of the following is a merit of Ni–Cd cell over lead storage battery?
(a) Ni–Cd cell can be re-used.
(b) Ni–Cd cell is comparatively economical to manufacture
(c) Ni–Cd cell has comparatively longer life
(d) All the above are the merits of Ni–Cd cell over lead storage battery.

13. Which of the following statements best describes how a catalyst works?
(a) A catalyst changes the potential energies of the reactants and products.
(b) A catalyst decreases the temperature of the reaction which leads to a faster rate.
(c) A catalyst lowers the activation energy for the reaction by providing a different reaction mechanism.
(d) A catalyst destroys some of the reactants, which lowers the concentration of the reactants.

14. Correct order of increasing basic character is
(a) $NH_3 < PhNH_2 < Et_2NH < EtNH_2 < Et_3N$ (b) $PhNH_2 < NH_3 < Et_3N < Et_2NH$
(c) $PhNH_2 < NH_3 < Et_2NH < Et_3N$ (d) $Et_3N < PhNH_2 < Et_2NH < NH_3$

In the following questions (Q. No. 15 - 18) a statement of assertion followed by a statement of reason is given. Choose the correct answer out of the following choices.
(a) Both assertion and reason are correct statements, and reason is the correct explanation of the assertion.
(b) Both assertion and reason are correct statements, but reason is not the correct explanation of the assertion.
(c) Assertion is correct, but reason is wrong statement.
(d) Assertion is wrong, but reason is correct statement.

15. **Assertion:** The two strands of DNA are complementary to each other
Reason: The hydrogen bonds are formed between specific pairs of bases.

16. **Assertion:** Ce^{4+} is used as an oxidising agent in volumetric analysis.
Reason: Ce^{4+} has the tendency of attaining + 3 oxidation state.

17. **Assertion:** Linkage isomerism arises in coordination compounds because of ambidentate ligand.
Reason: Ambidentate ligand like NO_2 has two different donor atoms i.e., N and O.

18. **Assertion:** Aldol condensation can be catalysed both by acids and bases.
Reason: β-Hydroxyaldehydes or ketones readily undergo acid-catalysed dehydration.

SECTION-B

This section contains 7 questions with internal choice in two questions. The following questions are very short answer type and carry 2 marks each.

19. Give (a) linkage isomer of $[Cr(CN)(H_2O)_5]^{2+}$
(b) ionisation isomer of $[PtCl_2(NH_3)_4]\,Br_2$

20. (a) Out of chlorobenzene and chloromethane, which is more reactive towards nucleophilic substitution reactions?
(b) Explain why thionyl chloride method is preferred for preparing alkyl chlorides from alcohols?

21. The vapour pressure of ethanol and methanol are 44.5 mm and 88.7 mm Hg respectively. A solution is prepared by mixing 60 g of ethanol and 40 g of methanol. Assuming the solution to be ideal, calculate the vapour pressure of the solution.

22. What happens when
(a) Propanone is treated with methylmagnesium iodide and then hydrolysed, and
(b) Benzene is treated with CH_3COCl in presence of anhydrous $AlCl_3$?

23. Give reasons :
(a) Ammonolysis of alkyl halides is not a good method to prepare pure primary amines.
(b) Aniline does not give Friedel-Crafts reaction.

24. Resistance of a conductivity cell filled with 0.1 M KCl is 100 ohm. If the resistance of the same cell when filled with 0.02 M KCl solution is 520 ohms, calculate the conductivity and molar conductivity of 0.02 M KCl solution. Conductivity of 0.1 M KCl solution is $1.29 \times 10^{-2}\ ohm^{-1}\ cm^{-1}$.

OR

For the cell: $Zn(s)\,|\,Zn^{2+}(2\,M)\,||\,Cu^{2+}(0.5\,M)\,|\,Cu(s)$
(a) Write equation for each half-reaction
(b) Calculate cell potential at 25°C.
[Given: $E^\circ_{Zn^{2+}|Zn} = -0.76\,V$; $E^\circ_{Cu^{2+}|Cu} = +0.34\,V$]

25. (a) Write the name of two monosaccharides obtained on hydrolysis of lactose sugar.
(b) Why Vitamin C cannot be stored in our body ?

OR

(a) What is the difference between a nucleoside and nucleotide ?
(b) Enzymes are least reactive at optimum temperature. "Justify the statement".

SECTION-C

This section contains 5 questions with internal choice in two questions. The following questions are short answer type and carry 3 marks each.

26. Calculate the emf of the following cell at 298 K :
$Fe(s)\,|\,Fe^{2+}(0.001\,M)\,||\,H^+(1\,M)\,|\,H_2(g)\,(1\,bar), Pt(s)$
(Given $E^\circ_{cell} = +0.44V$)

27. (a) What is the purpose of using salt bridge in electro chemical cell?
How would you account for any two of the following?
(b) Transition metals exhibit variable oxidation states.
(c) Zr (Z = 40) and Hf (Z = 72) have almost identical radii.
(d) Transition metals and their compounds act as catalyst.

OR

Complete any two of the following chemical equations :

(b) $Cr_2O_7^{2-} + 6Fe^{2+} + 14H^+ \longrightarrow$

(c) $2CrO_4^{2-} + 2H^+ \longrightarrow$

(d) $2MnO_4^- + 5C_2O_4^{2-} + 16H^+ \longrightarrow$

28. (a) Why aniline does not undergo Friedel-Crafts reaction?
(b) What is the basic structural difference between glucose and fructose?
(c) Write the products obtained after hydrolysis of lactose.

29. What is spectrochemical series? Explain the difference between a weak field ligand and a strong field ligand.

OR

Write the name, the structure and the magnetic behaviour of each one of the following complex:
(At no. of Ni = 28, Pt = 78)

(a) $[Pt(NH_3)_2Cl(NO_2)]$ (b) $Ni(CO)_4$

30. The following compounds are given to you:
2-Bromopentane, 2-Bromo-2-methylbutane, 1-Bromopentane
(a) Write the compound which is most reactive towards S_N2 reaction.
(b) Write the compound which is optically active.
(c) Write the compound which is most reactive towards β-elimination reaction.

SECTION-D

The following questions are case-based questions. Each question has an internal choice and carries 4 (1+1+2) marks each. Read the passage carefully and answer the questions that follow.

31. Alcohols and phenols are the most important compounds used in our daily life. Alcohols are prepared by hydration of alkenes, fermentation of glucose, reduction of aldehydes, ketones, carboxylic acids, and esters. Alcohols are soluble in water. Boiling points increase with the increase in molar mass and decrease with branching. Alcohols on dehydration give alkene at 443K, follow carbocation mechanism. Excess of alcohol at 413K on dehydration with conc. H_2SO_4 also follows the carbocation mechanism but gives diethyl ether. Alcohols undergo nucleophilic substitution reactions, esterification with carboxylic acids, and derivatives like amides, acid halides, acid anhydride. Phenol is prepared from cumene, diazonium salts, anisole, and chlorobenzene. Phenol is used to prepare salicylaldehyde, salicylic acid, aspirin, methyl salicylate, *p*-benzoquinone. Phenol undergoes electrophilic substitution reaction at *o* & *p*-position.

Answer the following questions :

(a) The IUPAC name of $CH_3-\underset{OH}{\underset{|}{CH}}-CH_2-\overset{CH_3}{\overset{|}{\underset{OH}{\underset{|}{C}}}}-CH_3$?

(b) What happens when Acid catalyzed hydration of alkenes except ethene takes place?
(c) Alcohols react as nucleophiles in the reactions involving cleavage of O–H bond—Justify.

OR

How do you distinguish between solicylic acid and phenol?

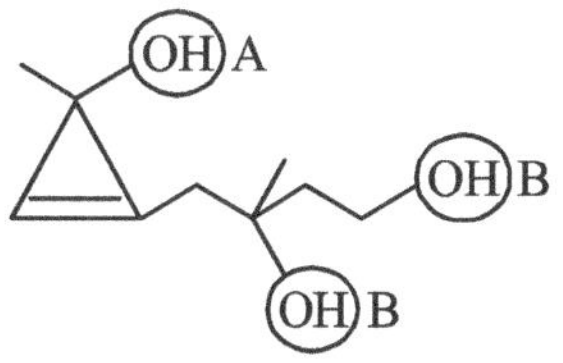

(OH)A (OH)B (OH)B

Explain the under of basic character of hydroxy groups in the above molecule.

32. The normal boiling point of a substance is the temperature at which the vapour pressure equals 1 atm. If a nonvolatile solute lowers the vapour pressure of a solvent, it must also affect the boiling point. Because the vapour pressure of the solution at a given temperature is less than the vapour pressure of the pure solvent, achieving a vapour pressure of 1 atm for the solution requires a higher temperature than the normal boiling point of the solvent. Thus the boiling point of a solution is always greater than that of the pure solvent. The magnitude of the increase in the boiling point is related to the magnitude of the decrease in the vapour pressure. The decrease in the vapour pressure is proportional to the concentration of the solute in the solution. Hence the magnitude of the increase in the boiling point must also be proportional to the concentration of the solute.

Answer the following questions :

(a) Assume three samples of juices A, B and C have glucose as the only sugar present in them. The concentration of sample A, B and C are 0.1M, .5M and 0.2 M respectively. Which one will have the highest freezing point?

(b) What happen to the boiling point and freezing pointof water when a non volatile solid is added to pure water?

(c) Polar solutes dissolve in a polar solvent and non-polars in non-polar solvents—Explain.

OR

Scuba drivers may experience a condition called Bends. To avoid this, the tanks used by scuba drivers are filled with air diluted with helium—Explain this phenomenon.

SECTION-E

The following questions are long answer type and carry 5 marks each. Two questions have an internal choice.

33. (a) Write the products formed when benzaldehyde reacts with the following reagents:

(i) CH_3CHO in presence of dilute NaOH

(ii) $H_2N-NH-C_6H_5$

(iii) Conc. NaOH

(b) Distinguish between the following:

(i) $CH_3-CH=CH-CO-CH_3$ and $CH_3-CH_2-CO-CH=CH_2$

(ii) Benzaldehyde and benzoic acid.

OR

(a) Write the final products in the following:

(i) $(CH_3)_2C=O \xrightarrow[\text{Conc. HCl}]{\text{Zn/Hg}}$

(ii) $C_6H_5-COONa \xrightarrow[D]{\text{NaOH/CaO}}$

(iii) $CH_2=CH-CH_2-CN \xrightarrow[(b)H_3O^+]{(a)DIBAL-H}$

(b) Arrange the following in the increasing order of their reactivity towards nucleophilic addition reaction:

CH_3COCH_3, HCHO, CH_3CHO, $C_6H_5-COCH_3$

(c) Draw the structure of 2, 4-DNP derivative of acetaldehyde.

34. (a) Consider the reaction $R \rightarrow P$ for which the change in concentration of R with time is shown by the following graph:

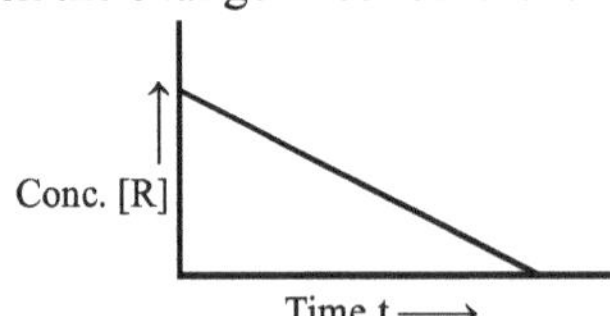

(i) Predict the order of reaction.

(ii) What does the slope of the curve indicate?

(b) The rate of reaction quadruples when temperature changes from 293 K to 313 K. Calculate E_a assuming that it does not change with time. $[R = 8.314\ JK^{-1}\ mol^{-1}]$

OR

(a) Draw the plot of *ln k* vs 1/T for a chemical reaction. What does the intercept represent? What is the relation between slope and E_a?

(b) A first order reaction takes 30 minutes for 20% decomposition. Calculate $t_{1/2}$ [log 2 = 0·3010]

35. (a) Explain why:

(i) Zn^{2+} salts are colourless while Ni^{2+} salts are coloured.

(ii) Why is copper sulphate pentahydrate coloured?

(iii) +2 oxidation state of manganese is quite stable while the same is not true for iron.

(b) The electronic configuration of an element is $3d^5 4s^1$. Write its

(i) most stable oxidation state, and (ii) most oxidising state.

SOLUTIONS

SAMPLE PAPER-1

1. **(d)** Due to inter-molecular hydrogen bonding in alcohols boiling point of alcohols is much higher than ether.

2. **(b)** $\underset{|}{CH_2Cl}$ CH_2Cl (*vic*-dihalide) $\quad$ $CHCl_2$ | CH_3 (*gem*-dihalide)

3. **(c)** Among the green elements, manganese has the highest oxidation state of + 7 in $KMnO_4$. Chromium, vanadium and iron has the highest oxidation state of +6 ($K_2Cr_2O_7$), +5 (V_2O_5) and +3 (Fe_2O_3) respectively. (1 mark)

4. **(c)** For zero order,
$A = A_0 - kt$
$$t_{1/2} = \frac{A_0}{2k}$$
$$t_{1/4} = \frac{A_0}{4k}$$
$$\frac{t_{1/2}}{t_{1/4}} = \frac{2}{1}$$

5. **(b)** Ag gets oxidized at anode and Br^- gets reduced at cathode.

6. **(b)** $3A \longrightarrow 2B$
Rate of appearance of B is equal to rate of disappearance of A.
$$\frac{1}{2}\frac{d[B]}{dt} = -\frac{1}{3}\frac{d[A]}{dt} \Rightarrow \frac{d[B]}{dt} = -\frac{2}{3}\frac{d[A]}{dt}$$ (1 mark)

7. **(d)** $\underset{\text{Alkyl isocyanide}}{R-N\equiv C} \xrightarrow{4[H]} \underset{\text{Secondary amine}}{RNH-CH_3}$

8. **(c)** [Structures: Cl–Co(en)$_2$–Cl complex and its mirror image, each with Cl above and below Co and en on both sides]

In complex (c), the mirror image is superimposable. So, they are not different compounds.

9. **(b)** Since the compound is formed by hydration of an alkene, to get the structure of alkene remove a molecule of water from the alcohol.
$$\underset{\text{Isopropyl alcohol}}{CH_3\underset{\underset{OH}{|}}{C}HCH_3} \xrightarrow{-H_2O} \underset{\text{Propylene}}{CH_2{=}CHCH_3}$$

10. **(b)** Nitrobenzene (NO_2) $\xrightarrow[30\%HCl]{Fe}$ Aniline (NH_2) $\xrightarrow[CH_3Br]{excess}$ N,N-dimethylaniline ($N(CH_3)_2$)

11. **(c)**

12. **(a)** $k = \frac{0.693}{t_{1/2}} = \frac{0.693}{480} = 1.44 \times 10^{-3} s^{-1}$

13. **(b)** $\mu = \sqrt{n(n+2)}$
$1.73 = \sqrt{n(n+2)} \Rightarrow n = 1$
No. of unpaired electrons = 1, hence its configuration will be, V(23) = [Ar] $3d^3 4s^2$
V^{4+} = [Ar]$3d^1 4s^0$
∴ Its chloride has the formula VCl_4.

14. **(b)** Compounds having $-\overset{\overset{O}{\|}}{C}-CH_3$ group show positive iodoform.
Hence, $CH_3-CH_2-CH_2-\underset{\underset{O}{\|}}{C}-CH_3$ (pentanone-2) gives this test.

15. **(b)** *ter*-butyl bromide and sodium methoxide reacts to form 2-methylpropene and ethanol (elimination reaction).
$$CH_3-\underset{\underset{CH_3}{|}}{\overset{\overset{CH_3}{|}}{C}}-Br + CH_3ONa \longrightarrow CH_3-\overset{\overset{CH_3}{|}}{C}=CH_2$$

16. **(a)** α-amino acids have a basic–NH_2 group and an acidic–COOH group. In neutral solution they exists as an internal salt which is also called as zwitter ion. This zwitter ion is formed due to the reason that proton of –COOH group is captured by –NH_2 group having lone pair of electrons.
$$H_2\ddot{N}-\overset{\overset{R}{|}}{C}H-COOH \longrightarrow \underset{\text{zwitter ion (dipolar ion)}}{H_3\overset{+}{N}-\overset{\overset{R}{|}}{C}H-COO^-}$$

17. **(c)** Cu^+ (cuprous ion) does not have any unpaired electron while cupric ion (Cu^{2+}) has one unpaired electron in 3*d* shell.
$Cu^+ = 3d^{10} 4s^0$; $Cu^{2+} = 3d^9 4s^0$
Cu^+ is colourless because it does not have any unpaired electron but Cu^{2+} ion is blue in aqueous solution due to the formation of complex with water molecules.

18. **(c)** The correct reason is : The overall electron deficiency in *m*-nitroaniline is much less (due to –R effect of NO_2 group and +R effect of NH_2 group) than in *m*-dinitrobenzene (–R effect of the two NO_2 groups) and hence does not accept additional electrons from a weak reducing agent such as $(NH_4)_2S$ and thus further reduction is prevented.

19. $k = 2{\cdot}2 \times 10^{-5}\ sec^{-1}$, t = 90 min = 90 × 60 = 5400 sec.

$$k = \frac{2{\cdot}303}{t} \log \frac{a}{(a-x)}$$ (½ mark)

$$2{\cdot}2 \times 10^{-5} = \frac{2{\cdot}303}{5400} \log \frac{a}{(a-x)}$$

$$\log\left(\frac{a}{a-x}\right) = \frac{2{\cdot}2 \times 10^{-5} \times 5400}{2{\cdot}303} = 0{\cdot}05158$$ (½ mark)

Taking antilog of both the sides, we get

$$\frac{a}{a-x} = 1{\cdot}126$$

$$a = 1{\cdot}126\,a - 1{\cdot}126\,x$$

$$x = \frac{0{\cdot}126}{1{\cdot}126}\,a = 0{\cdot}1119a$$

If a = 100 then x = 0·1119 × 100 = 11·19

Hence, the percentage decomposition of SO_2Cl_2 = 11·19 % (1 mark)

20. Chemical components of nucleotides are
(a) a nitrogenous base (purine or pyrimidine)
(b) a pentose sugar (ribose or 2-deoxyribose)
(c) a phosphoric acid group. (1 mark)

Functions of nucleotides:
(a) Nucleotides are precursors of nucleic acids in the cell.
(b) They are source of chemical energy, viz. ATP (adenosine triphosphate) and ADP (adenosine diphosphate). (1 mark)

OR

(i) **Glycosidic linkage:** A linkage between two monasaccharide units through O-atom is called glycosidic linkage. It is formed when two monosaccharide units are joined together through an ethereal or oxide linkage by loss of a H_2O molecule. (1 mark)

(ii) **Invert sugar:** An equimolar mixture of glucose and fructose is called invert sugar. (1 mark)

21. (a)

$$CH_3CH_2COOAg \xrightarrow{Br_2} CH_3CH_2Br \xrightarrow[KOH]{Alc.} CH_2 = CH_2$$

1-Bromoethane Ethene (1 mark)

(b) $CH_3{-}\underset{|\atop Br}{CH}{-}CH_3 \xrightarrow{Alc.KOH}$

2-Bromopropane Propane

$$CH_3 - CH = CH_2 \xrightarrow[peroxide]{HBr} CH_3 - CH_2 - CH_2 - Br$$

1-Bromopropane (1 mark)

22. Coordination number of cobalt is 6. NH_3 and Cl both are monodenate ligand. From the given information, it is clear that cobalt is in + 3 oxidation state and forms coordination sphere with four NH_3 and two Cl^- and third Cl^- forms ionisation sphere, *i.e.,* formula of complex is $[Co(NH_3)_4Cl_2]Cl$. (1 mark)

Its IUPAC name is tetrammine dichlorido cobalt (III) chloride. (1 mark)

OR

Transition metals/ions have empty *d*-orbitals into which the electron pairs can be accomodated which are donated by ligands containing π-electrons, *e.g.,* $CH_2 = CH_2$, C_5H_5, C_6H_6, etc. The presence of empty *d*-orbitals in the transition metal enables them to form π-complexes. (2 marks)

23. (a) This occurs due to the cathodic protection in which magnesium metal is oxidised (or corroded) in preference to iron since its reduction potential is lower. It acts as anode and protects iron from getting rusted.

$Mg^{2+}(aq) + 2e^- \rightarrow Mg(s);\ E^\circ = -2.37\ V$

$Fe^{2+}(aq) + 2e^- \rightarrow Fe(s);\ E^\circ = -0.44\ V$ (1 mark)

(b) With decrease in the concentration or upon dilution, the number of ions present per unit volume of the solution also decrease. As a result, the conductivity of the soluton decreases. (1 mark)

24. $$\log \frac{k_2}{k_1} = \frac{E_a}{2{\cdot}303\,R}\left[\frac{T_2 - T_1}{T_1 T_2}\right]$$

$$E_a = \frac{2{\cdot}303\,R \times T_1 T_2}{T_2 - T_1} \log \frac{k_2}{k_1}$$ (½ mark)

$$= \frac{2{\cdot}303 \times 8{\cdot}314 \times 298 \times 308}{308 - 298} \log \frac{14 \times 10^{-5}}{3.5 \times 10^{-5}}$$ (½ mark)

$= 175740{\cdot}12 \log 4 = 175740{\cdot}12 \times 0{\cdot}6020$

$= 105795\ J = 105{\cdot}795\ kJ.$ (1 mark)

25. (a) Addition of H_2O to ethenylbenzene (styrene) is presence of dil. H_2SO_4.

$$C_6H_5{-}CH=CH_2 + H-OH \xrightarrow{dil.\ H_2SO_4} C_6H_5{-}\underset{|\atop OH}{CH}{-}CH_3$$

(Styrene) 1-Phenylethanol

(1 mark)

(b) Hydrolysis of cyclohexylmethyl bromide by aqueous NaOH gives cyclohexylmethanol.

$$C_6H_{11}{-}CH_2Br + NaOH \xrightarrow[S_N2,\ hydrolysis]{\Delta} C_6H_{11}{-}CH_2OH + NaBr$$

Cyclohexylmethyl Bromide Cyclohexyl methanol

(1 mark)

26. (a) Lucas regent (anhyd. $ZnCl_2$ + HCl) is added to both and shaken. 2-propanol produces cloudiness in about 3-5 minutes at room temperature while 1-propanol does not give cloudiness even after a long time at room temperature. (1 marks)

(b) It is because of the poisonous substance (phosgene) which is formed due to its reaction with air in presence of light. (1 mark)

(c) $CH_3-\underset{\underset{Cl}{\downarrow}}{CH}\leftarrow\overset{O}{\overset{\|}{C}}\leftarrow O\leftarrow H > \underset{\underset{Cl}{\downarrow}}{CH_2}\leftarrow CH_2\leftarrow\overset{O}{\overset{\|}{C}}\leftarrow O\leftarrow H$

α-Chloropropanoic acid β-Chloropropanoic acid

Electron withdrawing effect (– I effect) decrease with increase in distance of electron withdrawing group from carboxyl group. (1 mark)

27. (a) A - $[Co(NH_3)_5SO_4]Cl$ (1 mark)
B - $[Co(NH_3)_5Cl]SO_4$ (1 mark)
(b) Ionisation isomerism (½ mark)
(c) IUPAC name of A is Pentaamminesulphatocobalt (III) chloride, IUPAC name of B is Pentaammine chlorocobalt (III) sulphate. (½ mark)

28. $K_f = 1.85\ K\ mol^{-1}\ kg$, $\Delta T_f = 6K$, $m = 62$,
$W = 4\ kg = 4 \times 10^3\ g$, w = wt. of solute

Now we know that $\Delta T_f = \dfrac{1000 \times K_f \times w}{W \times m}$

$$6 = \frac{1000 \times 1.85 \times w}{4 \times 10^3 \times 62}$$

On usual calculations, $w = 804.32$ g (3 marks)

29. (a) $C_6H_5N_2^+Cl^- + KI \longrightarrow C_6H_5I + KCl + I_2$

Benzene diazonium chloride → Iodobenzene (1 mark)

(b) Aniline $\xrightarrow{Br_2/H_2O}$ 2,4,6-Tribromoaniline (1 mark)

(c) Aniline (NH₂) $+ (CH_3CO)_2O \longrightarrow$ Acetanilide ($NHCOCH_3$) (1 mark)

(d) Aniline (NH_2) $\xrightarrow{HCl}$ Anilinium chloride ($NH_3^+Cl^-$) (1 mark)

30. (a) All are primary alkyl halides and their structural formulae are:

(I) $C_2H_5-\overset{CH_3}{\underset{H}{C}}-CH_2Br$

(II) $CH_3-\overset{CH_3}{\underset{CH_3}{C}}-CH_2Br$

(III) $C_4H_9-\overset{H}{\underset{H}{C}}-Br$

The order of reactivity is : (III) > (I) > (II) (½ mark)
The S_N2 reactions are sensitive to steric hindrance. Greater the steric hindrance to the attacking nucleophile, lesser will be the reactivity. (1 mark)

(b) $CH_3F < CH_3Cl < CH_3Br < CH_3I$ (½ mark)
In the nucleophilic substitution reactions, the nucleophile is to displace the halide ion (X^-). Greater the bond dissociation enthalpy of the C—X bond, lesser will be the reactivity. The order of bond dissociation enthalpy of different C—X bond is
C—F > C—Cl > C—Br > C—I
The order of reactivity towards S_N2 reactions is the reverse. (1 mark)

OR

(a) Allyl chloride readily undergoes ionization to produce resonance stabilized allyl carbocation. Since carbocations are reactive species, therefore, allyl cation readily combines with OH^- ions to form allyl alcohol. Corresponding formation of n-propyl carbocation is not easy because of its less stability. So, n-propyl chloride does not hydrolyse easily.

$$\underset{\text{Allyl chloride}}{CH_2=CH-CH_2-Cl} \xrightarrow[\text{Slow}]{\text{Ionization}} CH_2=CH-\overset{+}{C}H_2 + Cl^- \longleftrightarrow \underset{\text{Allyl carbocation}}{\overset{+}{C}H_2-CH=CH_2}$$

$$\underset{\text{Allyl carbocation}}{\overset{+}{C}H_2-CH=CH_2} \xrightarrow[\text{Fast}]{OH^-} \underset{\text{Allyl alcohol}}{CH_2=CH-CH_2OH}$$

(1 mark)

(b) Vinyl chloride may be represented as a resonance hybrid of the following two structures:

$$CH_2=CH-\ddot{\underset{..}{Cl}}: \longleftrightarrow :\bar{C}H_2-CH=\overset{+}{\underset{..}{Cl}}:$$

As a result of resonance, the carbon-chlorine bond acquires some double bond character. In contrast, in ethyl chloride the carbon-chlorine bond is a pure single bond. Thus, vinyl chloride undergoes hydrolysis more slowly than ethyl chloride. (1 mark)

(c) This is because in $CHCl_3$ all the three chlorine atoms are bonded to carbon atom by covalent bonds and there is no free chloride ions. $AgNO_3$ gives white precipitate when free chloride ions are present in solution. (1 mark)

31. (a) 0.05 [1 molecule will require 5 molecules of HIO_4. Hence 10^{-2} moles will require 5×10^{-2} moles of HIO_4.] (1 mark)
(b) Tartaric and glycolic acid. (1 mark)
(c) Glucose on oxidation with conc. HNO_3 produces dibasic acid, So, basicity will be two. (2 mark)

OR

Red P/ HI and $LiAlH_4$ can be used for reduction of both glucose and fructose. (2 mark)

32. (a) By adding nonvolatile solute vapour pressure of the solution dcrease. (1 mark)

(b) Plot I because methanol is a volatile compound. (1 mark)

(c) Because methanol is more volatile than water. (2 marks)

OR

$T_3 - T_2$ (2 marks)

33. (a) Mg is more electropositive than Ag, so the cell is Mg $|Mg^{2+}||Ag^{+}(aq)|$ Ag.

The net cell reaction is given by,

$Mg + 2Ag^{+} \longrightarrow Mg^{2+} + 2Ag$ (½ mark)

Here $n = 2$ (½ mark)

The Nernst equation for this cell is,

$$E_{cell} = E^{\circ}_{cell} - \frac{2{\cdot}303\,RT}{nF}\log\frac{[Mg^{2+}]}{[Ag^{+}]^2} \quad \text{(½ mark)}$$

$$2{\cdot}96 = E^{\circ}_{cell} - \frac{2{\cdot}303 \times 8{\cdot}31 \times 298}{2 \times 96500}\log\frac{0{\cdot}130}{(1\times10^{-4})^2} \quad \text{(½ mark)}$$

$$\therefore E^{\circ}_{cell} = 2{\cdot}96 + \frac{2{\cdot}303 \times 8{\cdot}31 \times 298}{2 \times 96500}\log\frac{0{\cdot}130}{(1\times10^{-4})^2} \quad \text{(½ mark)}$$

$$= 2{\cdot}96 + 0{\cdot}0295 \times 7{\cdot}114 = 2{\cdot}96 + 0{\cdot}21$$

$E^{\circ}_{cell} = 3{\cdot}17$ V. (½ mark)

(b) No, we cannot use a copper vessel to store $AgNO_3$ solution. This is because the reduction potential of Ag^{+}/Ag electrode is higher than that of Cu^{2+}/Cu electrode, *i.e.*, copper is more reactive than silver.

$2Ag^{+}(aq) + Cu(s) \longrightarrow 2Ag(s) + Cu^{2+}(aq)$. (2 marks)

OR

(a) An aqueous solution of NaCl contains Na^{+}, Cl^{-}, H^{+} and OH^{-} ions (produced by the dissociation of H_2O). When this solution is electrolysed, the cations (Na^{+} and H^{+}) migrate towards the cathode whereas anions (Cl^{-} and OH^{-}) migrate towards the anode.

Since the reduction potential of Na is less than that of H_2, H_2 is reduced in preference to Na at cathode.

$2H_2O\,(l) + 2e^{-} \longrightarrow H_2\,(g) + 2OH^{-}$

At anode, the following reactions take place:

$2Cl^{-}(aq) \longrightarrow Cl_2(g) + 2e^{-}; E^{\circ} = 1{\cdot}36$ V

$2H_2O\,(l) \longrightarrow O_2(g) + 4H^{+}(aq) + 4e^{-}; E^{\circ} = 1{\cdot}23$ V

The reaction at the anode with lower value of E° is preferred and water should get oxidised in preference to $Cl^{-}(aq)$. But $Cl^{-}(aq)$ is oxidised in preference to H_2O because of over potential of oxygen. (2 marks)

The overall reaction may be written as,

$$NaCl\,(aq) + H_2O\,(l) \longrightarrow Na^{+}(aq) + OH^{-}(aq) + \frac{1}{2}H_2\,(g) + \frac{1}{2}Cl_2\,(g).$$ (1 mark)

(b) Reduction potential, $E^{\circ}_{I_2,I^-}$ is lower than that of $E^{\circ}_{F_2,F^-}$. Iodide ion (I^{-}) will be oxidised and F_2 will be reduced to F^{-}, *i.e.*, the following reaction will take place:

$F_2 + 2I^{-} \longrightarrow 2F^{-} + I_2$ (2 marks)

34. (a) Ethanal to lactic acid :

$$\underset{\text{Ethanal}}{CH_3CH = O} \xrightarrow{HCN} \underset{\text{Ethanal cyanohydrin}}{CH_3CH(OH)CN} \xrightarrow{2H_2O/H^+} \underset{\text{Lactic acid}}{CH_3CH(OH)COOH}$$ (1 mark)

(b) Ethanol to butan-2-one :

$$\underset{\text{Ethanol}}{CH_3CH_2OH} \xrightarrow[-H_2O]{\text{Oxidation}} \underset{\text{Ethanal}}{CH_3CHO} \xrightarrow{C_2H_5MgBr} \underset{\text{Addition compound}}{CH_3CH(OMgBr)C_2H_5} \xrightarrow{H_2O} \underset{\text{Butan-2-ol}}{CH_3C(H)(OH)C_2H_5} \xrightarrow[-H_2O]{\text{Oxidation}} \underset{\text{Butan-2-one}}{CH_3COCH_2CH_3}$$ (1 mark)

(c) Acetone to *tert*-butyl alcohol :

$$\underset{\text{Acetone}}{CH_3COCH_3} \xrightarrow{CH_3MgBr} \underset{\text{Addition compound}}{\left[(H_3C)_2C(OMgBr)CH_3\right]} \xrightarrow{H_2O} \underset{tert\text{-Butyl alcohol}}{(H_3C)_2C(OH)CH_3}$$ (1 mark)

(d) Propene to propanone :

$$\underset{\text{Propene}}{CH_3CH = CH_2} \xrightarrow{H_2O/H^+} \underset{\text{Propan-2-ol}}{CH_3-CH(OH)-CH_3} \xrightarrow{K_2Cr_2O_7/H^+} \underset{\text{Propanone}}{CH_3-C(=O)-CH_3}$$ (1 mark)

(e) Benzaldehyde to benzophenone :

$$\underset{\text{Benzaldehyde}}{C_6H_5CHO} \xrightarrow{\text{Oxidation}} \underset{\text{Benzoic acid}}{C_6H_5COOH} \xrightarrow[\text{heat}]{Ca(OH)_2} \underset{\text{Cal. benzoate}}{(C_6H_5COO)_2Ca} \xrightarrow{\text{Distill.}} \underset{\text{Benzophenone}}{C_6H_5COC_6H_5}$$

(1 mark)

OR

(a) (i) $\underset{\text{Formaldehyde}}{6HCHO} + 4NH_3 \longrightarrow \underset{\text{Urotropine}}{(CH_2)_6N_4} + 6H_2O$ (1 mark)

(ii) $$\underset{\text{2,2-Dimethylpropanal}}{2CH_3-\overset{CH_3}{\underset{CH_3}{C}}-CHO} + NaOH \xrightarrow[\text{Cannizzaro reaction}]{\text{Heat}} \underset{\text{Sod. 2, 2-Dimethylpropanoate}}{CH_3-\overset{CH_3}{\underset{CH_3}{C}}-COONa} + \underset{\text{2, 2-Dimethylpropan-1-ol}}{CH_3-\overset{CH_3}{\underset{CH_3}{C}}-CH_2OH}$$ (1 mark)

(b) (i) Grignard reagents form ketones with acid chlorides but the reaction does not stop at this stage. Ketones further take part in the reactions with Grignard reagents to give tertiary alcohols. Therefore, dialkyl cadmium is used which reacts with only acid chlorides and not with ketones. (1½ mark)

(ii) Hydrazones are formed by reacting carbonyl compounds with hydrazine ($\ddot{N}H_2-\ddot{N}H_2$) which acts as a nucleophile. In the strongly acidic medium, hydrazine gets protonated and, therefore, it is not in a position to act as nucleophile. As a result, hydrazones of aldehydes and ketones are not prepared in strongly acidic medium. (1½ mark)

35. (a) (i) None. Both V_2O_5 and CrO_3 are acidic oxides. (1 mark)

(ii) Ti (Z = 22) has electronic configuration $[Ar]^{18}\ 3d^2\ 4s^2$. It shows + 4 as most stable oxidation state in which it (Ti^{4+}) has configuration of argon. (1 mark)

(iii) In copper sulphate pentahydrate, $CuSO_4\cdot5H_2O$, Cu^{2+} ion has unpaired electron in 3*d*-orbital. Due to this, Cu^{2+} ion can have *d* – *d* transition when exposed to visible radiation. (1 mark)

(b) (i) Mn^{2+} is more stable $(4s^0\ 3d^5)$, because of half-filled *d*-orbitals than Mn^{3+} $(4s^0\ 3d^4)$ while Fe^{3+} $(4s^0\ 3d^5)$ is more stable than Fe^{2+} $(4s^0\ 3d^6)$ again because of half filled *d*-orbitals. Therefore, Mn^{3+} can be easily reduced to Mn^{2+} whereas Fe^{3+} is not easily reduced to Fe^{2+}, rather Fe^{2+} is more easily oxidised to Fe^{3+}. (1 mark)

(ii) Ce^{4+} is more stable than Ce^{3+} because of stable electronic configuration and higher hydration energy of Ce^{4+}, hence Ce^{3+} is easily oxidised to Ce^{4+}. (1 mark)

1. **(c)** For ideal solution,
$\Delta V_{mixing} = 0$ and $\Delta H_{mixing} = 0$.

2. **(b)** The solubility of alcohols depend on number of C-atoms of alcohols. The solubility of alcohols in water decreases with the increase in number of C-atoms of alcohol. As resulting molecular weight increases, the polar nature of – OH bond decreases and hence strength of hydrogen bond decreases.

3. **(d)** Atomic radii follows the order, Ce > Ho > Lu

4. **(b)** $Pd/BaSO_4$ is used as a catalyst in rosenmund reduction.

5. **(b)** **Chlorine;** because rate of formation of $\dot{C}H_3$ (one of the propagating steps) is high when $\dot{X}$ is Cl.
$CH_4 + \dot{X} \longrightarrow \dot{C}H_3 + H-X$

6. **(b)** The attraction between HCl and H_2O molecules is stronger, so the escaping tendency from the solution to the vapour phase will be smaller. Then, the partial vapour pressure will be smaller than predicted by Raoult's law and the system will exhibit a negative deviation.

7. **(a)** $2Cr^{3+} + 7H_2O \rightarrow Cr_2O_7^{2-} + 14H^+$
O.S. of Cr changes from +3 to +6 by loss of electrons. At anode oxidation takes place.

8. **(b)** Hinsberg's reagent is $C_6H_5SO_2Cl$ which is used to distinguish between primary, secondary and tertiary amines.

9. **(c)** As $\alpha-D-(+)-$glucose and $\beta-D-(+)$ glucose differ in configuration at C – 1 atom so they are colled anomers.

10. **(d)** Order of reaction $= 1 + \frac{1}{2} = 1.5$
Molecularity of the reaction = 1 + 1 = 2
As, $\frac{dx}{dt} \propto [Br_2]^{1/2}$;
so, the rate of reaction will be doubled if concentration of Br_2 is increased by 4 times.

11. **(a)** Given $\mu = 3.9$ BM
$\mu = \sqrt{n(n+2)}$ BM; $3.9 = \sqrt{n(n+2)}$; $n = 3$
So, the central metal ion has 3 unpaired electrons.
∴ Configuration is either d^3 or d^7 as H_2O is a weak field ligand.
V^{2+} has d^3 configuration.
Co^{2+} has d^7 configuration.

12. **(c)** $E^0_{cell} = \frac{2.303\,RT}{nF} \log K_{eq} = \frac{0.0591}{n} \log K_{eq}$
$= \frac{0.0591}{2} \log 10^6 = 0.0591 \times 3 = 0.1773$ V

13. **(a)** Plots of conc. [A] Vs time, t

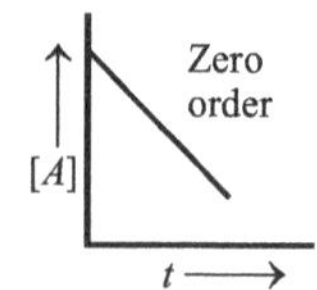

14. **(b)** $[Pt(NH_3)_4Cl_2]Br_2$ and
$[Pt(NH_3)_4ClBr]Cl.Br$: Ionization isomer

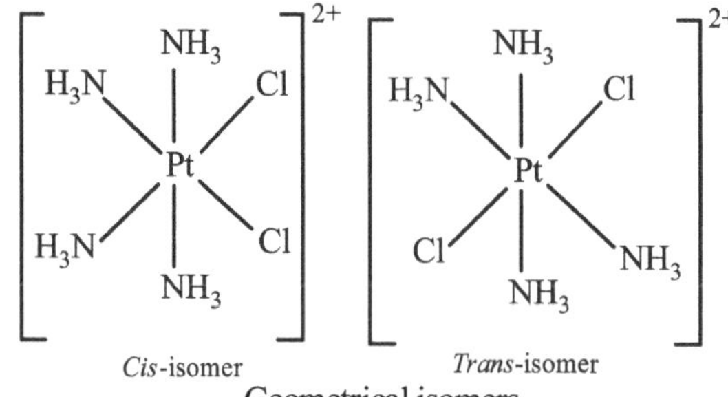

Geometrical isomers

15. **(c)** Anilinium chloride is more acidic than ammonium chloride as it easily looses proton to form aniline (resonance stabilized).
Anilinium ion does not show resonance because charge dispersion at ring may involve unstable pentavalent nitrogen structure.

16. **(b)** Due to denaturation, a protein molecule uncoils and, form a more random conformation and ultimately precipitates from the solution. Also, during denaturation protein molecule loses its biological activity.
Thus, reason is correct but it is not the correct explanation of assertion.

17. **(c)** Aryl halides do not undergo nucleophilic substitution under ordinary conditions due to resonance. Due to resonance the carbon–halogen bond acquires partial double bond character, which is shorter and stronger and thus, cannot be substibuted by nucleophiles.

18. **(b)** Phenol is a stronger acid than ethanol because phenoxide ion is resonance stabilised.
Groups having +M effect present at *p*-position (like halide group), decreases the acidity of phenols.

19. Cu^{2+} $[Ar]_{18}\,3d^9\,4s^0$
Cr^{2+} $[Ar]_{18}\,3d^4\,4s^0$
As can be seen from the electronic configuration, above that additional five electrons in Cu^{2+} are present in the same 3*d*-orbitals as compared to Cr^{2+}. Thus, there are greater attractive forces in Cu^{2+} ion between nucleus and 3*d*-electron as compared to Cr^{2+} ion. (2 marks)

20. $(Rate)_1 = k[A]^m[B]^n$; $(Rate)_2 = k(2[A])^m([B]/2)^n$

Hence, $\frac{(rate)_2}{(rate)_1} = 2^m \times \left(\frac{1}{2}\right)^n = 2^{m-n}$ (2 marks)

OR

Assuming I[st] order, i.e., $k = \frac{2.303}{t} \log_{10} \frac{a}{(a-x)}$, where

a = 0.12 M (½ mark)

For case I : $k = \frac{2.303}{10} \log_{10} \frac{0.12}{0.06} = 0.069\ hr^{-1}$

for t = 10 hr; (a-x) = 0.06M (½ mark)

For case II : $k = \frac{2.303}{20} \log_{10} \frac{0.12}{0.03} = 0.069\ hr^{-1}$

for t = 20 hr; (a-x) = 0.03M (½ mark)

Reaction is of I[st] order and rate constant $k = 0.069\ hr^{-1}$ (½ mark)

21. $\lambda_m^\infty(NH_4OH) = \lambda_m^\infty(NH_4^+) + \lambda_m^\infty(OH^-)$

Using Kohlrausch law of independent migration of ions, $\lambda^\infty(NH_4OH)$

$= [\lambda_m^\infty(NH_4^+) + \lambda_m^\infty(Cl^-)] + [\lambda_m^\infty(Na^+) + \lambda_m^\infty(OH^-)]$

$- [\lambda_m^\infty(Na^+) + \lambda_m^\infty Cl^-]$ (1 mark)

$= \lambda_m^\infty(NH_4Cl) + \lambda_m^\infty(NaOH) - \lambda_m^\infty NaCl$

$= 150 + 248{\cdot}1 - 126{\cdot}4 = 271{\cdot}7\ S\ cm^2\ mol^{-1}$. (1 mark)

22. Here, $x_1 = x$ and $x_2 = 2x$ and $p_1^\circ = p$ and $p_2^\circ = 2p$

So, $p_1 = x_1 \times p_1^\circ$

and $p_2 = x_2 \times p_2^\circ$

$p_1 = x \times p$; $p_2 = 2x \times 2p$

$p_1 = x \times p = xp$; $p_2 = 4xp$

$p_{total} = p_1 + p_2 = xp + 4xp = 5xp$ (1 mark)

Mole fraction of component 1 in vapour phase

$y_1 = \frac{p_1}{p_{total}} \Rightarrow y_1 = \frac{xp}{5xp} = 0.2$ (1 mark)

23. (a) Due to presence of lone pair of electrons on oxygen, alcohols behave as Bronsted base (proton acceptors). (1 mark)

(b) Alcohol molecules are capable of forming H–bonds with each other. On the other hand ether molecules do not form H–bonds and thus they do not exhibit association, hence their boiling point are lower than the isomeric alcohols. (1 mark)

OR

(a) Greater acidity of phenol than an alcohol is due to possibility of resonance in phenol which leads to electron-deficient oxygen atom. Presence of electron-deficient oxygen atom (see structures II, III and IV) in turn weakens the $-\overset{+}{O}\leftarrow H$ bond, and thus facilitates release of proton.

Such structures are not possible in alcohols. (1 mark)

(b) Amino group, being electron releasing, intensifies the negative charge if present at *ortho* and *para* positions (but not *meta* position) and thus makes the phenoxide less stable and thus the parent phenol (*o*-amino phenol) less acidic than phenol. However, when present at *meta* position, it is not involved in the intensification of charge and thus has no additional effect on stability of the corresponding phenoxide ion and hence on acidity of the corresponding phenol (*m*-amino phenol), i.e. it is as acidic as phenol and hence more acidic than *o*-aminophenol. (1 mark)

24. (a) Stability of the corresponding conjugate acids.

$(CH_3)_2\overset{+}{N}H_2$	> $CH_3\overset{+}{N}H_3$	> $(CH_3)_3\overset{+}{N}H$	> NH_4^+
Most stable due to solvation as well as inductive (2 CH_3 gps) effects	Less stable due to one +I gp.	Lesser stable due to less solvation	Least stable due to absence of +I gp.

Thus the relative basic strength of the four parent compounds is

$(CH_3)_2NH > CH_3NH_2 > (CH_3)_3N > NH_3$ (1 mark)

(b) Increasing order of basic strength in gas phase is (1 mark)

CH_3NH_2	< $C_2H_5NH_2$	< $(C_2H_5)_2NH$	< $(C_2H_5)_3N$
Least +I effect due to CH_3 group	Lesser +I effect due to 1 ethyl group	Lesser +I effect due to 2 ethyl groups	Max. +I effect due to 3 ethyl groups

25. When proteins dissolved in water is heated above 80 °C, rearrangement of secondary and tertiary structures occurs, as simple heating can cause disruption of these comparatively weaker forces of attraction. However, primary structure remains unaffected as it involves stronger covalent bonds between various amino acid units. (2 marks)

26. (a) Raoult's law: According to Raoult's law, for a solution of volatile liquids, the partial vapour pressure of each component of the solution is directly proportional to its mole fraction pressent in the solution (1 mark)

(b) Acc. to relative lowering of vapour pressure

$$\frac{p^\circ - p}{p^\circ} = \frac{w/m}{w/m + W/M}$$

Here, $p^\circ = 640$ mm Hg, $p = 600$ mm Hg, $w = 2.175$g, $W = 39.0$ g, $M = 78$, m = Molecular weight of solute

Substituting the various values in the above equation,

$$\frac{640-600}{640} = \frac{2.175/m}{2.175/m + 39/78}$$ (1½ marks)

$m = 65.25$ (½ mark)

OR

(a) Mass of H_2SO_4 in 100 mL of 93% H_2SO_4 solution = 93g
∴ Mass of H_2SO_4 in 1000 mL of the H_2SO_4 solution = 930g
Mass of 1000 mL H_2SO_4 solution = 1000 × 1.84 = 1840g
Mass of water in 1000 mL of solution = 1840 – 930 = 910 g

$$\text{Moles of } H_2SO_4 = \frac{\text{Wt. of } H_2SO_4}{\text{Mol Wt. of } H_2SO_4} = \frac{930}{98}$$ (1 mark)

$$\text{Molality (m)} = \frac{\text{Moles of } H_2SO_4}{\text{Mass of water (in kg)}}$$

$$\text{Molality (m)} = \frac{930}{98} \times \frac{1000}{910} = 10.43 \text{ mol kg}^{-1}$$

∴ Molality of 1 litre solution = 10.43 (1 mark)

(b) Increased temperature causes an increase in kinetic energy. the higher energy causes more motion in the gas molecules which break intermolecular bonds and escape from solution. Therefore, as the temperature increases, the solubility of a gas in a liquid decreases. (1 mark)

27. (a) Though the energy possessed by molecules is more than the threshold energy and the reaction should proceed at a reasonable rate yet in some cases the reaction is slow. It is due to the fact that in such cases the reacting molecules are not properly oriented. Due to this the number of effective collision decreases and so the reaction is slower than expected rate. (1 + 1 = 2 mark)

(b) A bimolecular reaction may be kinetically of the first order by taking one of the reactants in large excess so that it may not contribute towards the order of reaction. (1 mark)

28. (a) $2C_2H_5OH \xrightarrow[415K]{\text{conc. } H_2SO_4} C_2H_5—OC_2H_5 + H_2O$

(1 mark)

(b) $CH_3CH_2CH_2CH_2OH \xrightarrow[\text{Oxidation}]{KMnO_4/\text{dil}H_2SO_4}$
$CH_3CH_2CH_2COOH$ (1 mark)

(c) Aldehydes forms silver mirror with Tollen's reagent and forms red precipitate with Fehling solution, and restore the pink colour of Schiff's reagent. Ketones do not respond to any of these tests. (1 mark)

29. (a) $CH_3–\overset{O}{\overset{\|}{C}}–CH_2CH_3 \xrightarrow[\text{or Ni}/H_2]{LiAlH_4,\ NaBH_4} CH_3–\overset{OH}{\overset{|}{C}H}–CH_2CH_3$

Butan-2-one → Butan-2-ol

(1 mark)

(b) $(CH_3)_2C = O \xrightarrow[-H_2O]{NH_2OH} (CH_3)_2C = NOH$

Acetone → Acetoxime

$\xrightarrow[\text{Reduction}]{LiAlH_4} (CH_3)_2CHNH_2$ (1 mark)

Isopropylamine

(c) Benzaldehyde (C_6H_5CHO) $\xrightarrow{\text{Oxidation}}$ Benzoic acid (C_6H_5COOH) $\xrightarrow[\text{(Heat)}]{NH_3}$

Benzamide ($C_6H_5CONH_2$) $\xrightarrow[-H_2O]{(P_2O_5/\text{heat})}$ Cyanobenzene (C_6H_5CN) (1 mark)

30. (a) Amylose and Amylopectin

Amylose: It is a linear polymer of α-D glucose having approximately 200 –1000 α-D-glucose units. C-1 of one α-D glucose is attached to C-4 of another α-D glucose with glycosidic bond. It is water soluble and it forms 15-20% part of starch and give blue colour with I_2.

Amylopectin: It is a branched chain polymer of α-D glucose which is constituted by hundreds of small chain having 20-30 α-D glucose unit. In it small chain are formed by glycosidic bonds between C-1 and C-4. These chain are joined by $C_1—C_6$ bonds. This fraction does not give blue colour with I_2. (1 mark)

(b) Peptide linkage and Glycosidic linkange

The bond conecting two or more similar or different amino acid in protein is commonly called *peptide bond* or *peptide linkage*. In the formation of peptide bond —NH_2 group of one amino acid is condensed with —COOH of adjacent amino acid to form —CONH linkage. When —OH group of hemiacetal carbon of one monosaccharide is condensed with — OH group of another, glycosidic bond is formed, which links two monosacharide together. (1 mark)

(c)

Fibrous Proteins	Globular Proteins
(i) Proteins which are made up of linear, thread like molecules are called fibrous protein. In these molecules, poly-peptide chains are held together with H bonds.	(i) In these proteins poly-peptides attain spherical shape and poly-peptides are held together with relatively weaker-H-bonds.
(ii) They are insoluble in water but soluble in strong acid and bases. **Example:** Keratin, Myosin	(ii) They are soluble in water, alkalies, salt solutions and acid solutions. **Example:** Globulin, Pepsin

(1 mark)

OR

(a) Glucose on heating with HI and red phosphorous at 100°C, it forms *n*-hexane. This proves the presence of straight chain of six carbon atom in glucose. (1 mark)

(b) Glucose forms pentaacetyl derivatives with acid chloride and acid anhydride in the presence of anhydrous zinc chloride. It proves that one molecule of glucose contains five —OH groups. (1 mark)

(c) Glucose reacts with hydrogen cyanide to form, cyanohydrin. This reaction proves the presence of carbonyl group. (1 mark)

31. (a) $2I^- + Cl_2 \longrightarrow I_2 + 2Cl^-$

$E° = E^o_{I^-/I_2} + E^o_{Cl_2/Cl^-} = -0.54 + 1.36\,; E° = 0.82V$ (1 mark)

E° is positive hence, iodide ion is oxidized by chlorine.

(b) The precipitate formed in this reaction is of $Fe_4[Fe(CN)_6]_3$ (1 mark)

(c) No, oxygen cannot oxidised chloride ion because reduction potential of chloride ion is higher than oxygen. (2 marks)

OR

Reduction potential of Mn^{+3}/Mn^{+2} is higher than that of O_2. Therefore Mn^{+3} undergo reduction and water is oxidised to O_2. (2 marks)

32. (a) Compound "A" will be ZnO. (1 mark)

(b) B is $ZnCl_2$ (1 mark)

(c) It is amphoteric in nature. (2 marks)

OR

$$\underset{\text{"A"}}{ZnO} + 2NaOH(aq) \longrightarrow \underset{\text{"C"}}{Na_2ZnO_2} + H_2O$$

"C" + $H_2S \rightarrow ZnS$ (2 marks)

33. (a) (i) $[Cr(C_2O_4)_3]^{3-} \Rightarrow [Cr(ox)_3]^{3-}$

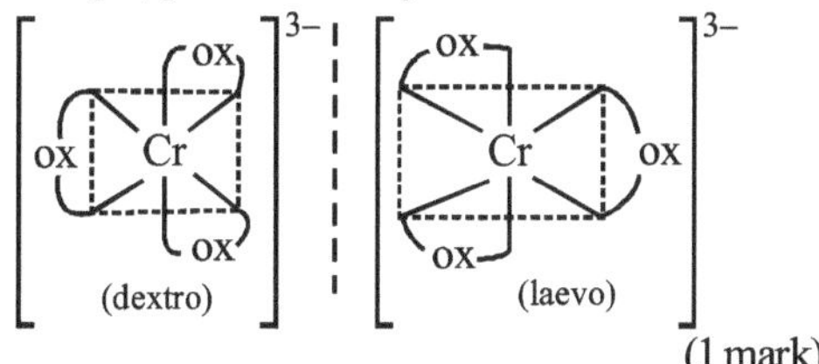

(1 mark)

(ii) cis - $[PtCl_2(en)_2]^{2+}$

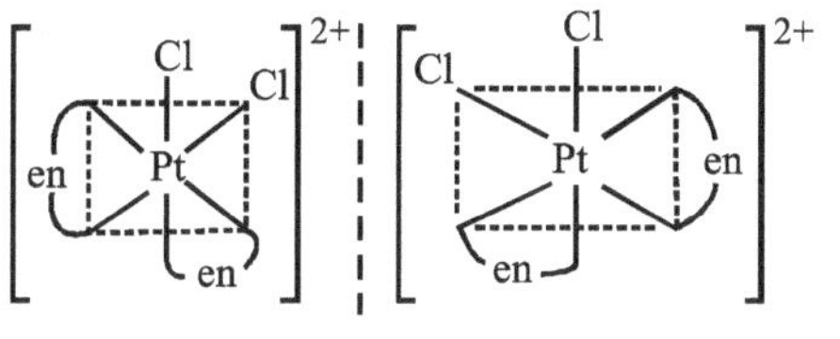

(1 mark)

(iii) cis - $[Cr(NH_3)_2Cl_2(en)]^+$

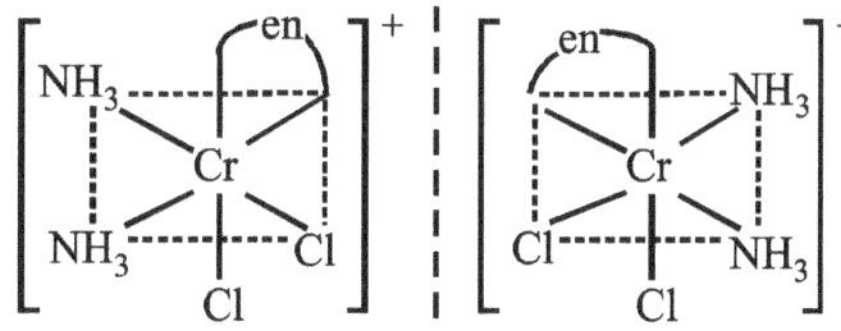

(1 mark)

(b) The spin magnetic moment, μ of the complex is 1.73 BM.

$\mu = \sqrt{n(n+2)} = 1.73 \Rightarrow n = 1$

It means that nucleus of the complex, chromium ion **has one unpaired electron**. So the ligand NO is **unit positively** charged. (½ mark)

IUPAC name :

Potassium amminetetracyanonitrosochromate (I). (½ mark)

Electronic configuration of Cr^+ :

Electronic configuration of Cr^+ under the influence of strong field ligand CN^-

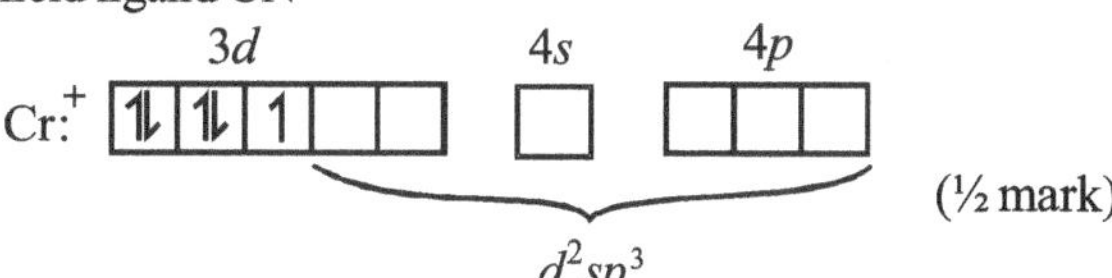

(½ mark)

So, Hybridisation : d^2sp^3

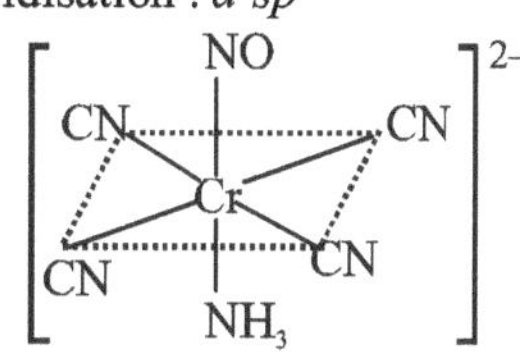

Shape : Octahedral (½ mark)

OR

(a) (i) Diamminechloridonitrito-N-platinum (II) (½ mark)

(ii) Potassium trioxalatochromate (III) (½ mark)

(b) In $Ni(CO)_4$, Ni is in zero oxidation state whereas in $NiCl_4^{2-}$, it is in +2 oxidation state. In the presence of CO ligand, the unpaired *d*-electrons of Ni pair up but Cl^- being a weak ligand is unable to pair up the unpaired electrons. (1 mark)

(c) (i) For octahedral complexes, coordination number should be 6. Since, nickel has $[Ar]3d^84s^2$ configuration *i.e.*, only one *d*-orbital is empty, so it can only form high spin octahedral complexes. (1 mark)

(ii) The transition metals/ions contain vacant *d*-orbitals to accomodate the electron pair donated by ligands containing π-electrons while the other metals do not have empty *d*-orbitals hence π complexes are formed by only transition metal atoms/ions. (1 mark)

(iii) In the presence of a strong field ligand such as CN^- ion, crystal field splitting energy is more than the third ionisation enthalpy (Δ_iH_3) for the oxidation of Co^{2+} to Co^{3+} ion. Therefore, Co^{2+} is easily oxidised to Co^{3+}. (1 mark)

34. (a) (i) $\overset{4}{H_3C}$–$\overset{3}{C}H$=$\overset{2}{C}H$–$\overset{1}{C}H_2Br$ (1 mark)

1-Bromobut-2-ene

(ii) $\overset{4}{Cl}\overset{3}{CH_2C} \equiv \overset{2}{C}\overset{1}{CH_2}Br$ (1 mark)

1-Bromo-4-chlorobut-2-yne.

(b) (i) In aqueous solution, KOH is almost completely ionised to give OH^- ions which being a strong nucleophile leads to substitution reaction to form alcohols. In case of alcoholic solution of KOH ($C_2H_5OH + KOH \rightarrow C_2H_5O^- + K^+$), alkoxide ($RO^-$) ions are present which being much stronger base than OH^- ions causes elimination of a molecule of HCl leading to alkenes. (2 marks)

(ii) 3° Alkyl halide (former one) reacts faster than the 2° alkyl halide (latter one) due to greater stability of 3° carbocations over 2° carbocations. (1 mark)

OR

(a) (i) For a given alkyl group, the order of reactivity is R–I > R–Br > R–Cl > R–F. This is due to C–X bond energy, C–I bond dissociation enthalpy is minimum, while the C–F bond dissociation enthalpy is maximum. Hence R – I is most reactive, while R–F is least reactive. (1½ marks)

(ii) In neopentyl chloride, carbon bearing chlorine is sterically hindered due to bulky $(CH_3)_3C-$ group, hence not attacked easily by nucleophile to form transition state (S_N2 mechanism).

$$(CH_3)_3C{-}CH_2{-}Cl \xrightarrow[S_N2]{Nu:} \text{Transition state not formed}$$

(1½ marks)

(b) (i) $CH_3CH_2CH=CH_2 + HBr \xrightarrow[\text{anti-markov. addition}]{\text{Peroxide}}$

$CH_3CH_2CH_2CH_2Br$ (1 mark)

(ii) $H_2C=CH_2 + Br_2 \xrightarrow{CCl_4} BrCH_2-CH_2Br$ (1 mark)

35. (a) $\underset{\text{Butan-l-ol}}{CH_3CH_2CH_2CH_2OH} \xrightarrow{\text{Acidified } K_2Cr_2O_7} \underset{\text{Butanoic acid}}{CH_3CH_2CH_2COOH}$ (1 mark)

(b) $\underset{\text{Benzyl alcohol}}{C_6H_5CH_2OH} \xrightarrow{HBr} \underset{\text{Benzyl bromide}}{C_6H_5CH_2Br} \xrightarrow{KCN} \underset{\text{Benzyl cyanide}}{C_6H_5CH_2CN} \xrightarrow{\Delta,\ H_3O^+} \underset{\text{Phenylethanoic acid}}{C_6H_5CH_2COOH}$ (1 mark)

(c) 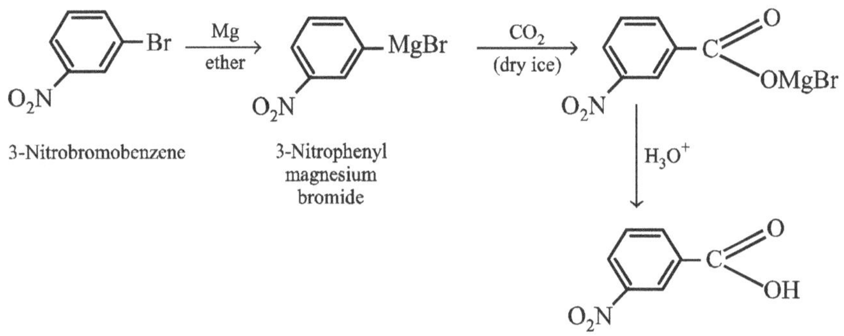 3-Nitrobromobenzene $\xrightarrow[\text{ether}]{Mg}$ 3-Nitrophenyl magnesium bromide $\xrightarrow[\text{(dry ice)}]{CO_2}$ m-$O_2N{-}C_6H_4{-}COOMgBr$ $\xrightarrow{H_3O^+}$ m-$O_2N{-}C_6H_4{-}COOH$ (3-Nitrobenzoic acid) (1 mark)

(d) 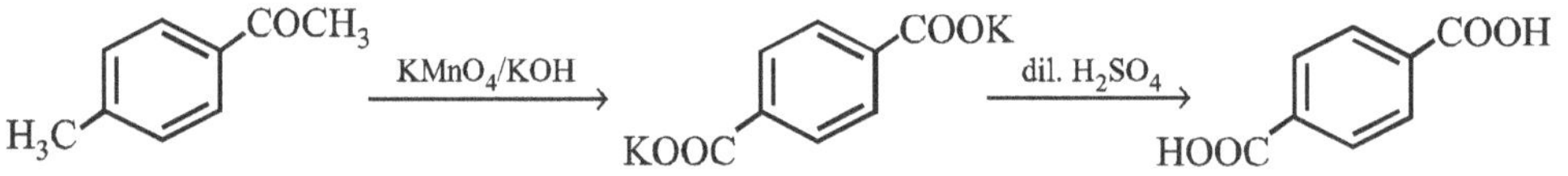 4-Methylacetophenone ($H_3C{-}C_6H_4{-}COCH_3$) $\xrightarrow{KMnO_4/KOH}$ Dipotassium benzene 1,4-dicarboxylate ($KOOC{-}C_6H_4{-}COOK$) $\xrightarrow{\text{dil. } H_2SO_4}$ Benzene-1, 4-dicarboxylic acid (terephthalic acid) ($HOOC{-}C_6H_4{-}COOH$) (1 mark)

(e) $\underset{\text{Butanal}}{CH_3CH_2CH_2CHO} \xrightarrow[\text{(tollen's reagent)}]{\text{Ammoniacal } AgNO_3} \underset{\text{Butanoic acid}}{CH_3CH_2CH_2COOH}$ (1 mark)

1. (b) The process of conversion of alkyl halides into alcohols involves substitution reaction.

$$\underset{\text{Alkyl halide}}{R—X} \xrightarrow{OH^-} \underset{\text{Alcohol}}{R—OH}$$

2. (b) The chemical formula of pentamminenitrochromium (III) chloride is $\left[Cr(NH_3)_5NO_2\right]Cl_2$
It can exist in following two structures
$\left[Cr(NH_3)_5NO_2\right]Cl_2$ and $\left[Cr(NH_3)_5ONO\right]Cl_2$
Therefore the type of isomerism found in this compound is linkage isomerism as nitro group is linked through N as $-NO_2$ or through O as $-ONO$.

3. (d) All aliphatic primary amines give N_2 with nitrous acid ($NaNO_2 + HCl$).

4. (c) For high v.p. concentration of solute should be low and temperature should be high.

5. (a) $k = \dfrac{0.693}{t_{1/2}} = \dfrac{0.693}{480} = 1.44 \times 10^{-3} s^{-1}$

6. (d) The two components should be $(CH_3)_3CONa$ + $(CH_3)_3CBr$. However, tert-alkyl halides tend to undergo elimination reaction rather than substitution leading to the formation of an alkene, $Me_2C = CH_2$

7. (b) Benzoic acid is the strongest acid as the benzoate ion is stablised by resonance effect. +I effect of $-CH_3$ or $-OCH_3$ group reduces the possibility of ionisation of H^+ from COOH.

8. (b) Insulin is a biochemically active peptide hormone secreted by pancreas.

9. (a) $Ag^+ + e^- \rightarrow Ag$

$$E_{cell} = E°_{cell} - \frac{0.0591}{1} \log \frac{1}{[Ag^+]}$$

$$E_{cell} = 0.80 - \frac{0.0591}{1} \log \frac{1}{0.1} = 0.80 - 0.0591 = 0.741 \text{ V}$$

10. (a) With increase in atomic numbers ionisation energy also increases. But the trend is irregular among some *d*-block elements.

Zn : $1s^2 2s^2 p^6 3s^2 p^6 d^{10} 4s^2$

Fe : $1s^2 2s^2 p^6 3s^2 p^6 d^6 4s^2$

Cu: $1s^2 2s^2 p^6 3s^2 p^6 d^{10} 4s^1$

Cr : $1s^2 2s^2 p^6 3s^2 p^6 d^5 4s^1$

On the basis of electronic configuration, the IE_1 follows the order : Zn > Fe > Cu > Cr.

11. (d) Neohexyl chloride is a primary halide as in it Cl-atom is attached to a primary carbon.

$$CH_3—\underset{CH_3}{\overset{CH_3}{\underset{|}{\overset{|}{C}}}}—CH_2—CH_2Cl$$

12. (c) $CH_3—\overset{O}{\overset{\|}{C}}—H + HCN \longrightarrow CH_3—\underset{CN}{\overset{OH}{\underset{|}{\overset{|}{C}}}}—H$

$$\underset{\text{2-Hydroxy propanoic acid}}{CH_3—\underset{OH}{\underset{|}{CH}}—COOH} \xleftarrow{\text{Hydrolysis}}$$

(As it has a chiral C-atom thus it is optically active)

13. (a) Reduction of alkyl isocyanides in presence of $LiAlH_4$ yields secondary amines containing methyl as one of the alkyl group.

$$R - N \equiv C + 4[H] \xrightarrow{LiAlH_4} \underset{2°\text{amine}}{R - NH - CH_3}$$

e.g., $CH_3 - N \equiv C + 4[H] \xrightarrow{LiAlH_4} \underset{\text{dimethyl amine}}{CH_3 - NH - CH_3}$

whereas, alkyl cyanides give 1° amine on reduction.

14. (a) Solubility decreases and K_H increases with increase in temperature.

15. (a) All α-amino acids have $-NH_2$ and $-COOH$ groups. Since $-NH_2$ group is basic and $-COOH$ group is acidic, in neutral solution it exists as internal salt which is also called as zwitter ion. This zwitter ion is formed due to the reason that proton of $-COOH$ group is transferred to $-NH_2$ group.

$$\underset{\alpha\text{–Amino acid}}{H_2\ddot{N}—\underset{|}{\overset{R}{CH}}—COOH} \xrightarrow{\text{in water}} H_2\ddot{N}—\overset{R}{\underset{|}{CH}}—COO^- + H^+ \longrightarrow \underset{\substack{\text{Zwitter ion}\\ \text{(dipolar ion)}}}{H_3\overset{+}{N}—\overset{R}{\underset{|}{CH}}—COO^-}$$

Hence assertion and reason both are true and reason is the correct explanation of assertion.

16. **(a)** If a reactant is present in excess, order with respect to that reactant is zero.

17. **(b)** Due to larger surface area and variable valencies shown by transition metals, they are used as catalysts.

18. **(d)** The specific conductivity decreases while equivalent and molar conductivities increase with dilution.

19. (a)

$$\underset{\text{Ethanol}}{CH_3CH_2OH} \xrightarrow[\text{dil. } H_2SO_4]{KMnO_4} CH_3COOH \xrightarrow{Ca(OH)_2}$$

$$(CH_3COO)_2Ca \xrightarrow[(-CaCO_3)]{\text{dry distillation}} \underset{\text{Acetone (propanone)}}{CH_3COCH_3}$$

(1 mark)

(b) $\underset{\text{Benzene}}{C_6H_6} + CH_3COCl \xrightarrow[\text{Friedel-Craft reaction}]{\text{anhy. } AlCl_3} \underset{\text{Acetophenone}}{C_6H_5COCH_3}$

(1 mark)

OR

(a) Toulene ($C_6H_5CH_3$) + CrO_2Cl_2 (Chromyl chloride) $\xrightarrow{CS_2}$ $C_6H_5CH(OCrOHCl_2)_2$ (Chromium Complex) $\xrightarrow{H_3O^+}$ C_6H_5CHO (Benzaldehyde)

(1 mark)

(b)

$$2CH_3-\underset{\underset{CH_3}{|}}{CH}-I \xrightarrow[\text{Wurtz reaction}]{2\,Na,\text{ Dry ether}} CH_3-\underset{\underset{CH_3}{|}}{CH}-\underset{\underset{CH_3}{|}}{CH}-CH_3$$

(1 mark)

20. An important alloy of lanthanoids is Mischmetal. It contains Lanthanoids (94–95%), iron (5%) and traces of S, C, Si, Ca and Al. (1 mark)

Uses:

(i) Mischmetal is used in cigarettes and gas lighters.

(ii) It is used in tracer bullets and shells. (1 mark)

21. Rate constant, $k = \dfrac{\text{Rate}}{(\text{Conc.})^n}$ (1 mark)

Thus, rate constant (k) is defined as the rate of reaction when the concentration of reactants is taken to be unity.

As $k = \dfrac{\text{Rate}}{(\text{Conc.})^n} = \dfrac{\text{mol L}^{-1}\text{ s}^{-1}}{(\text{mol L}^{-1})^n} = (\text{mol L}^{-1})^{1-n}\text{s}^{-1}$

∴ Units of k for (i) zero order reaction: mol L^{-1} s^{-1} (½ mark)

(ii) first order reaction : s^{-1} (½ mark)

OR

Rate of reaction, $-\dfrac{d[A]}{dt} = k[A][B]^2$

$= 5{\cdot}1 \times 10^{-3} \times [0{\cdot}01][0{\cdot}02]^2 \text{ mol L}^{-1}\text{ s}^{-1}$ (1 mark)

$= 20{\cdot}4 \times 10^{-9} = 2{\cdot}04 \times 10^{-8} \text{ mol L}^{-1}\text{ s}^{-1}$. (1 mark)

22. Phenol is more acidic than cyclohexanol. In phenol, the carbon atom that bears the hydroxyl group is sp^2 hybridized whereas in cyclohexanol it is sp^3 hybridized. Because of greater s-character, sp^2 hybridized carbon atoms are more electronegative that sp^3 hybridized carbon atoms and hence more acidic. Also, phenoxide ion is a resonance stabilized whereas there is no resonance in cyclohexanol or its anion. (2 marks)

23. Given for 0.01 N solution

$R = 210$ ohm, $\dfrac{\ell}{A} = 0.88 \text{ cm}^{-1}$

Specific conductance

$\therefore \ \kappa = \dfrac{1}{R} \times \dfrac{\ell}{A}$ (½ mark)

$\kappa = \dfrac{1}{210} \times 0.88 = 4.19 \times 10^{-3} \text{ mho cm}^{-1}$ (½ mark)

$\Lambda_{eq} = \dfrac{\kappa \times 1000}{N} = \dfrac{4.19 \times 10^{-3} \times 1000}{0.01}$

$= 419 \text{ mho cm}^2\text{eq}^{-1}$ (1 mark)

24. (a) This is because if acetic anhydride is not used, benzoic acid is formed instead of benzaldehyde. So acetic anhydride stops further oxidation of C_6H_5CHO. (1 mark)

(b) For any alkyl group attached to benzene ring to be oxydized to –COOH group, at least one α-hydrogen atom must be present in the group that is attached to the ring. Since, no α-hydrogen atom is present in *tert*-butyl group that is attached to the benzene ring in *tert*-butyl benzene so it does not give benzoic acid when oxidised with $KMnO_4$. (1 mark)

25. (a) **Molality** is defined as the number of moles of solute dissolved per kg of the solvent. It is denoted by m.

$$m = \frac{\text{No. of moles of solute}}{\text{Mass of solvent in kg}}$$

The unit of molality is mol kg^{-1}. (1 mark)

(b) **Osmotic Pressure:** The pressure which need to be applied to a solution to prevent the flow of solvent into the solution through the semi-permeable membrane is called osmotic pressure. (1 mark)

26. $K_f = 1.85 \text{ K mol}^{-1}\text{ kg}$, $\Delta T_f = 6\text{K}$, $m = 62$, $W = 4 \text{ kg} = 4 \times 10^3 \text{ g}$, w = wt. of solute

Now we know that $\Delta T_f = \dfrac{1000 \times K_f \times w}{W \times m}$

$6 = \dfrac{1000 \times 1.85 \times w}{4 \times 10^3 \times 62}$

On usual calculations, $w = 804.32$ g (3 marks)

27. (a) $\underset{\text{Propanal (1° alcohol)}}{CH_3CH_2CH_2OH} \xrightarrow{PCC} \underset{\text{Propanal (an aldehyde)}}{CH_3CH_2CHO}$

(1 mark)

PCC is pyridinium chlorochromate (a complex of Cr_2O_3 with pyridine and HCl). It does not oxidise C=C, if present.

(b) Tollen's reagent is a weak oxidizing agent not capable of breaking the C-C bond in ketones . Thus ketones cannot be oxidized using Tollen's reagent itself gets reduced to Ag. (1 mark)

(c) In case of chlorobenzene, the C—Cl bond is quite difficult to break as it acquires a partial double bond character due to conjugation.

So Under the normal conditions, ammonolysis of chlorobenzene does not yield aniline. (1 mark)

28. (a) $CH_3-COOH + NH_3 \longrightarrow CH_3COO^-NH_4^+ \xrightarrow[-H_2O]{\Delta}$

$\underset{(A)}{CH_3-CO-NH_2} \xrightarrow{NaOBr} \underset{(B)}{CH_3-NH_2}$

(½ + ½ = 1 mark)

Note

Conversion of A to B is Hofmann Degradation reaction.

Step 1:

$R-CO-NH-H \underset{}{\overset{OH^-}{\rightleftharpoons}} R-CO-\bar{N}-H \xrightarrow{Br-Br} R-CO-N(Br)-H + Br^-$

Step 2:

$R-CO-N(Br)-H \overset{OH^-}{\rightleftharpoons} R-CO-\ddot{\bar{N}}-Br \xrightarrow{-Br^-} \underset{\text{Isocyanate}}{R-N=C=O}$

Step 3: $R-N=C=O \xrightarrow{OH^-} R-\bar{N}-C(OH)=O \rightleftharpoons R-NH-C(=O)-O^- \xrightarrow{H^+} R-NH_2 + CO_2$

(b) $\underset{}{C_6H_5NO_2} \xrightarrow{Fe/HCl} \underset{(A)}{C_6H_5NH_2} \xrightarrow[0°–5°C]{NaNO_2 + HCl} \underset{(B)}{C_6H_5N^+\equiv NCl^-}$

(½ + ½ = 1 mark)

(c) $C_6H_5N_2^+Cl^- \xrightarrow[\Delta]{CuCN} \underset{(A)}{C_6H_5CN} \xrightarrow{H_2O/H^+} \underset{(B)}{C_6H_5COOH}$

(½ + ½ = 1 mark)

OR

(a) (i) Aniline and ethanamine can be distinguished by the azo-dye test.

An orange dye is obtained when aniline reacts with ($NaNO_2$ + dil. HCl) at 0°–5°C followed by a reaction with alkaline solution of 2-naphthol. Ethanamine gives a brisk effervescences with the same solution due to evolution of N_2 gas.

(ii) $C_6H_5NH_2$ — Aniline (1° Amine); $C_6H_5NHCH_3$ — N-Methylaniline (2° Amine)

Only primary amines react with ($CHCl_3$ + KOH) to give a foul odour of isocyanide (carbylamine reaction). Hence, aniline will give this test but N-methylaniline will not. Also, aniline will form azo dye as in (i), but N-methylaniline will not form dye.

(1 + 1 = 2 marks)

(b) $CH_3-CH_2-CH_2-CH_2-OH$ (butanol)
$CH_3-CH_2-CH_2-CH_2-NH_2$ (butanamine)
$CH_3-CH_2-CH_2-CH_3$ (butane)

Due to hydrogen bonding, the decreasing order of boiling point is:

Butanol > Butanamine > Butane (1 mark)

29. (a) Alcohols and amines combine with anhydrous $CaCl_2$ to form complexes. For example, with C_2H_5OH it gives a complex of molecular formula, $CaCl_2.3C_2H_5OH$. Therefore, it cannot be used as a drying agent.

(1 mark)

(b) Grignard reagents form coordination complexes with ethers but not with benzene since the former has lone pairs of electrons but the latter does not. Grignard reagent and ether form a complex where Mg acts as a Lewis acid and ether act as a Lewis base. This makes Grignard reagent soluble in ether. (1 mark)

(c) This is because the nucleophile attack by the halide ion on the carbon of the benzene ring does not occur. Oxygen of ether is in resonance with ring. Also the C of ring is sterically more hindered. (1 mark)

OR

(i) $CH_3CH_2CH_2CH_2OH \xrightarrow[\text{Oxidation}]{[O]} \underset{\text{Butanoic acid}}{CH_3CH_2CH_2COOH}$

(1 mark)

(ii) $\underset{\text{2-butanol}}{CH_3-CH(OH)-CH_2CH_3} \xrightarrow[\text{Oxidation}]{[O]} \underset{\text{2-butanone}}{CH_3-C(=O)-CH_2CH_3}$

(1 mark)

(iii) $CH_3-\underset{CH_3}{\overset{H}{C}}-CH_2OH \xrightarrow[\text{Oxidation}]{[O]} CH_3-\underset{CH_3}{\overset{H}{C}}-COOH$

2-methylpropanoic acid

(1 mark)

30. The reaction is of first order with respect to H_2O_2

$\therefore$ Rate = k $[H_2O_2]$

k = 1.01×10^{-2} min^{-1}

$[H_2O_2] = 0{\cdot}4$ mol L^{-1}.

(i) Rate = $(1{\cdot}01 \times 10^{-2}\ \text{min}^{-1}) \times (0{\cdot}4\ \text{mol L}^{-1})$

$= 4{\cdot}04 \times 10^{-3}$ mol L^{-1} min^{-1}. (1 mark)

(ii) When $[H_2O_2] = 0{\cdot}15$ mol L^{-1}.

Rate = $(1{\cdot}01 \times 10^{-2}\ \text{min}^{-1}) \times (0{\cdot}15\ \text{mol L}^{-1})$

$= 1{\cdot}5 \times 10^{-3}$ mol L^{-1} min^{-1}. (1 mark)

(iii) To obtain concentration of H_2O_2 when rate = $1{\cdot}12 \times 10^{-2}$ mol L^{-1} min^{-1},

$$[H_2O_2] = \frac{\text{Rate}}{k} = \frac{1{\cdot}12 \times 10^{-2}\ \text{mol L}^{-1}\ \text{min}^{-1}}{1{\cdot}01 \times 10^{-2}\ \text{min}^{-1}}$$

$= 1{\cdot}11$ mol L^{-1}. (1 mark)

31. (a) Manganese is having lower melting point as compared to chromium, as it has highest number of unpaired electrons, strong interatomic metal bonding, hence no delocalisation of electrons. (1 mark)

(b) Tungsten (1 mark)

(c) There is much more frequent metal – metal bonding in compounds of the heavy transition metals i.e 4*d* and 5*d* series, which accounts for lower melting point of 3*d* series. (2 marks)

OR

(c) Due to the presence of completely filled d-orbitals $[(n-1)d^{10}ns^2]$ in Zn, Cd, Hg, the interaction with adjacent atoms is weaker in comparison to that other transition elements which are having unpaired d-electrons. (2 marks)

32. (a) On dilution, number of ions per millilitre decreases but per mole increases. (1 mark)

(b) Conductivity of solutions of different electrolytes in the same solvent and at a given temperature is different. It also depend on charge and size in which they dissociate. (1 mark)

(c) Electrons are not tightly held but are free to flow. Instead, kernels start vibrating which create hinderance to the flow of electrons. In case of electrolytes, dissociation and ionic mobilities increase with temperature. (2 marks)

OR

The percent dissociation of a strong electrolyte is already very high. Thus, on dilution, molar conductivity increases slowly. (2 mark)

33. (a)

	Coordination compound	Coordination entity	Counter ions
(*i*)	$[Cr(NH_3)_6]Cl_3$	$[Cr(NH_3)_6]^{3+}$	Cl^-
(*ii*)	$K_4[Fe(CN)_6]$	$[Fe(CN)_6]^{4-}$	K^+
(*iii*)	$K_2[PtCl_4]$	$[PtCl_4]^{2-}$	K^+
(*iv*)	$[Ni(CO)_4]$	$[Ni(CO)_4]$	Nil
(*v*)	$K_2[Ni(CN)_4]$	$[Ni(CN)_4]^{2-}$	K^+

(b) (*i*) Fe.

(*ii*) $[Fe(C_2O_4)_3]^{3-}$.

(*iii*) $(K_3)^{3+}$ or $3K^+$.

(*iv*) Six (each oxalate ion is bidentate).

(*v*) +3.

OR

(a) The d-orbitals present in metal have the same energy in the free state. This is called degenerate state of d-orbital. But, when a complex is formed the ligands destroy the degeneracy of these orbitals. The d-orbitals gets split into two sets one with lower and one with higher energy. The difference of energy between two sets is called crystal field splitting energy.

(i) When $\Delta_0 > P$, the d^4 has configuration ◯◯ e_g

i.e., $t_{2g}^4 e_g^0$ (↑↓)(↑)(↑) t_{2g}

(ii) When $\Delta_0 < P$, the d^4 has configuration (↑)◯ e_g

i.e., $t_{2g}^3 e_g^1$ (↑)(↑)(↑) t_{2g}

(b) Splitting will be larger in 4d-orbitals.

[Note: The splitting of 4d-orbitals is about 1.45 times as large as the splitting of 3d-orbitals.]

(c) $H_2N—NH_2$ (both N → Ⓜ)

Although hydrozine has two lone pairs of electrons of each 'N' atom, it cannot donate both the lone pairs of electrons to the metal as it forms highly strained 3-membered ring as shown in the figure, it is unstable.

34. (a) (i)

$C_6H_5Cl + CH_3Cl \xrightarrow[\text{dry ether}]{2Na} C_6H_5CH_3 + 2NaCl$

Wurtz-Fitting reaction

(1 mark)

(ii) 1-bromo-1-methylcyclohexane (H_3C, Br on the same ring carbon) $\xrightarrow[\text{KOH}]{\text{alc.}}$ 1-methylcyclohexene (CH_3) + methylenecyclohexane (CH_2)

(major) (minor)

(This is in accordance with the Saytzeff's rule) (1 mark)

(b) (i) 1-Bromopentane is most reactive towards S_N2 reaction. It is a primary halide. (1 mark)

Note

Primary halides are more reactive towards S_N2 reaction and tertiary halides are more reactive towards S_N1 reaction.

(ii) 2-Bromopentane $CH_3-\overset{\overset{Br}{|}}{\underset{*}{C}}H-CH_2CH_2CH_3$

(1 mark)

(iii) 2-Bromo-2-methylbutane is most reactive towards β-elimination reaction. (1 mark)

$$CH_3-\underset{\underset{Br}{|}}{\overset{\overset{CH_3}{|}}{C}}-CH_2-CH_3 \xrightarrow[\text{alc.}]{\text{KOH}} CH_3-C=CH_2CH_3$$

(Highly substituted alkene)

35. (a) (i) **Polysaccharides:** Carbohydrates which yield a large number of monosaccharide units on hydrolysis are called polysaccharides. *Example:* Starch (1 mark)

(ii) **Denatured protein:** When a protein is subjected to physical change like change in pH, the hydrogen bonds are disturbed. Due to this, globules unfold and helix get uncoiled and protein loses its biological activity. This form is called 'denatured protein'. *Example:* Coagulation of egg white on boiling

(1 mark)

Note: *Denaturation destroys secondary and tertiary structures of protein, but primary structure remains intact.*

(b) (i) Proteins which are found in a biological system with unique 3D-structure and biological activity are called native proteins. When a native protein is subjected to physical and chemical change, it loses its biological activity and are called as denatured protein. (1 mark)

(ii) Lactose is a disaccharide. (1 mark)

(iii) Vitamin K is responsible for the coagulation of blood. (1 mark)

Note

Deficiency of vitamin K is rare, but, in severe cases, it can increase clotting time, leading to the hemorrhage and excessive bleeding.

The nine essential amino acids are histidine, isoleucine, leucine, lysin, methionine, phenylalanine, threonine, tryptophan and valine.

OR

(a) When glucose reacts with conc HNO_3, saccharic acid is formed.

$$\begin{matrix} CHO \\ | \\ (CHOH)_4 \\ | \\ CH_2OH \\ \text{glucose} \end{matrix} \xrightarrow[HNO_3]{\text{Conc.}} \begin{matrix} COOH \\ | \\ (CHOH)_4 \\ | \\ COOH \\ \text{saccharic acid} \end{matrix}$$

(1 mark)

(b) Amino acids show amphoteric behaviour in zwitter ionic form as they react both with acids and bases. Due to presence of both acidic (carboxyl group) and basic (amino group) in same molecule, amino acids exist as zwitter ion form and can react with acids as well bases. (1 mark)

(c) **α-Helix:** The polypeptide chains twist into a right handed screw with –NH group of amino acid hydrogen bonded with $>C=O$ group of an adjacent turn of the helix.

β-pleated: The polypeptide chains strech to maximum extension and lay side by side in a zig-zag manner to form a flat sheet. Each chain is held to two neighbouring chains by hydrogen bond. (1 mark)

(d) (i) **Fibrous protein:** When the polypeptide chains run parallel and are held together by hydrogen and disulphide bonds, then fibre like structure is formed. Such type of proteins are called 'fibrous proteins' *Example:* Keratin (1 mark)

(ii) **Essential amino acids** : These amino acids cannot be synthesised in the body and must be obtained through diet.

For ex : Valine, leucine, lysine (1 mark)

1. (a) $CH_3-CN + RMgX \longrightarrow CH_3-\overset{\overset{R}{|}}{C}=N-MgX$
Methyl cyanide

$\xrightarrow{2H_2O} CH_3-\overset{\overset{R}{|}}{C}=O + Mg\begin{smallmatrix}X\\OH\end{smallmatrix}$
Ketones

2. (c) (a) High spin with d^6 configuration

t_{2g}^4 and e_g^2 CFSE $= -0.4\Delta_0$

(b) Low spin with d^4 configuration

t_{2g}^4 and e_g^0 CFSE $= -1.6\Delta_0$

(c) Low spin with d^5 configuration

t_{2g}^5 and e_g^0 CFSE $= -2.0\Delta_0$

(d) High spin with d^7 configuration

t_{2g}^5 and e_g^2 CFSE $= -0.8\Delta_0$

3. (a) For example, decrease in the vapour pressure of water by adding 1.0 mol of sucrose to one kg of water is nearly similar to that produced by adding 1.0 mol of urea to the same quantity of water at the same temperature.

4. (c) The given data explains that Fe^{3+} is the strongest oxidising agent. More the positive value of E°, more will be the tendency to get oxidized.

5. (b) The ionic radii of trivalent lanthanides decreases progressively with increase in atomic number which is also termed as lanthanide contraction.

6. (b) A molecule having a plane of symmetry but having chiral carbons will have *meso* form.

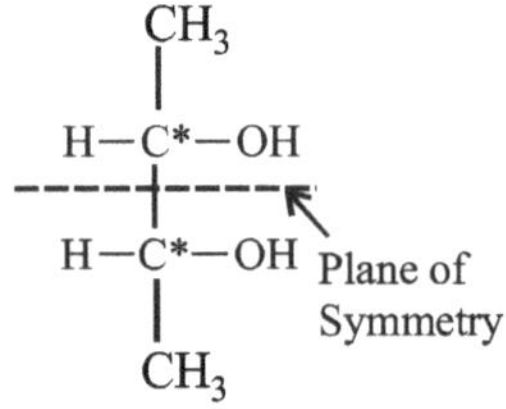

7. (c) HCl + An. $ZnCl_2$ is known as lucas reagent. It is used to determine degree of an alcohol.
The reaction follow nucleophilic substitution reaction in which — OH group is replaced by — Cl. In this reaction carbocation is formed as intermediate. Higher the stability of intermediate carbocation higher will be the reactivity of reactant molecule. Since 3° carbocation is more stable than 2° carbocation as well as 1° carbocation, so the order of reactivity of alcohols is 3° > 2° > 1°.

8. (b) aniline.

9. (a) Given $r = k\,[A]^{3/2}\,[B]^{-1/2}$

Order $= 3/2 - 1/2 = \frac{3-1}{2} = \frac{2}{2} = 1$

10. (d)

11. (b) This reaction is known as Rosenmund's reduction.

$C_6H_5COCl \xrightarrow{Pd/BaSO_4} C_6H_5CHO$

12. (d) $\frac{1}{2}$

$X \longrightarrow Y$

$r_1 = R \propto [X]^n$

$r_2 = 2R \propto [4X]^n \Rightarrow \frac{2R}{R} = \frac{[4X]^n}{[X]^n} \Rightarrow 2 = 4^n \Rightarrow n = \frac{1}{2}$

13. (c)

14. (b) Order of basicity in aqueous solution for amines :

2° > 1° > 3° > NH_3

15. (a) According to Kohlrausch law, "limiting molar conductivity of an electrolyte can be represented as the sum of the individual contributions of the anion and cation of the electrolyte." That is,

$\Lambda^\circ_{NaCl} = \lambda^\circ_{Na^+} + \lambda^\circ_{Cl^-}$

16. (b) On adding a non-volatile solute in a liquid the vapour pressure decreases. The solution has more randomness (entropy) than the pure liquid and hence has lesser tendency to evaporate.

17. (b) Due to denaturation, a protein molecule uncoils and, form a more random conformation and ultimately precipitates from the solution. Also, during denaturation protein molecule loses its biological activity.
Thus, reason is correct but it is not the correct explanation of assertion.

18. (c) Assertion is true and reason is false.

19. The following precautions must be taken in preservation of $CHCl_3$:
(i) It must be stored in dark coloured bottles to protect it from sunlight; the bottles must be filled up to brim and stoppered properly to keep out air. (1 mark)
(ii) A small amount of ethyl alcohol (0·6 to 1%) must be added to the bottle of chloroform. It converts the poisonous phosgene, if formed, to non-toxic and harmless diethyl carbonate. (1 mark)

20. (a) Ni^{2+} 3*d* [⇅][⇅][⇅][↑][↑] 4*s* [ ] 4*p* [ ][ ][ ]
In some complexes, the two unpaired 3*d* electrons pair up and the hybridisation is *dsp*^{2}. Thus, no unpaired electron is left. The nature of complex depends on the type of

hybridisation of the central metal atom (Ni). dsp^2 hybridisation gives square planar complexes and sp^3 hybridisation gives tetrahedral complexes i.e., diamagnetic or paramagnetic complexes respectively. Strong ligands like NH_3, CN^-, CO forms diamagnetic complexes while paramagnetic complexes are formed by weak field ligands like Cl^-, Br^-. (2 marks)

21. (a) $\underset{\text{Ethyl alcohol}}{CH_3CH_2OH} \xrightarrow[\text{NaBr + H}_2\text{SO}_4]{\text{HBr}} CH_3CH_2Br$

$\xrightarrow[\text{Step-up reaction}]{\text{KCN}} CH_3CH_2CN \xrightarrow{4H\,(LiAlH_4)} \underset{\text{n-Propyl amine}}{CH_3CH_2CH_2NH_2}$ (1 mark)

(b) Phenol $\xrightarrow[\Delta]{\text{Zn dust}}$ Benzene $\xrightarrow{CH_3Cl/AlCl_3}$ Toluene ($C_6H_5CH_3$) $\xrightarrow[KMnO_4/H_2SO_4]{\text{Oxidation}}$ Benzoic acid (C_6H_5COOH) (1 mark)

OR

(a) $\underset{\text{1-Propoxy propane}}{CH_3CH_2CH_2—O—CH_2CH_2CH_3} \xrightarrow[373K]{HI}$

$\underset{\text{Propanol}}{CH_3CH_2CH_2—OH} + \underset{\text{Iodopropane}}{CH_3CH_2CH_2I}$ (1 mark)

(b) Methoxybenzene ($C_6H_5OCH_3$) $\xrightarrow{\text{HI, 373 K}}$ Phenol (C_6H_5OH) $+ CH_3—I$ (1 mark)

22. (a) $8MnO_4^- + 3S_2O_3^{2-} + 2H_2O \longrightarrow$

$8MnO_2 + 6SO_4^{2-} + 2OH^-$ (1 mark)

(b) $Cr_2O_7^{2-} + 6Fe^{2+} + 14H^+ \longrightarrow$

$2Cr^{3+} + 6Fe^{3+} + 7H_2O$ (1 mark)

23. (a) Vapour pressure of a liquid is constant at constant temperature. This is beacuse it reaches a state of equilibrium where rate of evaporation becomes equal to rate of condensation. (1 mark)

(b) B will show greater lowering of vapour pressure

because $\frac{p^\circ - p_s}{p^\circ} = \frac{w_2 \times M_1}{w_1 \times M_2}$ (1 mark)

24. Nucleotides are monomers of nucleic acids. A nucleotide is made of three components a nitrogen containing heterocyclic base, five carbon pentose sugar and a phosphoric acid residue. (1 mark)

The two classes of nitrogen containing bases found in nucleotides are:

(i) Purine (ii) Pyrimidine (1 mark)

25. Given : $C = 0.02$ M, $\kappa = 2.428 \times 10^{-3}\ \Omega^{-1}\ cm^{-1}$

To find : Molar conductivity

Formula : Molar conductivity $= \frac{1000\kappa}{C}$ (½ mark)

Calculation :

Molar conductivity $= \frac{1000\kappa}{C} = \frac{1000 \times 2.428 \times 10^{-3}}{0.02}$

$= 121.4\ \Omega^{-1}\ cm^2\ mol^{-1}$ (1 mark)

Molar conductivity of 0.02 M $AgNO_3$ solution at 25 °C is $121.4\ \Omega^{-1}\ cm^2\ mol^{-1}$. (½ mark)

OR

Given : Conductivity (κ) $= 6.23 \times 10^{-5}\ \Omega^{-1}\ cm^{-1}$

Resistance (R) $= 13710\ \Omega$

Distance between electrodes (l) = 0.7 cm

To find: Area of cross-section of the electrode (a)

Formula: $\kappa \times R = \frac{l}{a}$ (½ mark)

Calculation : From formula,

$a = \frac{l}{\kappa \times R} = \frac{0.7}{6.23 \times 10^{-5} \times 13710} = 0.82\ cm^2$ (1 mark)

The cross-sectional area of the given electrode is $0.82\ cm^2$. (½ mark)

26. (a) Due to presence of lone pair of electrons on oxygen, alcohols behave as Bronsted base (proton acceptors). (1 mark)

(b) Alcohol molecules are capable of forming H–bonds with each other. On the other hand ether molecules do not form H–bonds and thus they do not exhibit association, hence their boiling point are lower than the isomeric alcohols. (1 mark)

(c) In *ortho*-hydroxy benzaldehyde, intramolecular H-bonding takes place due to which it exists as a liquid, whereas, in para-hydroxy benzaldehyde, intermolecular H-bonding takes place. Due to intermolecular H-bonding, the molecules of *p*-hydroxy benzaldehyde associate and hence, it is a high melting solid. In the *ortho* isomer due to intramolecular H-bonding, melting point is low, so it is liquid. (1 mark)

27. **Step I.** Calculation of volume of the solution.

Mass of solution = 100 g ; Density of solution $= 1.06\ g\ cm^{-3}$

Volume of solution $= \frac{\text{Mass of solution}}{\text{Density}}$ (½ mark)

$= \frac{(100\ g)}{(1.06\ g\ cm^{-3})} = 94.34\ cm^3$ (½ mark)

Step II. Calculation of molarity of the solution

Molarity of solution (M) =

$\frac{\text{Mass of KCl/Molar mass of KCl}}{\text{Volume of solution in dm}^3}$ (½ mark)

Mass of KCl = 10 g ; Molar mass of KCl = 39 + 35.5 $= 74.5\ g\,mol^{-1}$ (½ mark)

Volume of solution = $94.34\ cm^3 = \frac{94.34}{1000} = 0.0943\ dm^3$

Molarity (M) = $\frac{10\ g/(74.5\ g\ mol^{-1})}{(0.0943\ dm^3)} = 1.42\ mol\ dm^{-3}$

(1 mark)

= 1.42 M

Alternative:

Molarity of solution can also be obtained by applying the formula :

Molarity=

$$\frac{\%\ \text{Strength of solution} \times \text{Density of solution} \times 10}{\text{Molar mass of KCl}}$$

$$\text{Molarity} = \frac{10 \times 1.06 \times 10}{74.5} = 1.42\ M$$

OR

For dilute solutions, $\frac{P^\circ - P_s}{P^\circ} = \frac{W_2 M_1}{W_1 M_2}$ (1 mark)

$\frac{\Delta P}{P^\circ} = \frac{W_2 M_1}{W_1 M_2}$

For same P°, *i.e.*, P° constant and M_1 is also constant.

$W_2 = W_A = W_B = 2\ g$

$W_1 = W_C = 20\ g$ (1 mark)

Hence $\frac{\Delta P_A}{\Delta P_B} = \frac{M_B}{M_A}$.

As $M_A > M_B$, therefore, $\Delta P_B > \Delta P_A$. (1 mark)

It means B will show greater lowering of vapour pressure.

28. (a) (i) Zwitter ion (½ mark)

(ii) Polypeptide (½ mark)

(iii) Denaturation (½ mark)

(iv) Fibrous proteins. (½ mark)

(b) It indicates that the –OH group at carbon next to the terminal (or penultimate) carbon atom is towards right.

(1 mark)

29. In this cell, Cu/Cu^{2+} electrode acts as anode, and Ag^+/Ag electrode acts as cathode. (¼ + ¼ = ½ mark)

(a) Standard electrode potential,

$$E^\circ_{cell} = E^\circ_{cathode} - E^\circ_{anode} = 0{\cdot}80\ V - 0{\cdot}34\ V = 0{\cdot}46\ V.$$

(½ mark)

(b) The net cell reaction is $Cu + 2Ag^+ \longrightarrow Cu^{2+} + 2Ag$

(½ mark)

Here n = 2.

By Nernst equation,

$$E_{cell} = E^\circ_{cell} - \frac{2{\cdot}303\,RT}{nF}\log\frac{[Cu^{2+}]}{[Ag^+]^2}$$ (½ mark)

$$\therefore E_{cell} = 0{\cdot}46\ V - \frac{2{\cdot}303 \times 8{\cdot}314 \times 298}{2 \times 96500}\log\frac{2}{(0{\cdot}05)^2}$$

$$= 0{\cdot}46 - \frac{0{\cdot}0591}{2}\log\frac{2 \times 10^4}{25}$$

$$= 0{\cdot}46 - 0{\cdot}086 = 0{\cdot}37\ V.$$ (1 mark)

30. Since **'A'** gives a white precipitate with $AgNO_3$ and this precipitate is soluble in NH_3, so in **'A'** Cl is present in the ionisation sphere.

Since **'B'** gives a pale yellow precipitate with $AgNO_3$ and this precipitate is soluble in concentrated NH_3, so in **'B'** Br is present in the ionisation sphere.

The formula of these two isomers can be written as

$$\underset{'A'}{\left[Cr(NH_3)_4ClBr\right]Cl} \quad \text{and} \quad \underset{'B'}{\left[Cr(NH_3)_4Cl_2\right]Br}$$

(1 mark)

Hybridisation of chromium in both the isomers is d^2sp^3 (the C.N. of chromium in both isomers is 6) (1 mark)

Calculation of Magnetic moment

In both the isomers chromium is present in +3 oxidation state.

3*d*

Cr^{3+} | ↿ | ↿ | ↿ | | |

Thus, it has three unpaired electrons in +3 state.

Hence magnetic moment = $\sqrt{n(n+2)}$ B.M.

(n = number of unpaired electrons)

$= \sqrt{3(3+2)}$ B.M. $= \sqrt{15}$ B.M.

= 3.87 B.M. (1 mark)

OR

In Fe^{2+} ion all the 3*d*-orbitals have same energy because of their degenerate nature.

3*d*

Fe^{2+} | ⇅ | ↿ | ↿ | ↿ | ↿ |

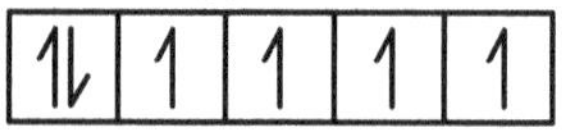

When CN^- ion approach these *d*-orbitals, the five *d*-orbitals split up into two groups (i.e. e_g and t_{2g}). The t_{2g} group containing three *d*-orbitals $d_{xy}, d_{yz}\ d_{zx}$ has lower energy than those of e_g group containing two orbitals ($d_{z^2}, d_{x^2-y^2}$). This splitting is caused by CN^- ions in an octahedral field and as a result the rearrangement occurs in electronic structure of Fe^{2+} when it forms complex with CN^-. The six 3*d*-electrons of Fe^{2+} will tend to pair in three lower energy levels in violation of Hund's rule.

Fe^{2+} in $[Fe(CN)_6]^{4-}$

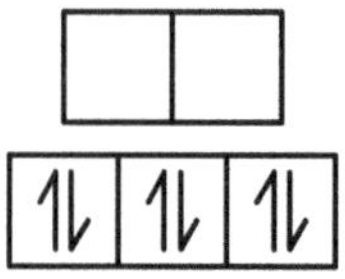

| | | e_g orbitals

| ⇅ | ⇅ | ⇅ | t_{2g} orbitals

In $[Fe(H_2O)_6]^{2+}$ the separation is smaller because neutral H_2O molecule repels electrons less than negatively charged CN^- ions. In this case the electron distribution in Fe^{2+} is retained.

Fe^{2+} in $[Fe(H_2O)_6]^{2+}$

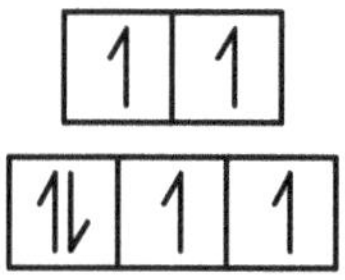

| ↿ | ↿ | e_g orbitals

| ⇅ | ↿ | ↿ | t_{2g} orbitals

Since, $[Fe(H_2O)_6]^{2+}$ has unpaired electrons so it is paramagnetic, whereas in $[Fe(CN)_6]^{4-}$ there is no unpaired electron so it is diamagnetic. (3 marks)

31. (a) Carbon chain decreases by one carbon atom. (1 mark)

(b) 1° Amine or primary amine. (1 mark)

(c) CO_2 (2 marks)

OR

$-NO_2$ (electron withdrawing group) (2 marks)

32. (a) The *tert*-butoxide ion, being large in size faces difficulty in attacking the carbon atom of isopropyl cation, which thus loses proton to form propene (A), E2 reaction. (1 mark)

(b) $CH_3-\underset{\displaystyle Ch_3}{\underset{|}{C}H}Br \xrightarrow{t\text{-}BuO^-} \underset{(A)}{CH_3CH=CH_2}$ (1 mark)

(c) $CH_2=CH-CH_3 \xrightarrow[\text{Cold}]{KMnO_4(\text{dil.})} \underset{\text{OH}}{\underset{|}{CH_2}}-\underset{\text{OH}}{\underset{|}{CH}}-CH_3$ Diol

OR

2-Ethoxypropane : $H_3C-\overset{\displaystyle CH_3}{\overset{|}{C}H}-OC_2H_5$ (2 marks)

33. (a) The rate law may be expressed as :

Rate $= k[A]^p[B]^q$

$(Rate)_1 = k[0.1]^p[1.0]^q = 2.1\times10^3$ .... (i) (½ mark)

$(Rate)_2 = k[0.2]^p[1.0]^q = 8.4\times10^{-3}$ .... (ii) (½ mark)

$(Rate)_3 = k[0.2]^p[2.0]^q = 8.4\times10^{-3}$ .... (iii) (½ mark)

Dividing equation (iii) by (ii),

$$\frac{(Rate)_3}{(Rate)_2}=\frac{k[0.2]^p[2.0]^q}{k[0.2]^p[1.0]^q}=\frac{8.4\times10^{-3}}{8.4\times10^{-3}}$$ (½ mark)

$[2]^q=[2]^0;\ q=0$

Dividing equation (ii) by (i),

$$\frac{(Rate)_2}{(Rate)_1}=\frac{k[0.20]^p[1.0]^q}{k[0.10]^p[1.0]^q}=\frac{8.4\times10^{-3}}{2.1\times10^{-3}}=4$$

$[2]^p=[2]^2;\ p=2$ (½ mark)

Order w.r.t. A = 2 ; B = 0 ; Overall order = 2. (½ mark)

(b) Rate of reaction $= k[NO]^2[H_2]$ (1 mark)

Order of reaction = 2 + 1 = 3. (1 mark)

OR

(a) Use the equation for first order.

20% complete means $[A] = 0.8\,[A]_0$

$$k=\frac{2.303}{t}\log\frac{[A]_0}{[A]}=\frac{2.303}{20}\log\frac{[A]_0}{0.8[A]_0}$$ (½ mark)

or $k=\dfrac{2.303}{20}\log\dfrac{5}{4}=\dfrac{2.303}{20}(\log5-\log4)$

$$k=\frac{2.303}{20}(0.6990-0.6021)=\frac{2.303}{20}\times0.0969\,\text{min}^{-1}$$ (1 mark)

80% complete means $[A] = 0.2\,[A]_0$

$$t=\frac{2.303}{k}\log\frac{[A]_0}{[A]}=\frac{2.303}{k}\log\frac{[A]_0}{0.2[A]_0}$$ (½ mark)

or $t=\dfrac{2.303}{2.303}\times\dfrac{20}{0.0969}\log5$

$=\dfrac{20}{0.0969}\times0.6990=144.2\,\text{min}.$ (1 mark)

(b) Those reactions which are bimolecular but their order is found to be one are called pseudo unimolecular reactions. (1 mark)

(i) $CH_3COOC_2H_5 \xrightarrow{H^+} CH_3COOH + C_2H_5OH + H_2O$ (½mark)

(ii) $C_{12}H_{22}O_{11}+H_2O \xrightarrow{H^+} C_6H_{12}O_6 + C_6H_{12}O_6$ (½ mark)

34. (a) (i) Formation of ammonia derivatives (oximes, hydrazone, semi-carbazone, etc.) proceeds via the attack of carbonyl carbon with proton to form the conjugate acid.

$$>C=\ddot{O}+H^+\longrightarrow >C=\overset{+}{O}H$$

Therefore, presence of an acid is must for preparing these derivatives. However, in strongly acidic medium, the proton attacks the unshared pair of electrons on nitrogen to form the species $R\overset{+}{N}H_3$ which cannot attack the carbonyl carbon.

$$H^+ + :NH_2R \longrightarrow \overset{+}{N}H_3R$$

In basic medium, there is no protonation of carbonyl group, and hence no reaction.

$>C=O \xrightarrow{\text{Basic medium}}$ No protonation (No reaction)

Therefore, preparation of ammonia derivatives requires slightly acidic medium (pH ≃ 3·5) and its careful control is essential. (2 marks)

(ii) Due to resonance between lone pairs of electrons on the O-atom of the OH group and C = O, the carboxyl carbon is less electrophilic than carbonyl carbon in aldehyde and ketones. Therefore, nucleophilic addition of NH_2OH to the C = O group of carboxylic acids does not occur and hence carboxylic acids do not form oximes. (1 mark)

(b) (i) $C_6H_6 \xrightarrow[\text{Anhy. }AlCl_3/CuCl]{CO/\ HCl} C_6H_5CHO$ (1 mark)

(ii) $2C_6H_5CHO \xrightarrow{\text{Conc. NaOH}} C_6H_5CH_2OH + C_6H_5COONa$ (1 mark)

OR

(a) HCOOH has an aldehydic (CHO) group in addition to carboxyl group (COOH). Therefore, it is expected to behave as reducing agent and also reduces Tollen's reagent to form a shining mirror.

$$\underset{\text{Formic acid}}{HCOOH} + \underset{\text{Tollen's reagent}}{2[Ag(NH_3)_2]^+OH^-} \longrightarrow$$

$$\underset{\text{Silver mirror}}{2Ag} + 2H_2O + CO_2 + 4NH_3$$ (1 mark)

(b) In the carboxylic acids, the carboxylic groups are involved in the intermolecular hydrogen bonding resulting in the formation of dimer. However, it is absent in the aldehydes and ketones. Therefore, aldehydes and ketones have lower boiling point than the corresponding acids of comparable molecular mass. (1 mark)

(c) The K_a value of benzoic acid (6.3×10^{-5}) is more than that of acetic acid (1.75×10^{-5}). Actually, C_6H_5 group with –I effect facilitates the release of H^+ from benzoic acid while CH_3 group with + I effect tends to retard it. Therefore, benzoic acid is stronger acid than acetic acid. (1 mark)

(d) (i) 3-Methylbutanoyl chloride (1 mark)

(ii) Ethanoic propanoic anhydride (1 mark)

35. (a) (i) *d*-orbitals are influenced more by ligands as they can project out and so they have greater tendency to form complexes. Comparatively, *f*-orbitals lie deep inside the atom and thus, *f*-electrons do not come in contact with ligands. Therefore, *f*-block elements form lesser complexes. (2 marks)

(ii) Molybdenum, Mo. (1 mark)

(b) (i) *d*-orbitals are influenced more by ligands as they can project out and so they have greater tendency to form complexes. Comparatively, *f*-orbitals lie deep inside the atom and thus, *f*-electrons do not come in contact with ligands. Therefore, *f*-block elements form lesser complexes. (1 mark)

(ii) The strength of metallic bond in transition metals depend upon number of unpaired electrons in valence shell, *i.e.*, $(n - 1)d$ and ns orbitals. As there are no unpaired electrons in these metals, the bond strength is quite weak and thus they are soft and have very low melting points. Hg is liquid at ordinary temperature. (1 mark)

SAMPLE PAPER-5

1. (a) With increase in dilution, the conductivity of a weak electrolyte increases due to increase in ionisation. The conductivity of strong electrolytes remain constant at all dilution because they are completely ionised under all dilutions.

2. (a) The sequence in which the α-amino acids are linked to one another in a protein molecule is called its primary structure.

3. (a) $\Delta T_f = K_f \dfrac{1000\ W_2}{M_2 W_1} = \dfrac{1.86 \times 1000 \times 68.5}{342 \times 1000}$

$= 0.372$

$T_f = T°\Delta_f - \Delta T_f \Rightarrow T_f = -0.372°C$

4. (c) $Mn(25) = 1s^2\, 2s^2\, 2p^6\, 3s^2\, 3p^6\, 3d^5\, 4s^2$

Mn has maximum number of oxidation states from +1 to +7 due to $3d^5 4s^2$.

5. (c) $[Cr(H_2O)_6]Cl_3$

This compound dissociates to $[Cr(H_2O)_6]^{3+}$ and $3Cl^-$ ions. Thus, it will give white precipitate of AgCl on reacting with $AgNO_3$.

6. (b) This method is not applicable for the preparation of aryl halides because the C–O bond in phenol has a partial double bond character and is difficult to break being stronger than a single bond.

7. (c) $\wedge = \wedge_0$ as $C \to 0$

$\wedge = \wedge_0 - A\sqrt{C}$

when $C = 0$, $\wedge = \wedge_0$

8. (a) Cyclic structures of monosaccharides which differ in structure at carbon -1 are known as anomers.

Here, I and II are anomer because they differ from each other at carbon-1 only.

*8. (b) The two isomeric forms (α – and β –) of D–glucopyranose differ in configuration only at C-1. Hence these are called anomers.

9. (c) Molality (m)

$$= \frac{\text{Molarity}}{\text{Density} - \dfrac{\text{Molarity} \times \text{Molecular mass}}{1000}}$$

$$= \frac{18}{1.8 - \dfrac{18 \times 98}{1000}} = 500 \text{ mol kg}^{-1}$$

10. $\dfrac{r_{100°C}}{r_{10°C}} = 2^{\left(\frac{T_2 - T_1}{10}\right)} = 2^{\left(\frac{100-10}{10}\right)} = 2^9 = 512$ (where 2 is temperature coefficient of reaction)

11. (c) RNA does not contain thymine.

12. (b) Due to greater electronegativity of sp^2-hybridized carbon atoms of the benzene ring, diaryl ethers are not attacked by nucleophiles like I^-.

13. (c) The phenyl esters on treatment with on anhydrous $AlCl_3$ undergoes rearrangement to give *o*– and *p*–hydroxyketones (Fries rearrangement).

C_6H_5–O–$COCH_3$ (phenyl acetate) $\xrightarrow[\Delta]{AlCl_3}$ *o*-hydroxy acetophenone (OH, $COCH_3$) + *p*-hydroxy acetophenone (OH, $COCH_3$)

*13. (b) $LiAlH_4$ reacts with the benzoic acid and reduces the – COOH group to – CH_2OH group.

$C_6H_5COOH \xrightarrow{LiAlH_4} C_6H_5CH_2OH + H_2O$ (1 mark)

14. (a) Mn^{2+}–5 unpaired electrons; Fe^{2+}–4 unpaired electrons Ti^{2+}–2 unpaired electrons; Cr^{2+}–4 unpaired electrons

Hence, maximum no. of unpaired electron is present in Mn^{2+}.

Magnetic moment ∝ number of unpaired electrons

15. (d) Conductivity of an electrolyte decreases with decrease in concentration because number of ions per unit volume decreases on dilution.

16. (a) Aniline is a better nucleophile than anilium ion. Anilium ion contain positive charge, which reduces its tendency to donate lone pair of electrons of nitrogen $C_6H_5\overset{+}{N}H_3$ (anilium ion).

17. (d) $[Ni(en)_3]Cl_2$ is more stable than $[Ni(NH_3)_6]Cl_2$ because ethylenediamine is a bidentate ligand, hence it forms chelating ring with Ni^{2+} ion. In $[Ni(en)_3]Cl_2$, the geometry of Ni is octahedral.

18. (d) Aryl halides do not undergo nucleophilic substitution reaction under ordinary conditions.

19. (i) $\underset{\text{D-glucose}}{OHC—(CHOH)_4—CH_2OH} \xrightarrow{(CH_3CO)_2O}$

$\underset{\text{Glucose pentaacetate}}{OHC—(CHOCOCH_3)_4—CH_2OCOCH_3}$ (1 mark)

(ii)

$$HOH_2C—(CHOH)_4—CHO \xrightarrow{HCN}$$
D-glucose

$$HOH_2C—(CHOH)_4—CH(OH)CN$$ (1 mark)
Glucose cyanohydrin

20. Calculation of molality of solution
$\Delta T_f = K_f \times m$ or $m = \Delta T_f / K_f$ (½ mark)
$\Delta T_f = 273 - 272.07 = 0.93$ K; $K_f = 1.86$ K kg mol^{-1}. (½ mark)

$$m = \frac{(0.93K)}{(1.86K\ kg\ mol^{-1})} = 0.5\ mol\ kg^{-1} = 0.5\ m$$ (½ mark)

Calculation of boiling point of solution
$\Delta T_b = K_b \times m$
$= 0.512$ K/m × 0.5 m
$= 0.256$ K
Boiling point of solution = (373 K + 0.256 K) = 373.256 K (½ mark)

OR

Molarity of solution on mixing :

$$M_3 = \frac{M_1V_1 + M_2V_2}{(V_1 + V_2)}$$ (½ mark)

According to available data :
$M_1 = 0.5$ M, $V_1 = 2.5$ L; $M_2 = 2$M, $V_2 = 500$ mL $= 0.5$ L (½ mark)

$\therefore M_3 =$

$$\frac{(0.5M \times 2.5L) + (2\ M \times 0.5\ L)}{(2.5\ L + 0.5\ L)} = \frac{(2.25\ ML)}{(3.0\ L)} = 0.75\ M$$ (1 mark)

21. Tetrahedral complexes do not show geometrical isomerism because the relative position of the ligands attached to the central metal atom are same with respect to each other. (2 marks)

OR

$[Co(NH_3)_3Cl_3] < [Co(NH_3)_4Cl_2]Cl < [Co(NH_3)_5Cl]Cl_2 < [Co(NH_3)_6]Cl_3$ (2 marks)

22. When the concentration of a weak electrolyte becomes very low, its degree of ionisation rises sharply. This results in a sharp increase in the number of ions in solution. Thus, the molar conductivity of a weak electrolyte rises steeply at low concentrations. (2 marks)

23. (a) Rate $= k[NO]^2[O_2]$ (½ mark)
Suppose initially, moles of NO = a, moles of O_2 = b, volume of the vessel = V L. Then

$$[NO] = a/V\ M, [O_2] = b/V\ M$$

$$\therefore \quad \text{Rate } (r_1) = k\left(\frac{a}{V}\right)^2\left(\frac{b}{V}\right) = k\frac{a^2b}{V^3}$$ ....(i) (½ mark)

New volume = V/3.

$\therefore$ New concentrations : $[NO] = \frac{a}{V/3} = \frac{3a}{V}$

$[O_2] = \frac{b}{V/3} = \frac{3b}{V}$

$\therefore$ New rate

$$(r_2) = k\left(\frac{3a}{V}\right)^2\left(\frac{3b}{V}\right) = \frac{27\,k\,a^2b}{V^3}$$ ...(ii) (½ mark)

$\therefore \quad \frac{r_2}{r_1} = 27$ or $r_2 = 27\,r_1$, i.e., rate becomes 27 times

There is no effect on the order of reaction. (½ mark)

24. (i) Carbylamine reaction: Both aliphatic and aromatic primary amines when warmed with chloroform and an alcoholic solution of KOH, produces isocyanides or carbylamines which have very unpleasant odours. This reaction is called carbylamine reaction.

$$R—NH_2 + CHCl_3 + 3KOH\,(alc) \longrightarrow R—N \equiv C + 3KCl + 3H_2O$$ (1 mark)

(ii) Hoffmann's bromamide reaction: When an amide is treated with bromine in alkali solution, it is converted to a primary amine that has one carbon atom less than the starting amide. This reaction is known as Hoffmann's bromamide degradation reaction.

$$C_6H_5CONH_2 \xrightarrow{Br_2 + NaOH} C_6H_5NH_2$$ (1 mark)

25. The reactions of glucose with Fehling's solution and phenyl hydrazine are characteristic of a –CHO group. In aqueous solution open chain, aldehyde form is in equilibrium with the cyclic hemiacetal form. Since these reactions are irreversible, the equilibrium shifts towards the open chain and eventually all the glucose reacts.
The addition reaction of an aldehyde with bisulphite is reversible reaction. It means that enough aldehyde should remain in equilibrium with the bisulphite adduct to satisfy the equilibrium with the cyclic form. At equilibrium the concentration of open chain form is very low. Consequently, there is no reaction. (2 marks)

26. (a) Electrode potential value, E° depend upon following factors:
(a) Energy of sublimation of metal, ΔH_{sub},
(b) Ionisation energy $(IE_1 + IE_2)$, and
(c) Hydration energy, ΔH_{hyd}.
There is no regular trend in values of E° for transition elements because there is no definite value of above mentioned three factors. These factors are irregular due to variation in atomic size, ionic size, etc of transition metals. (1 mark)

(b) The complex $[Ni(CN)_4]^{2-}$ is square planar while $[Ni(CO)_4]$ is tetrahedral in nature. But since all the electrons in the orbitals of the central metal atom/ion in these complexes are paired, both are therefore, diamagnetic in nature. (1 mark)
(c) In square planar complexes MX_2L_2, the two identical ligands (X or L) can occupy either adjacent positions or opposite positions in the co-ordination polyhedron representing square plane. Therefore, *cis* and *trans* isomers are possible. In tetrahedral complexes, all the four positions are identical and no spatial isomerism can be shown. (1 mark)

27. (a) In S_N2 reaction, transition state is formed, so alkyl halide whose halogen is less sterically hindered and also a better leaving group will follow preferably S_N2 path.
2° alkyl halide is less sterically [structure: pentyl chain]Cl (1 mark)

(b) I_2/NaOH or Fehling solution CH_3CHO will give positive test with these reagents (1 mark)

(c) I_2/NaOH $C_6H_5COCH_3$ will give positive iodoform test. (1 mark)

28. $m = 0.01$; $\Delta T_f = 0.068°C$; $K_f = 1.86$ K kg mol^{-1}
If i is the van't Hoff factor for the aqueous solution of $AlCl_3$, then

$$\Delta T_f = i.K_f.m \quad (½ \text{ mark})$$

$$\Rightarrow \quad i = \frac{\Delta T_f}{K_f.m}$$

$$\Rightarrow \quad i = \frac{0.068}{1.86 \times 0.01} \quad (½ \text{ mark})$$

$$\Rightarrow \quad i = 3.66 \quad (½ \text{ mark})$$

$AlCl_3$	$\rightleftharpoons$	Al^{3+}	+	Cl^-	(½ mark)
1		0		0	initial
$1-x$		x		$3x$	at equilibrium

$$i = \frac{(1-x)+x+3x}{1} \quad (½ \text{ mark})$$

$\Rightarrow \quad 3.66 = 1 + 3x$
$\Rightarrow \quad x = 0.89$
x is degree of dissociation.
$\therefore$ Percentage of dissociation = 89%. (½ mark)

29. (a) The given cell reaction is the net result of the following half cell reactions.

$$Mg(s) \longrightarrow Mg^{2+}(aq) + 2e^-$$
$$2Ag^+(aq) + 2e^- \longrightarrow 2Ag(s)$$
$$\overline{Mg(s) + 2Ag^+(aq) \longrightarrow Mg^{2+}(aq) + 2Ag(s)}$$

The cell may be represented as:
$Mg \mid Mg^{2+}(0.130\,M) \mid\mid Ag^+(1.0 \times 10^{-4}\,M) \mid Ag$
Anode Cathode

$$E^\circ_{cell} = E^\circ_{cathode} - E^\circ_{anode} = E^\circ_{Ag^+/Ag} - E^\circ_{Mg^{2+}/Mg}$$
(½ mark)

$$= +0.80\,V - (-2.37\,V) = 0.80\,V + 2.37\,V = +3.17\,V$$
(½ mark)

(b) Applying Nernst equation,

$$E_{cell} = E^\circ_{cell} - \frac{0.0591\,V}{2}\log\frac{[Mg^{2+}(aq)]}{[Ag^+(aq)]^2} \quad [\because [Mg(s)] = [Ag(s)] = 1 \text{ and } T = 298\,K] \quad (½ \text{ mark})$$

Or, $$E_{cell} = +3.17 - \frac{0.0591}{2}\log\frac{0.130}{[1.0\times10^{-4}]^2} \quad (½ \text{ mark})$$

$$= +3.17 - \frac{0.0591}{2}\log 0.130 \times 10^8$$
$$= +3.17 - 0.02955 \times (8 - 0.886) \quad (½ \text{ mark})$$
$$= +3.17 - 0.02955 \times 7.114$$
$$= +3.17 - 0.21\,V = 2.96\,V \quad (½ \text{ mark})$$

OR

(a) The cell reactions are
$Zn(s) \longrightarrow Zn^{2+}(aq) + 2e^-$ (anode)
$Cu^{2+}(aq) + 2e^- \longrightarrow Cu(s)$ (cathode) (1 mark)

(b) $E^\circ_{cell} = E_{cathode} - E_{anode} = 0.34 - (-0.76)$
$= 0.34 + 0.76 = 1.10\,V$ (½ mark)
from Nernst equation

$$E_{cell} = E^\circ_{cell} - \frac{0.059}{n}\log\frac{[Zn^{2+}]}{[Cu^{2+}]} \quad (½ \text{ mark})$$

$$E_{cell} = 1.1 - \frac{0.059}{2}\log\frac{[2]}{[0.5]} \quad (½ \text{ mark})$$

$$= 1.1 - \frac{0.059}{2}(\log 20 - \log 5)$$

$$= 1.1 - \frac{0.059}{2} \times 0.6021$$

$$= 1.1 - 0.0177 = 1.09\,V \quad (1 \text{ mark})$$

30. (a) Aniline is basic in nature. It does not undergo Friedal-Crafts reaction due to salt formation with aluminium chloride, the Lewis acid, which is used as a catalyst. Anilinium ion is formed in which nitrogen of aniline acquires positive charge and hence acts as a strong deactivating group for further reaction. (1 mark)

(b) Aromatic primary amines cannot be prepared by Gabriel phthalimide synthesis because aryl halides do not undergo nucleophilic substitution with the anion formed by phthalimide. (1 mark)

(c) Aliphatic amines are stronger bases than ammonia due to + I effect of alkyl groups leading to high electron density on the nitrogen atom. (1 mark)

(d) Diazonium salts are present in ionic form in their aqueous solution, e.g. $RN_2^+HSO_4^-$, $RN_2^+BFO_4^-$ etc. Ionic solutions are good conductors of electricity.

31. (a) One (1 mark)
(b) Rate = k_1[A] (1 mark)
(c) Slowest step (step-1) of the reaction. (1 mark)
(d) Two (1 mark)

OR

For the given reaction, the rate of reaction is

$$= -\frac{1}{2}\frac{d[N_2O_5]}{dt} = \frac{1}{4}\frac{d[NO_2]}{dt} \quad (1 \text{ mark})$$

$$= \frac{d[O_2]}{dt}$$

32. (a) Inversion occurs more than retention, leading to partial racemization. (1 mark)

(b) Polarimeter (½ mark)

(c) Iodoform (CHI_3) is used as a disinfectant. (½ mark)

(d) (2 marks)

2-bromopentane $\xrightarrow{\text{alc.KOH}}$ pent-2-ene (major product)

OR

anisole + HI ⟶ phenol + CH_3-I (2 marks)

33. (a) (i) Phenol to anisole

Phenol + NaOH ⟶ Sodium phenoxide (O^-Na^+)

$\xrightarrow{CH_3Br}$ Anisole (OCH_3) (1 mark)

(ii) Ethanol to propan-2-ol

$$CH_3-CH_2OH \xrightarrow[\text{oxidation}]{PCC} CH_3-\overset{O}{\overset{\|}{C}}-H + CH_3MgI$$

$$\xrightarrow[\text{ether}]{\text{Dry}} \left[CH_3-\overset{OMgI}{\overset{|}{CH}}-CH_3\right] \xrightarrow{H^+/H_2O}$$

$$CH_3-\overset{OH}{\overset{|}{CH}}-CH_3$$

(1 mark)

(b) $C_2H_5OH \xrightarrow[443K]{H_2SO_4} CH_2=CH_2 + H_2O$

Mechanism is as follows:

Step I: $CH_3CH_2\ddot{O}H + H-O-\overset{O}{\overset{\|}{\underset{O}{\underset{\|}{S}}}}-O-H$

$$\rightleftharpoons CH_3CH_2\overset{+}{O}H_2 + HSO_4^-$$

Step II: $CH_3CH_2-\overset{H}{\overset{|}{\underset{+}{O}}}-H \rightleftharpoons CH_3\overset{+}{C}H_2 + H_2O$

Step III: $H-\overset{H}{\overset{|}{\underset{H}{\underset{|}{C}}}}-\overset{+}{C}H_2 + {}^-O-\overset{O}{\overset{\|}{\underset{O}{\underset{\|}{S}}}}-O-H \rightleftharpoons$

$$CH_2=CH_2 + H_2SO_4$$

(2 marks)

(c) The rate of any electrophilic substitution reaction depends upon the electron density in the aromatic ring. Higher the electron density in the aromatic ring, higher is the rate of electrophilic substitution reaction. The presence of OH group in phenol, increases the electron density at ortho and para position by +R effect. Since the electron density is more in phenol than in benzene. Therefore phenol undergoes electrophilic substitution more easily than benzene. (1 mark)

OR

(a) (i) Ortho nitrophenol is more steam volatile than para nitrophenol because o-Nitrophenol has intra molecular hydrogen bonding where as para nitrophenol has intermolecular H-bonding. Energy is required to overcome attractive forces in the molecules of *p*-nitrophenol. This means that boiling point of *o*-nitrophenol is less and is steam volatile while that of *p*-nitrophenol is more, and is non-volatile. (1 mark)

(ii) Sodium methoxides is a strong nucleophile and a strong base. Thus elimination predominates substitution. In this reaction E_1 favored over S_N1. So t-butyl chloride on heating with sodium methoxide gives 2-methylpropene instead of t-butyl methyl ether. (1 mark)

Elimination reaction is favored under strong base condition while substitution reaction is favored under weak nucleophile condition.

(b) (i) 2 Phenol + $CHCl_3 \xrightarrow{3\text{ KOH}}$ *o*-Hydroxy benzaldehyde (major) $+ 3KCl + 2H_2O$

(1 mark)

(ii) Friedel Craft alkylation of phenol

In this reaction phenol react with alkyl halide in the presence of anhydrous $AlCl_3$ & forms *o*-methyl phenol, *p*-methyl phenol.

Phenol + $CH_3Cl \xrightarrow{\text{anhyd } AlCl_3}$

OH (p-cresol) + OH, CH_3 (o-cresol) (1 mark)

Phenols undergoes Friedel craft alkylation with very low yield due to the formation of complex with $AlCl_3$.

(c) Ethanol and phenol can be distinguished by idoform test.

$CH_3CH_2OH + 4I_2 + 6NaOH \rightarrow$ (ethanol) $CHI_3\downarrow + HCOONa + 5H_2O$ (Iodoform (yellow))

Phenol (OH) $+ I_2 + NaOH \rightarrow$ No reaction

(1 mark)

34. (a) These elements do not fulfill the condition or definition of a transition element . It is because neither, these elements nor their ions have incompletely filled *d*-orbitals. (1 mark)

(b) Transition metal atoms or their ions have generally partially filled *d*-orbitals and thus can undergo $d-d$ transitions by absorbing light from visible region and radiate complimentary colour. (1 mark)

(c) Zr and Hf exhibit almost similar properties because their atomic and ionic sizes are almost equal due to lanthanide contraction. (1 mark)

(d) 4 *f*-orbitals are progressively filled in lanthanides whereas in actinides 5 *f*-orbitals are progressively filled up. (1 mark)

(e) Atomic size does not vary much due to poor shielding effect of $(n-1)$ *d*-electrons on nucleus. Thus, effective nuclear charge does not vary much. Hence first ionisation energy also do not vary much. (1 mark)

OR

(a) Ce (III) is easily oxidised to Ce (IV) because Ce (IV) has more stable electronic configuration.

$\underset{(Z=58)}{Ce} \longrightarrow [Xe]_{54}\,4f^1\,5d^1\,6s^2$

$Ce(III) \longrightarrow [Xe]_{54}\,4f^1\,5d^0\,6s^0$

Ce (III) can further loose one $4f^1$ electron easily to acquire stable Ce(IV). (2 marks)

(b) The decrease in atomic and ionic size with the increase in atomic number in lanthanoids is called lanthanoid contraction. (1 mark)

It has the following effects:

(i) The ionisation energy in 5*d* series is more than that in 3*d* and 4*d* series. (1 mark)

(ii) There is resemblance between properties of elements of 4*d* and 5*d* transition series. (1 mark)

35. (a) Propiophenone from Propanenitrile: (1 mark)

$H_3C-CH_2-C\equiv N + C_6H_5MgI \xrightarrow[\text{ether}]{\text{Dry}}$ (Propanenitrile; Phenyl magnesium iodide)

$\left[H_3C-CH_2-\underset{C_6H_5}{\underset{|}{C}}=N-MgI\right] \xrightarrow{H_3O^+}$ (Adduct)

$H_3C-CH_2-\underset{C_6H_5}{C}=O + Mg(OH)I + NH_3$ (Propiophenone)

(b) 4-Chlorobenzaldehyde from 4-Chlorotoluene: (1 mark)

4-Chlorotoluene (CH_3, Cl) $\xrightarrow[273-278\,K]{CrO_3/(CH_3CO)_2O}$ $CH(OCOCH_3)_2$ (Cl) $\xrightarrow{H_3O^+\ (-2CH_3COOH)}$ CHO (Cl)

4-Chlorotoluene $\xrightarrow{CrO_2Cl_2 \text{ in } CS_2}$ $CH(OCrOHCl_2)_2$ (Cl) $\xrightarrow{H_2O}$ CHO (Cl) 4-Chlorbenzaldehyde

(c) Cyclohexanecarbaldehyde from Cyclohexylmethanol: (1 mark)

CH_2-OH (Cyclohexylmethanol) $+ [O] \xrightarrow[\text{dil. } H_2SO_4]{K_2Cr_2O_7}$ CHO (Cyclohexanecarbaldehyde) $+ H_2O$

(d) 4-Methoxyacetophenone from Anisole: (1 mark)

$O-CH_3$ (Anisole) $+ CH_3COCl \xrightarrow[\Delta]{\text{Anhydrous } AlCl_3}$ $O-CH_3$, $O=C-CH_3$ (4-Methoxyacetophenone)

(e) 4-Methylbenzaldehyde from Toluene: (1 mark)

CH_3 (Toluene) $\xrightarrow[\text{Anhyd.}AlCl_3 + CuCl_2]{CO.HCl}$ CH_3, CHO (4-Methylbenzaldehyde)

1. **(b)** An increase in temperature of the solution increases the solubility of a solid solute.
The amount of solute that dissolve depends on what type of solute it is.
For solids and liquid solutes, changes in pressure have practically no effect on solubility.

2. **(b)**

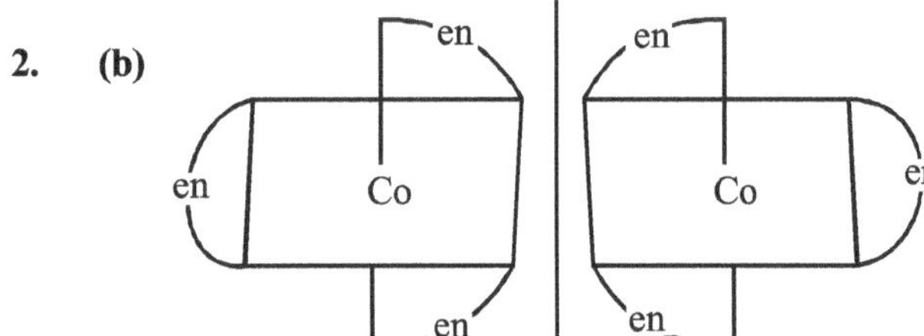

$[Co(en)_3]^{+3}$

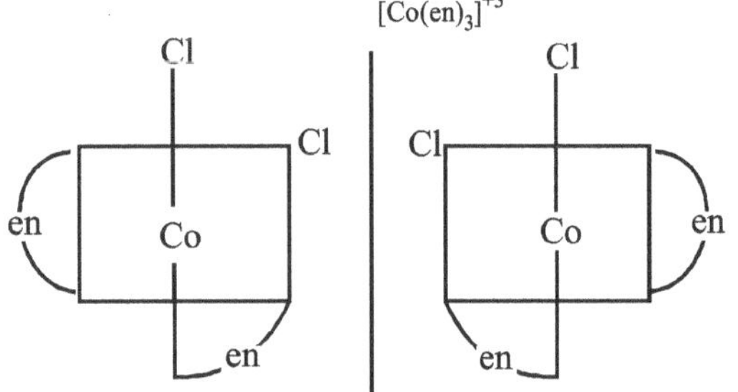

cis-$[Co(en)_2Cl_2]Cl$

These pairs are forming non-superimposable mirror images, so, they are optically active complexes.

3. **(b)** Electron withdrawing substituents increase the acidic strength of phenols. so, *p*-nitrophenol (II) and *m*-nitrophenol (IV) are stronger acid than phenol (I). If $-NO_2$ group is present at *p*-position, then it exerts both – I and – R effect, but if it is present at meta position, then it exerts only–I effect. Therefore, *p*-nitrophenol is stronger than *m*-nitrophenol.
On the other hand, electron releasing substituents decreases the acidic strength of phenol. If $-OCH_3$ group is present at meta position, it will exert – I effect only. But, if it is present at para position, it will exert + R and – I effect. Thus, *m* - methoxy benzyl alcohol is more acidic than *p*- methoxy phenol. Hence, the correct order of decreasing acidic strength will be :
II > IV > I > III > V.

4. **(c)** Reduction of CH_3COCH_3 to alkanes can be done by the action of HI. HI is a very strong reducing agent.
$$CH_3COCH_3 + 2HI \longrightarrow CH_3CH_2CH_3 + H_2O + I_2$$

5. **(c)** As the value of standard reduction potential decreases the reducing power increases *i.e.*,

$$\underset{(-3.0)}{Z} > \underset{(-1.2)}{X} > \underset{(+0.5)}{Y}$$

6. **(a)** $_{78}Pt = [Xe]\ 4f^{14}\ 5d^9\ 6s^1$ (Exceptional electronic configuration)

7. **(d)** 4-Bromobut-l-ene is not an allylic halide

$$BrH_2C{-}CH_2{-}CH{=}CH_2$$
4–Bromobut–1–ene

8. **(b)**

$C_6H_5CONH_2$ < o-nitroaniline < $C_6H_5NH_2$ < $C_6H_5CH_2NH_2$

e^- pair delocalised due to – C = O part; e^- pair delocalised due to weak – M and – I effects of – NO_2 group; e^- pair delocalised; e^- pair localised

(1 mark)

9. **(c)** Open chain structure is unstable and converted to cyclic.

10. **(b)** Rate of disappearance of reactants = Rate of appearance of products

$$-\frac{1}{2}\frac{d(N_2O_5)}{dt} = \frac{1}{4}\frac{d(NO_2)}{dt} = \frac{d(O_2)}{dt}$$

$$\frac{1}{2}k(N_2O_5) = \frac{1}{4}k'(N_2O_5) = k''(N_2O_5)$$

$$\frac{k}{2} = \frac{k'}{4} = k'' \Rightarrow k' = 2k,\ k'' = \frac{k}{2}$$

11. **(b)** C_4H_7Cl is a monochloro derivative of C_4H_8 which itself exists in three acyclic isomeric forms.

$CH_3CH_2CH = CH_2$ (I) (Its four C's are different)

$CH_3CH = CHCH_3$ (II) (It has 2 types of carbon)

$CH_3-\underset{}{\overset{CH_3}{\overset{|}{C}}}=CH_2$ (III) (It has 2 types of carbon)

Grand total of acyclic isomers = 6 + 4 + 2 = 12

12. **(a)** A strong nucleophile favours the S_N2 reaction and a weak nucleophile favours the S_N1 reaction.
First reaction is S_N1 reaction because C_2H_5OH is used as solvent which is a weak nucleophile.
Second reaction is S_N2 reaction because $C_2H_5O^-$ is strong nucleophile.

13. **(b)** Amino acids exist as zwitterions in which acidic character is due to $-NH_3^+$ and basic due to $-COO^-$ group.

$$H_3\overset{+}{N}\underset{}{\overset{R}{\overset{|}{C}}}HCOOH \xleftarrow{acid} H_3\overset{+}{N}\overset{R}{\overset{|}{C}}HCOO^-$$

$$\xrightarrow{base} H_2N\overset{R}{\overset{|}{C}}HCOO^-$$

14. **(b)** Aldehydes or ketones having α-hydrogen undergo aldol condensation in the presence of a base which abstracts α-H atom from them to form corresponding **carbanion** which is stabilised by resonance.

$$OH^- + H-CH_2-\overset{O}{\overset{||}{C}}-H \rightleftharpoons H_2O + [\bar{C}H_2-\overset{O}{\overset{||}{C}}-H \longleftrightarrow CH_2=\overset{O^-}{\overset{|}{C}}-H]$$

15. **(a)** Vapour pressure of liquid and solid are equal at freezing point. Reduction in V.P. occurs when solute is added.

16. **(a)** The rate expression, $\frac{dX}{dt} = k[A]^m[B]^n$ shows that the total order of reaction is $m+n+0=m+n$

The rate of reaction is independent of concentration of C, i.e., the order with respect to C is zero.

17. **(d)** $Ni(CO)_4$ has tetrahedral geometry and $[Ni(CN)_4]^{2-}$ has square planar geometry. $[Ni(CO)_4]$ possesses sp^3 hybridization whereas $[Ni(CN)_4]^{2-}$ has dsp^2 hybridization to show square planar geometry.

18. **(b)** Aldehydes which do not contain α-hydrogen undergo cannizzaro reaction.

19. In S_N2 reaction, transition state is formed, so alkyl halide whose halogen is less sterically hindered and also a better leaving group will follow preferably S_N2 path.

1° alkyl halide is less sterically hindered than 2° alkyl halide

(Cyclohexyl)$-CH_2Cl$ (2 marks)

20. (a) Greater acidity of phenol than an alcohol is due to possibility of resonance in phenol which leads to electron-deficient oxygen atom. Presence of electron-deficient oxygen atom (see structures II, III and IV) in turn weakens the $-\overset{+}{O}\leftarrow H$ bond, and thus facilitates release of proton.

I ⟷ II ⟷ III ⟷ IV

Such structures are not possible in alcohols. (1 mark)

(b) Amino group, being electron releasing, intensifies the negative charge if present at *ortho* and *para* positions (but not *meta* position) and thus makes the phenoxide less stable and thus the parent phenol (*o*-amino phenol) less acidic than phenol. However, when present at *meta* position, it is not involved in the intensification of charge and thus has no additional effect on stability of the corresponding phenoxide ion and hence on acidity of the corresponding phenol (*m*-amino phenol), i.e. it is as acidic as phenol and hence more acidic than *o*-aminophenol. (1 mark)

21. $$\lambda_m = \frac{K}{c} = \frac{7.8\times10^{-5}\,Scm^{-1}}{0.001\,mol\,L^{-1}} \times \frac{1000\,cm^3}{L} = 78.05\ cm^2\,mol^{-1}$$

$$\alpha = \frac{\lambda_m}{\lambda_m^0} = \frac{78.0\ Scm^2mol^{-1}}{390\ Scm^2mol^{-1}} = 0.2$$ (2 Marks)

22. (a) $Rate = k[P]^{1/3}[Q]^3 = k[8P]^{1/3}[2Q]^3$

$= k\,8^{1/3}[P]^{1/3} \times 2^3[Q]^3 = 16k[P]^{1/3}[Q]^3$

Therefore, on increasing the concentration of P to eight times and that of Q to two times, rate becomes 16 times. (1 mark)

(b) $Rate = k\,[A]^0[B]^0$ or $Rate = k$ (1 mark)

23. (a) It is because lanthanoids have similar ionic size, therefore, they occur together and their separation becomes difficult. (1 mark)

(b) The transition metals have voids in their crystal lattice into which small atoms like H, C, N, B etc. are trapped resulting in the formation of interstitial compounds. (1 mark)

OR

(a) Ce^{4+} has the noble configuration of Xe (Z = 54) but it has a strong urge to change to + 3 oxidation state which is the most common oxidation state of the elements belonging to lanthanoid family. Therefore, it acts as a strong oxidising agent in the volumetric analysis. (1 mark)

(b) Cu^{2+} ion ($3d^9$) has one half filled d-orbital. Therefore, it takes part in $d-d$ transition. Hence, the compounds containing Cu^{2+} ion (e.g., $CuSO_4.5H_2O$) are coloured. Zn^{2+} ion ($3d^{10}$) has completely filled d-orbitals and there is no scope for any electronic transition. Therefore Zn^{2+} salts are white and not coloured. (1 mark)

24. A is $KMnO_4/H^+$, B is $SOCl_2$ and C is CH_3COONa.

$$CH_3CHO \xrightarrow{KMnO_4/H^+} CH_3COOH \xrightarrow{SOCl_2}$$

$$CH_3COCl \xrightarrow{CH_3COONa} (CH_3CO)_2O$$

(½ + 1 + ½ = 2 marks)

25. In pure liquid water the entire surface of liquid is occupied by the molecules of water. When a non volatile solute, for example glucose, is dissolved in water the fraction of surface covered by the solvent molecules gets reduced because some positions are occupied by glucose molecules. As a result number of solvent molecules escaping from the surface also gets reduced, consequently the vapour pressure of aqueous solution of glucose is reduced. (2 marks)

OR

$$\left(\frac{P^\circ - P_s}{P^\circ}\right) = \frac{n}{N} = \frac{W_1}{M_1} \times \frac{M_2}{W_2}$$

Where, W_1 = wt of solute, W_2 = wt of solvent
M_1 = Mass of solute, M_2 = Mass of solvent
At 100 °C, $P^\circ = 760$ mm

$$\frac{760-732}{760} = \frac{6.5\times18}{M_1\times100}\ ;\ M_1 = 31.75\ \text{g mol}^{-1}$$

$$\Delta T_b = m\times K_b = \frac{W_1\times1000}{M_1\times W_2}\times K_b$$

$$\Delta T_b = \frac{0.52\times6.5\times1000}{31.75\times100} = 1.06\ °\text{C}$$

$\therefore$ boiling point of solution = 100°C + 1.06°C = 101°C

26. The structural formula of 2, 2, 5, 5-tetramethylhexane is

$$CH_3-\underset{CH_3}{\overset{CH_3}{\underset{|}{\overset{|}{C}}}}-CH_2-CH_2-\underset{CH_3}{\overset{CH_3}{\underset{|}{\overset{|}{C}}}}-CH_3$$

It suggest that compound A which gives the above compound during Wurtz reaction is

$$CH_3-\underset{CH_3}{\overset{CH_3}{\underset{|}{\overset{|}{C}}}}-CH_2Cl \quad \text{(1-chloro-2,2-dimethylpropane)}$$

The complete sequence of reaction is as follows:

$$CH_3-\underset{CH_3}{\overset{CH_3}{\underset{|}{\overset{|}{C}}}}-CH_2Cl \xrightarrow[\text{Wurtz reaction}]{\text{Na, ether}}$$

1–chloro–2,2–dimethyl propane
'A'

$$CH_3-\underset{CH_3}{\overset{CH_3}{\underset{|}{\overset{|}{C}}}}-CH_2-CH_2-\underset{CH_3}{\overset{CH_3}{\underset{|}{\overset{|}{C}}}}-CH_3 \xrightarrow[\text{reduction}]{\text{Zn/Cu}}$$

2, 2, 5, 5– tetramethyl hexane

$$CH_3-\underset{CH_3}{\overset{CH_3}{\underset{|}{\overset{|}{C}}}}-CH_3 \qquad (1+1+1=3\ \text{marks})$$

(Hydrocarbon with five carbon atoms)

27. Let 'w' be the required mass of ascorbic acid.

Molality of ascorbic and

$$m = \frac{w/176}{75/1000}\ ;\ m = \frac{w}{176}\times\frac{1000}{75} \qquad (½\ \text{mark})$$

$(k_f)_{\text{acetic}} = 3.9$ K kg mol^{-1} (1 mark)

$\Delta T_f = 1.5\ °\text{C} \Rightarrow \Delta T_f = 1.5$ K

$\Delta T_f = m.k_f$ (½ mark)

$$\Rightarrow\ 1.5 = \frac{w}{176}\times\frac{1000}{75}\times3.9$$

$\Rightarrow\ w = 5.08$ g (1 mark)

28. Rate = $k[A]^\alpha[B]^\beta$
Divide $(\text{Rate})_1$, and $(\text{Rate})_4$

$$\frac{(\text{Rate})_1}{(\text{Rate})_4} = \frac{k(0.1)^\alpha(0.1)^\beta}{k(0.4)^\alpha(0.1)^\beta}\ ;\ \frac{6\times10^{-3}}{2.40\times10^{-2}} = \left(\frac{0.1}{0.4}\right)^\alpha$$

$$\frac{1}{4} = \left(\frac{1}{4}\right)^\alpha$$

$\alpha = 1$ (½ mark)

$$\frac{(\text{Rate})_2}{(\text{Rate})_3} = \frac{k(0.3)^\alpha(0.2)^\beta}{k(0.3)^\alpha(0.4)^\beta} \Rightarrow \frac{7.2\times10^{-2}}{2.88\times10^{-1}} = \left(\frac{0.2}{0.4}\right)^\beta$$

$$\frac{1}{4} = \left(\frac{1}{2}\right)^\beta\ ;\ \left(\frac{1}{2}\right)^2 = \left(\frac{1}{2}\right)^\beta \qquad (½\ \text{mark})$$

$\beta = 2$
Rate = $k[A]^1[B]^2$
Order : $1+2=3$ (1 mark)
From experiment 1 :
$6\times10^{-3} = k(0.1)^1(0.1)^2$
$k = 6\times10^{-3}/1\times10^{-3} = 6\ \text{mol}^{-2}\ \text{L}^2\ \text{min}^{-1}$ (1 mark)

29. (a) Pentan-1-ol > 2-methyl butan-2-ol > 2methybutan-2-ol. As the branching increases the shape becomes more compact and spherical. As a result, there is less surface contact for van der Waal's attractive forces. Hence, boiling point decreases. (1 mark)

(b) The rate of reaction with Lucas Reagent follows the order: 3° alcohol > 2° alcohol > 1° alcohol
since carbocations are formed as intermediate, more stable the carbocations, higher will be the reactivity of the parent alcohol.

$$CH_3-\underset{CH_3}{\overset{CH_3}{\underset{|}{\overset{|}{C}}}}-OH \xrightarrow{H^+} H_3C-\underset{CH_3}{\overset{CH_3}{\underset{|}{\overset{|}{C}}}}-\overset{+}{O}H_2 \xrightarrow{-H_2O}$$

2-methylpropan-2-ol

$$(CH_3)_2\overset{\oplus}{C}-CH_3 \xrightarrow{Br^\ominus} CH_3-\underset{CH_3}{\overset{CH_3}{\underset{|}{\overset{|}{C}}}}-Br\ (1\ \text{mark})$$

3°-carbocation

(c) The process that involves the change in the optical rotation of either form of glucose (a – or b –) in aqueous solution to that of equilibrium mixture is known as mutarotation. This process of conversion of one anomeric form of glucose into the other in aqueous solution occurs through the open chain structure. The equilibrium mixture always contain a small amount of open chain form of glucose.

Specific rotation

α–glucose $\rightleftharpoons$ open chain form of glucose $\rightleftharpoons$ β – glucose
113° 52° 19°

(1 mark)

(d) Sucrose is dextrorotatory but on hydrolysis it gives an equimolar mixture of D – (+) –glucose and D – (–) – fructose, which is levorotatory. This change of specific rotation from dextro rotation to laevoration is called inversion of sugar. (1 mark)

30. The molecular formula of compound (B) and the characteristic odour of (A) suggest that (A) is an aromatic aldehyde, C_6H_5—CHO and (B) is an aromatic alcohol, $C_6H_5CH_2OH$. This view is further confirmed by the fact that (B) on oxidation gives back (A). (Primary alcohol on oxidation gives aldehydes). As (C) is a sodium salt of an acid and gives hydrocarbon (D) on heating with sodalime, (C) is sodium benzoate and (D) is benzene. The reaction involved are:

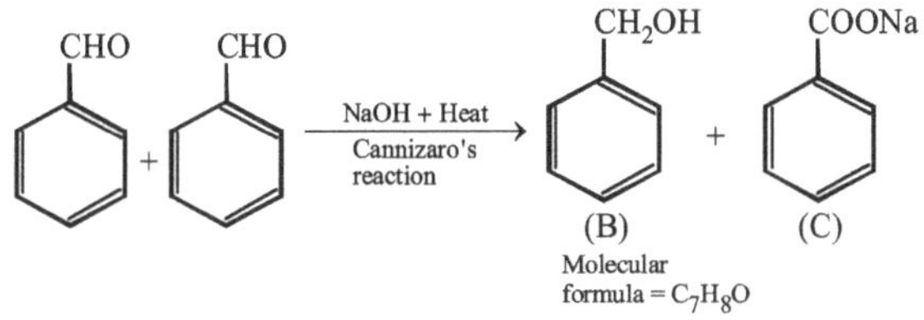

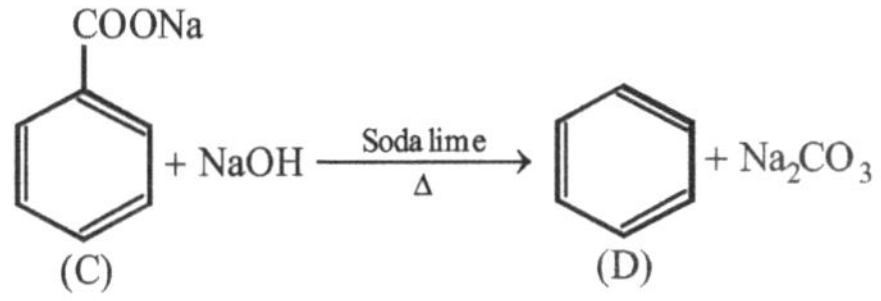

$$C_6H_5CHO + C_6H_5CHO \xrightarrow[\text{Cannizaro's reaction}]{\text{NaOH + Heat}} C_6H_5CH_2OH \text{ (B)} + C_6H_5COONa \text{ (C)}$$

(B) Molecular formula = C_7H_8O

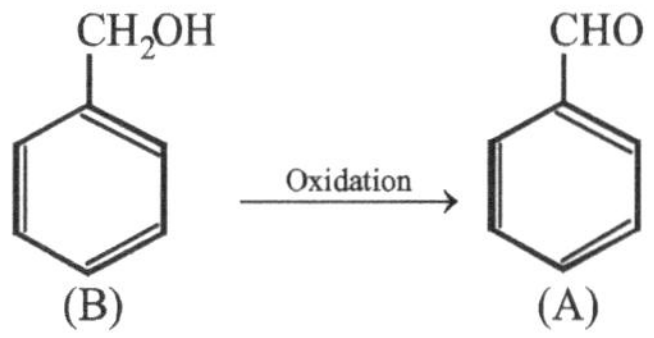

$$C_6H_5CH_2OH \text{ (B)} \xrightarrow{\text{Oxidation}} C_6H_5CHO \text{ (A)}$$

$$C_6H_5COONa \text{ (C)} + NaOH \xrightarrow[\Delta]{\text{Soda lime}} C_6H_6 \text{ (D)} + Na_2CO_3$$ (3 marks)

OR

Since the ketone (C) yields a mixture of ethanoic and propanoic acids on vigorous oxidation, it must be pentanone. The compound B must be butanol. The reactions are:

$$\underset{\text{(A)}}{CH_3CH_2-\underset{Br}{C}H CH_3} \xrightarrow{\text{aq NaOH}} \underset{\text{(B)}}{CH_3CH_2-\underset{OH}{C}H CH_3} \xrightarrow{[O]}$$

$$\underset{\text{(C)}}{CH_3-CH_2-\underset{\underset{O}{\|}}{C}-CH_2-CH_3} \xrightarrow[\text{oxidation}]{\text{Vigorous}}$$

$CH_3COOH + CH_3CH_2COOH$

(1 + 1 + 1 = 3 marks)

31. (a) $-NH_2$ group is present in amino acids as a basic group. (1 mark)

(b) Amino acids exist as anion in basic medium. (1 mark)

(c) Amino acids have both basic group ($-NH_2$) and acidic group (–COOH) in one molecule. In a molecule $-NH_2$ group accepts the proton from –COOH group of the same molecule and they form a dipolar molecule where $-\overset{+}{N}H_3$ and $-COO^-$ present in the same molecule in aqueous medium. This dipolar molecule is known as zwitter ion. (1 mark)

(d) Amino acids are highly polar molecule as it contains both cation and anion in the same molecule. (1 mark)

OR

The simplest amino acid – glycine. (1 mark)

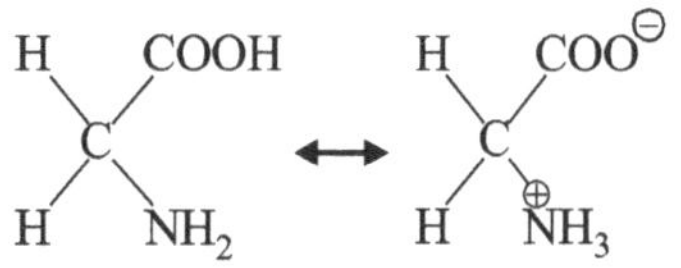

$$H_2C(NH_2)(COOH) \longleftrightarrow H_2C(\overset{\oplus}{N}H_3)(COO^{\ominus})$$

32. (i) oxalate ion $\Rightarrow$ $(O{=}C{-}O^-)_2$ (both O^- donate)

Ethylene diamine $\Rightarrow$ $H_2C(NH_2)-H_2C(NH_2)$ (both N donate)

Thiocyanato $\Rightarrow$ $S-C\equiv N^{\ominus}\rightarrow$ or $\leftarrow\overset{\ominus}{S}-C\equiv N$

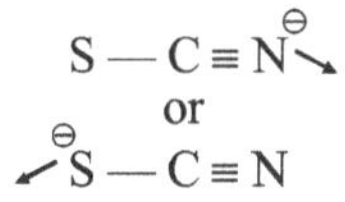

Nitrito $\Rightarrow$ $O{=}N{-}O^-\rightarrow$ or $\leftarrow N(=O)O^-$ (½ × 4 = 2 marks)

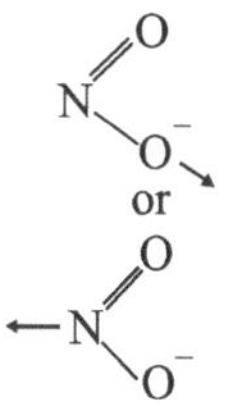

(ii) Oxalate ion and ethylene diamine are bidentate ligands Thiocyanato and nitrito are ambidentate digands. (2 marks)

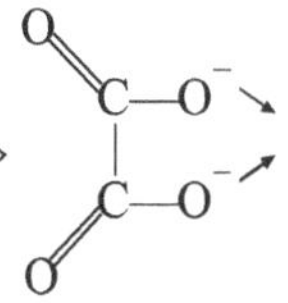

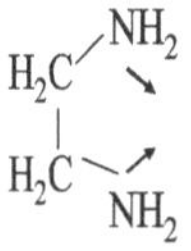

OR

d^6 system →

Octahedral splitting of d-orbitals

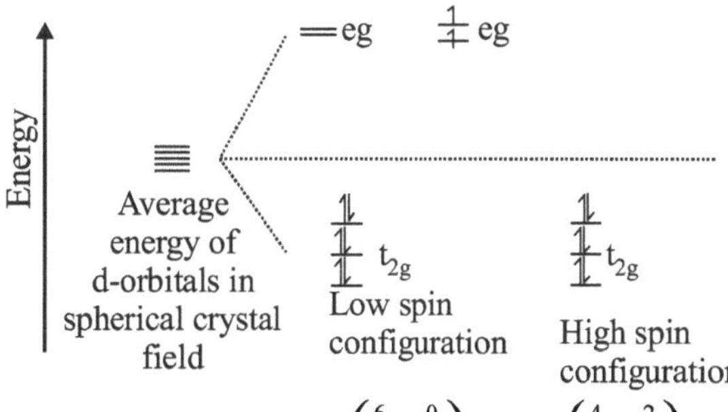

Energy ↑: Average energy of d-orbitals in spherical crystal field splits into eg (upper) and t_{2g} (lower).

Low spin configuration $(t_{2g}^6\, e_g^0)$ High spin configuration $(t_{2g}^4\, e_g^2)$

(2 marks)

33. (a) (i) $PhCH_2-\overset{O}{\overset{||}{C}}-NH_2 \xrightarrow{Br_2,NaOH} Ph\,CH_2\,NH_2$

Benzylamide — Benzyl amine (1 mark)

(ii) $PhCH_2I \xrightarrow[NH_3]{Excess} PhCH_2NH_2$ (1 mark)

Benzyl iodide — Benzylamine

(iii) Potassium phthalimide $\xrightarrow{PhCH_2I}$ N-benzylphthalimide ($N-CH_2Ph$) $\xrightarrow{Aq.\,NaOH}$ $C_6H_4(COONa)_2 + PhCH_2NH_2$ (Benzylamine)

(1 mark)

(b) Nitric acid is a strong oxidising agent and aniline gets easily oxidised. Therefore, aniline is converted to acetanilide before nitration. (1 mark)

(c) The alkyl halides on ammonolysis yield a mixture of primary amine, secondary amine, tertiary amine and a quaternary salt. This mixture cannot be easily separated into its constituents. Hence, it is difficult to get pure amines by ammonolysis of alkyl halides. (1 mark)

34. (a) (i) As $E^{\circ}_{Cr^{3+}/Cr^{2+}}$ is negative (– 0.4 V), this means that Cr^{3+} ions in solution cannot be reduced to Cr^{2+} ions or Cr^{3+} ions are very stable. As further comparison of E° values show that Mn^{3+} ions can be reduced to Mn^{2+} ion more readily than Fe^{3+} ions. Thus, the order of relative stabilities of different ions is: (1 mark)

$Mn^{3+} < Fe^{3+} < Cr^{3+}$.

(ii) From the E° values, the order of oxidation of the metal to the divalent cation is : $Mn > Cr > Fe$. (1 mark)

(b) (i) An ion is coloured in aqueous solution if it has unpaired electrons in its *d*-orbitals.

$_{47}Ag \longrightarrow {_{46}Ag^+}\ {_{36}Kr}\ 4d^{10}5s^0$

It has no unpaired electron is *d*-orbitals, thus it is colourless

$_{27}Co \longrightarrow {_{25}Co^{2+}}\ {_{18}Ar}\ 3d^7 4s^0$

It has three unpaired electrons in *d*-orbitals and hence it is coloured.

$_{22}Ti \longrightarrow {_{18}Ti^{4+}}\ {_{18}Ar}\ 3d^0\ 4d^0$

It has no unpaired electron in *d*-orbitals and thus colourless. (2 marks)

(ii) In the above given species, only Co^{2+}, when placed in magnetic field, it will be attracted and shows paramagnetism. The other two species Ag^+ and Ti^{4+} will not attract in magnetic field and thus are diamagnetic. (1 mark)

OR

(a) As the size decreases covalent character increases. Therefore La_2O_3 is more ionic and Lu_2O_3 is more covalent. (1 mark)

(b) As the size decreases from La to Lu, stability of oxosalts also decreases. (1 mark)

(c) Stability of complexes increases as the size of lanthanoids decreases. (1 mark)

(d) Radii of 4*d* and 5*d* block elements will be almost same. (1 mark)

(e) Acidic character of oxides increases from La to Lu. (1 mark)

35. (a) $Zn(s) + Cu^{2+}(aq) \longrightarrow Zn^{2+}(aq) + Cu(s)$

$E^o_{Cu^{2+}/Cu} = E^o_{cathode} = +0.34\ V$

$E^o_{Zn^{2+}/Zn} = E^o_{anode} = -0.76\ V$

$E^o_{cell} = E^o_{cathode} - E^o_{anode}$

$= 0.34 - (-0.76) = 1.1\ V$ (1 mark)

$n = 2$ (½ mark)

$F = 96500\ C\ mol^{-1}$

$\Delta G^o = -nF\ E^o_{cell}$ (½ mark)

$= -2 \times 96500 \times 1.1$

$= -212.27\ kJ\ mol^{-1}$ (1 mark)

(b) (i) Fuel cells produce electricity with an efficiency of about 70% as compared to thermal plants whose efficiency is about 40%.

(ii) Fuel cells are pollution free because the by-product of $H_2–O_2$ fuel cell is H_2O. (1 + 1 = 2 marks)

OR

(a) (i) Electrical conduction of metals decreases with increase in temperature. Thus, silver wire at 30°C will show greater conduction of electricity. (1 mark)

(ii) Conductance of solution increases on increase in dilution. Hence, 0.1 M CH_3COOH solution will allow greater conduction of electricity. (1 mark)

As the number of ions per litre of electrolyte increases with dilution, conductance also increases with dilution which implies less concentrated solution has greater conductance.

(iii) Increase in temperature increases the dissociation of an ionic compound. Thus, KCl solution at 50°C will show greater conduction of electricity. (1 mark)

(b)

	Electrochemical cell		Electrolytic cell
(i)	It generates electricity by chemical reactions.	(i)	Chemical reactions takes place by consuming electricity.
(ii)	Anode has negative and cathode has positive potential with respect to solution.	(ii)	Anode has positive and cathode has negative potential with respect to solution.

(1 + 1 = 2 marks)

1. **(c)** Lucas test is used to detect alcohols.

2. **(a)** $2AgCl(s) + H_2(g) \rightarrow 2HCl(aq) + 2Ag(s)$
The activities of solids and liquids are taken as unity and at low concentrations, the activity of a solute is approximated to its molarity.
The cell reaction will be

$$Pt(s) \mid H_2(g), 1bar \mid H^+(aq)1M \mid AgCl(aq)1M \mid Ag(s)$$

3. **(b)**

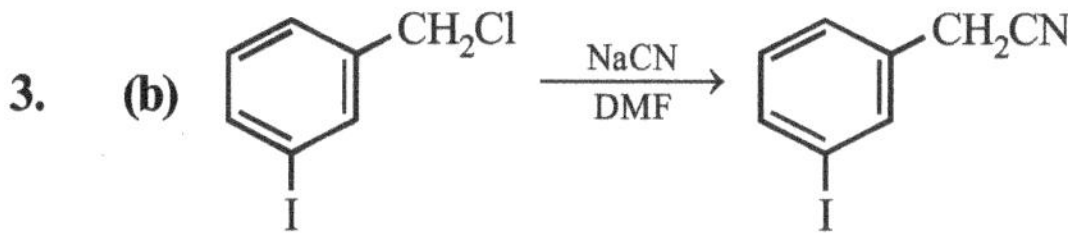

Nuclear substitution will not take place.

4. **(d)** Riemer-Tiemann reaction involves electrophilic substitution on the highly reactive phenoxide ring.

$$HCCl_3 + OH^- \longrightarrow H_2O + :\bar{C}Cl_3$$

$$:\bar{C}Cl_3 \longrightarrow Cl^- + \quad :CCl_2$$

Note the C has only a sextet of electrons

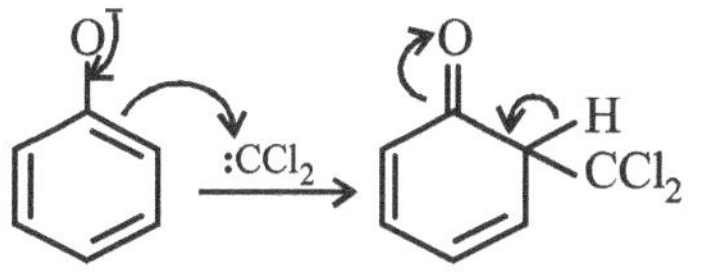

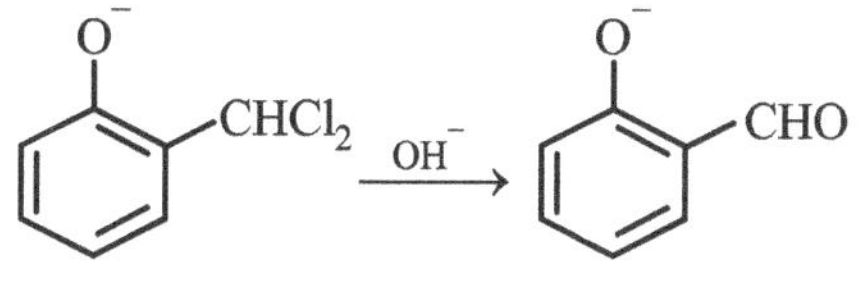

A benzal chloride

5. **(b)** A mixture of bromoethane and chloroethane is an example of ideal solution. For an ideal solution, the A—A or B—B type intermolecular interaction is nearly equal to A—B type interaction.
Chloroform and acetone mixture is an example of non-ideal solution having negative deviation while ethanol-acetone mixture shows positive deviation.

6. **(a)** Plots of conc. $[A]$ *Vs* time, t

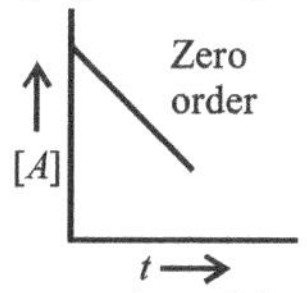

Zero order

7. **(c)** During denaturation 2° and 3° structures are destroyed but 1° structure remains intact.

8. **(d)** According to Henry's law

$$\frac{P_1}{P_2} = \frac{S_1}{S_2} \Rightarrow \frac{500}{750} = \frac{0.01}{S_2}$$

$$\therefore S_2 = \frac{750 \times 0.01}{500} = 0.015 \text{ g/L}$$

9. **(c)** S_N1 reactions involve the formation of carbocations, hence higher the stability of carbocation, more will be reactivity of the parent alkyl halide. Thus tertiary carbocation formed from (c) is stabilized by two phenyl groups and one methyl group, hence most stable.

10. **(c)** Due to lanthanide contraction, the size of Zr and Hf (atom and ions) become nearly similar.

11. **(d)** Phenol has active (acidic) hydrogen so it reacts with CH_3MgI to give CH_4, and not anisole

$$C_6H_5OH + CH_3MgI \longrightarrow CH_4 + C_6H_5OMgI$$

12. **(a)** (a) and (d) are L^- sugar but (a) gives an optically active dibasic acid.

OR

(d)

13. **(d)** $ohm^{-1}\, cm^{-1}$

14. **(c)** CH_3NC (methyl isocyanide) on reduction with $LiAlH_4$ gives secondary amine.

15. **(c)** Carboxyl group decreases the electron density at *m*-position relative to *o*- and *p*-positions.

16. **(d)** Daniell cell is a type of galvanic cell.

17. **(b)** The order of a reaction can have fractional value.
The order of a reaction cannot be written from balanced equation of a reaction because its value changes with pressure, temperature and concentration. It can only be determined experimentally. (1 mark)

18. **(a)** Acetaldehyde gives aldol condensation reaction because it contains α-hydrogen. (1 mark)

19. (a) Cr^{2+} is a stronger reducing agent because the more negative the electrode potential, greater is the reducing power of the electrode.

$$E^0_{Cr^{2+}/Cr} = -0.91 > E^0_{Fe^{2+}/Fe} = -0.44$$

(½ + ½ = 1 Mark)

(b) Mn^{2+} is the most stable ion because it ($Mn^{2+} - d^5$)

1	1	1	1	1

has half filled electronic configuration and it has most negative reduction potential

$$E^0_{Mn^{2+}/Mn} = -1.18V$$ (½ + ½ = 1 Mark)

20. The dry cell also known as Leclanche cell is used in transistors.

The reactions taking place at the anode and cathode are given below.

Cathode Reaction :

$$MnO_2 + NH_4^+ + e^- \longrightarrow MnO(OH) + NH_3$$

Anode Reaction:

$$Zn - 2e^- \longrightarrow Zn^{2+}$$

$$Zn^{2+} + 2NH_3 \longrightarrow [Zn(NH_3)_2]^{2+}$$

(1 + 1 = 2 Marks)

21. (a) Increasing order of acid strength is *p*-cresol < phenol < *p*-nitrophenol (1 Mark)

(b) Reaction :

$$CH_2 = CH_2 \xrightarrow{H_3O^+} CH_3 - CH_2^+ + H_2O$$

Mechanism :

$$H_2C = CH_2 + H - \overset{+}{\underset{..}{O}}(H) - H \rightleftharpoons H - \underset{H}{\overset{H}{C}} - \overset{+}{C}H_2 + H_2\ddot{O}$$

(1 Mark)

OR

(a) Secondary alcohol (butan-2-ol) on reaction with chromic anhydride (CrO_3) oxidises to ketone (butan-2-one).

$$\underset{\text{Butan-2-ol}}{CH_3 - CH_2 - \overset{OH}{\overset{|}{C}H} - CH_3} \xrightarrow{CrO_3} \underset{\text{Butan-2-one}}{CH_3 - CH_2 - \overset{O}{\overset{||}{C}} - CH_3}$$

(1 Mark)

(b) Butan-2-ol on treating with $SOCl_2$ forms 2-chlorobutane

$$\underset{\text{Butan-2-ol}}{CH_3 - CH_2 - \overset{OH}{\overset{|}{C}H} - CH_3} \xrightarrow{SOCl_2} \underset{\text{2-Chlorobutane}}{CH_3 - CH_2 - \overset{Cl}{\overset{|}{C}H} - CH_3R}$$

(1 Mark)

9. (i) The order of increasing basic strength is

$C_6H_5NH_2 < C_6H_5NHCH_3 < C_6H_5CH_2NH_2$

least basic most basic (1 Mark)

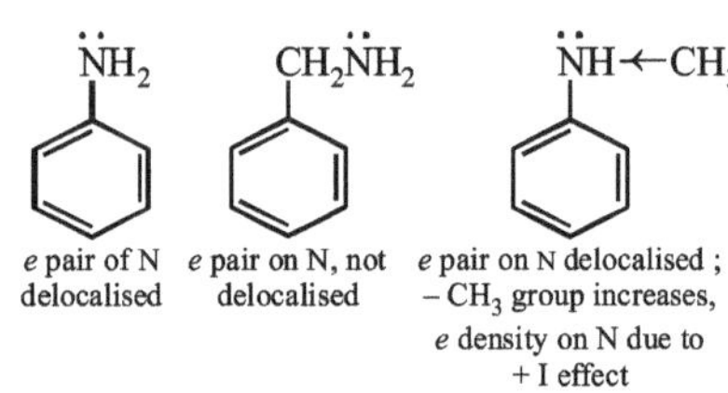

A pair of electron of nitrogen in $C_6H_5CH_2.NH_2$ is available for donation.

(ii) *p*-nitroaniline < aniline < *p*-toluidine

NO_2 least basic (*p*-nitroaniline) < (aniline) < CH_3 most basic (*p*-toluidine)

(1 Mark)

Nitro group is electron withdrawing hence reduces basic character, while methyl group is electron repelling hence increases basic character of aniline.

23. In acidic solution, an amino acid exists as a positive ion, $R - CH(\overset{+}{N}H_3) - COOH$. Therefore, when an electric field is applied, the amino acid migrates towards the cathode.

In alkaline solution, an amino acid exists as a negative ion, $R - CH(NH_2) - COO^-$. Therefore, when an electric field is applied, it migrates towards the anode. (2 marks)

24. Given reaction is $A + 2B \longrightarrow 3C + 2D$, thus rate of this reaction

$$\text{Rate} = -\frac{d[A]}{dt} = -\frac{1}{2}\frac{d[B]}{dt} = \frac{1}{3}\frac{d[C]}{dt} = \frac{1}{2}\frac{d[D]}{dt}$$

$$\frac{-d[B]}{dt} = 1 \times 10^{-2}\ \text{mol L}^{-1}\text{s}^{-1}\ \text{(given)}$$

$$\text{Rate} = \frac{-1}{2}\frac{d[B]}{dt} = \frac{1}{2} \times 1 \times 10^{-2} = 0.5 \times 10^{-2}\ \text{mol L}^{-1}\text{s}^{-1}$$

(1 mark)

$$\frac{-d[A]}{dt} = \frac{-1}{2}\frac{d[B]}{dt} = \frac{1}{2} \times (1 \times 10^{-2}) = 0.5 \times 10^{-2}\ \text{mol L}^{-1}\text{s}^{-1}$$

(½ mark)

$$\frac{d[C]}{dt} = \frac{-3}{2}\frac{d[B]}{dt} = \frac{3}{2} \times (1 \times 10^{-2}) = 1.5 \times 10^{-2}\ \text{mol L}^{-1}\text{s}^{-1}$$

(½ mark)

25. Bis(ethylene diamine) dichloro platinum (II)

Geometrical isomers

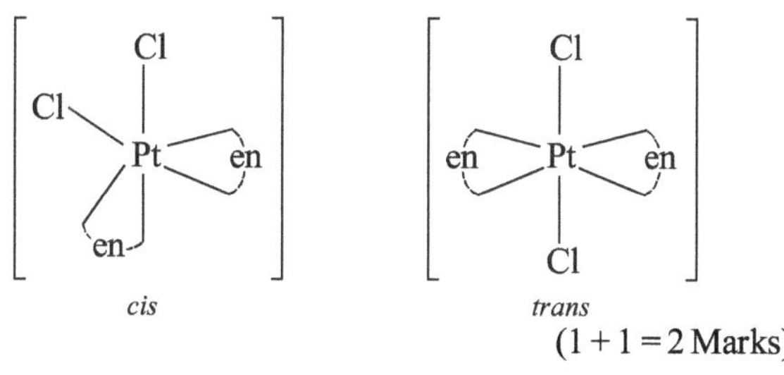

(1 + 1 = 2 Marks)

Note

cis-isomer of $[Pt(en)_2Cl_2]$ *has enantiomer pair i.e., d and l form while trans-isomer is opticaly inactive due to plane of symmetry in the molecule.*

OR

(i) Hexaamminecobalt (III) sulphate (1 Mark)
$[Co(NH_3)_6]_2(SO_4)_3$

(ii) Potassium trioxalatochromate (III) (1 Mark)
$K_3[Cr(C_2O_4)_3]$

26. (a) The C – X bond in haloarenes is quite strong due to partial double bond character and delocalisation of electrons in benzene ring. The negative charge centres get developed at ortho and para positions, and thus electrophile (positively charged species) can attack the benzene ring and then H^+ is removed to acquire stability.

(1 mark)

(b) Phenol $\xrightarrow{\text{Conc. } HNO_3}$ 2, 4, 6 Tritritrophenol (Picric acid) (1 Mark)

(c) $CH_3CH_2Cl + NaOC_2H_5 \xrightarrow{S_N2} CH_3CH_2OC_2H_5$
Diethyl ether

(1 Mark)

Note

When picric acid is hydrated then it is safe to handle, but it becomes a powerful explosive when dry (less than 10% H_2O*). Dry picric acid is highly sensitive to heat, shock and friction. The moistened solid is classified as a flammable solid.*

27. $Cd^{2+}(aq) + Zn(s) \longrightarrow Zn^{2+} + Cd(s)$

$E^0_{cell} = E^0_{Cd^{2+}/Cd} - E^0_{Zn^{2+}/Zn}$ (½ Mark)

$= -0.403 - (-0.763) = 0.36V$ (½ Mark)

$\Delta G^0 = -nFE^0_{cell}$

$n = 2$

$\Delta G^0 = -2 \times 96500 \times 0.36 = -69480\ J\ mol^{-1}$

$= -69.480\ kJ\ mol^{-1}$ (1 Mark)

$\Delta G^0 = -2.303\ RT \log K_c$ (½ Mark)

$$\frac{\Delta G^0}{-2.303\ RT} = \log K_c$$

$$\frac{-69480}{-2.303 \times 8.314 \times 298} = \log K_c$$

$12.17 = \log K_c$ (½ Mark)

Note

Relation between E^0_{cell} *and* K_c *might be calculated as given below which can used to determine the value of* K_c *directly from given value of* E^0_{cell}.

$\because \quad \Delta G = -nFE^0_{cell}$

$\because \quad \Delta G = -2.303\ RT \log K_c$

Now, $nFE^0_{cell} = 2.303\ RT \log K_c$

$$nE^0_{cell} = \frac{2.303\ RT}{F}.\log K_c$$

$$= \frac{2.303 \times 8.314 \times 298}{96500} \log K_c$$

$= 0.059 \log K_c$

$nE^0_{cell} = 0.059 \log K_c$

OR

$$m = \frac{\text{Atomic mass}}{n \times F} \times Q \quad (½ \text{ Mark})$$

where m = mass deposited
t = time

Atomic mass $=52\ g\ mol^{-1}$; $Q = 24000\ C$; $F = 96500\ C\ mol^{-1}$

$$\overset{+6}{CrO_3} \longrightarrow \overset{0}{Cr}$$

$n = 6$ (½ Mark)

$$m = \frac{52 \times 24000}{6 \times 96500} = \frac{12480}{5790} = 2.15\ g$$

(½ Mark)

2.15 g of Cr will be electroplated by 24000 C

$Q = i \times t$ (½ Mark)

$$m = \frac{\text{Atomic mass}}{n \times F} \times i \times t$$

$m = 1.5\ g;\ i = 12.5\ A,\ t = ?$

$$1.5 = \frac{52}{6 \times 96500} \times 12.5 \times t$$

$$t = \frac{1.5 \times 6 \times 96500}{52 \times 12.5}$$ (½ Mark)

$= 1336.15$ sec (½ Mark)

Note

$[Fe(H_2O)_6]^{2+}$ *complex.*

$Fe^{2+} - 3d^6$

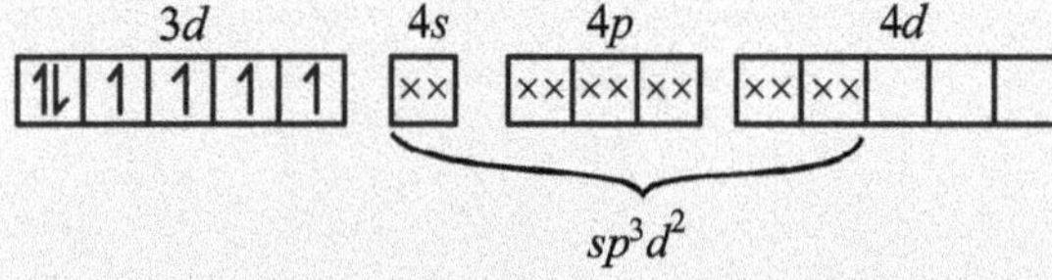

(H_2O *is a weak ligand does not lead to pairing of electrons). It will be a outer orbital complex.*

Magnetic character

$n = 4$ (4 unpaired e^- s), paramagnetic due to unpaired e^- s

$[Ni(CN)_4]^{2-}$ *complex.*

$Ni^{2+} - 3d^8$

Ni^{2+} 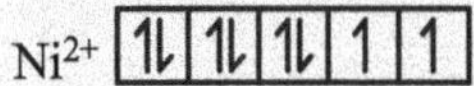

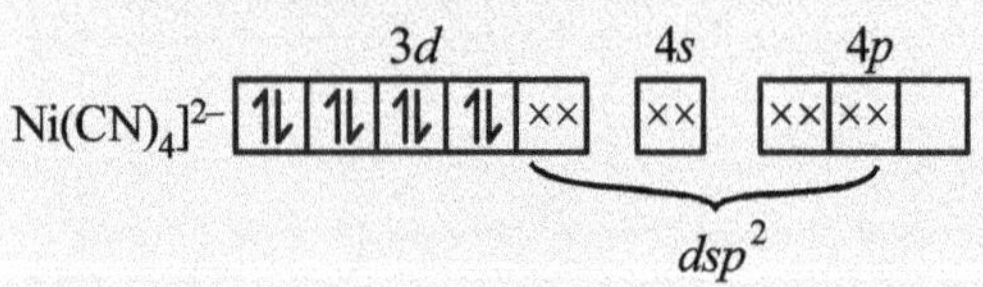

Pairing of electrons occurs due to strong CN^- ligand.

Magnetic nature

$n = 0$(no. unpaired electron). Diamagnetic

28.

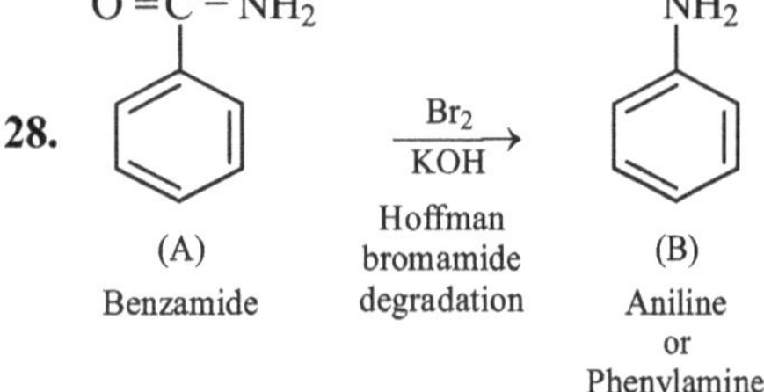

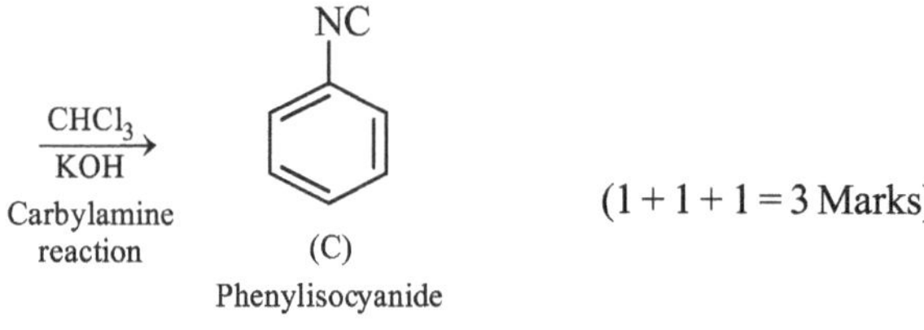

(1 + 1 + 1 = 3 Marks)

Note

Carbylamine reaction is given by aliphatic and aromatic primary amine only.

29. The reactions of glucose with Fehling's solution and phenyl hydrazine are characteristic of a –CHO group. In aqueous solution open chain, aldehyde form is in equilibrium with the cyclic hemiacetal form. Since these reactions are irreversible, the equilibrium shifts towards the open chain and eventually all the glucose reacts. The addition reaction of an aldehyde with bisulphite is reversible reaction. It means that enough aldehyde should remain in equilibrium with the bisulphite adduct to satisfy the equilibrium with the cyclic form. At equilibrium the concentration of open chain form is very low. Consequently, there is no reaction. (3 marks)

30. (a) At 300 s

For the first order reaction

$$k = \frac{2.303}{t}\log\frac{[A]_0}{[A]},$$ (½ Mark)

where $[A]_0$ is initial concentration & $[A]$ is final concentration

$$= \frac{2.303}{300}\log\frac{1.6 \times 10^{-2}}{0.8 \times 10^{-2}} = \frac{2.303}{300}\log 2$$

$= 2.31 ' 10^{-3}\ sec^{-1}$ (½ Mark)

At 600 s

$$k = \frac{2.303}{t}\log\frac{[A]_0}{[A]} = \frac{2.303}{600}\log\frac{1.6 \times 10^{-2}}{0.4 \times 10^{-2}}$$

$$= \frac{2.303}{600}\log 4 = \frac{2.303}{600} ' 0.6021$$

$= 2.31 ' 10^{-3}\ sec^{-1}$ (1 Mark)

In equal time interval, k is constant when using first order reaction, therefore it follows first order kinetics.

(b) $$t_{1/2} = \frac{0.693}{k}, k = 2.31 ' 10^{-3}$$

$$= \frac{0.693}{2.31 \times 10^{-3}} = 300\ sec$$ (1 Mark)

Half life is 300 sec.

OR

Given :

$P_i = 0.30$ atm

$P_t = 0.50$ atm

$C_2H_5Cl(g) \longrightarrow C_2H_4(g) + HCl(g)$

P_i	0	0	(At $t = 0$ s)
$P_i - x$	x	x	(At $t = 300$ s)

$\therefore \quad P_i - x + x + x = P_t$

$0.30 + x = 0.50$

$x = 0.20; P_i - x = 0.30 - 0.20$

$= 0.10$ atm　　(1 Mark)

For a first-order decomposition reaction, we know that

$$k = \frac{2.303}{t}\log\left(\frac{P_i}{P_i - x}\right) \quad (½ \text{ Mark})$$

$$= \frac{2.303}{300}\log\left(\frac{0.30}{0.10}\right) \quad (½ \text{ Mark})$$

$$= \frac{2.303 \times \log 3}{300} = \frac{2.303 \times 0.4771}{300}$$

$k = 0.0037\ s^{-1}$　　(1 Mark)

31. (a) $CH_3CH_2CH_2CH_2—Cl \xrightarrow[S_N2 \text{ mechanism}]{\text{alc. KOH}} CH_3CH_2CH_2CH_2—OH$

This reaction occurs through concerted mechanism (S_N2), not through the carbocation intermediate as the substrate is primary alkyl halide.　　(1 Mark)

(b) $CH_2(Cl)—CH_2—CH_2(Cl) \xrightarrow{\text{alc. KOH}} CH_2{=}CH_2$ (allene)

It is the nucleophilic elimination neaction.　(1 mark)

(c) Alkyl halides $\xrightarrow{\text{alc. KOH}}$ Elimination reaction

Alkyl halides $\xrightarrow{\text{aq. KOH}}$ Substitution reaction

In case of alcoholic KOH, the attacking reagent is RO^- whereas in aqucous KOH solution, it is OH^-. RO^- is stronger base than OH^- because OH^- is highly hydrated in aqueous medium, so it attacks the α-carbon of the alkyl halide directly.

In alcoholic medium RO^- being a stronger base takes up the β-hydrogen atom and results in the formation of alkene.

$CH_3—CH_2(H\leftarrow RO^-)—CH_2—Cl \xrightarrow{\text{alc. KOH}} CH_3—CH{=}CH_2 + ROH + Cl^-$

$CH_3—CH_2—CH_2—Cl\ (\bar{O}H) \xrightarrow{\text{alc. KOH}} CH_3—CH_2—CH_2—OH + Cl^-$ (2 marks)

OR

Inversion of configuration in the product occurs because the nucleophile attacks the α-carbon atom of alkyl halide on the side opposite to the one where the halogen atom is attachedc.

$H_3C(C_4H_9)C—Br + OH^- \xrightarrow{S_N2} HO—C(CH_3)(H)(C_4H_9) + Br^{\ominus}$

(–)-2-Bromohexane　　(+)-Hexan-2-ol

(2 marks)

32. (a) NF_3 is a weaker ligand due to high electronegativity of fluorine which withdraws electrons from N due to which the lone pair of electrons on N atom can't be ligated. $N(CH_3)_3$ is a strong ligand because CH_3 groups are electron releasing and thus increase electron availability on N atom.　(1 Mark)

(b) $[FeF_6]^{3-}$ is a high spin complex as F^- is a weak ligand.　(1 Mark)

(c) In potassium ferrocyanide, Fe is in the form Fe^{2+} and in potassium ferricyanide, Fe is in the form Fe^{3+}. CN^- is a strong field ligand. So, it will pair up all the $3d^6$ electrons of Fe^{3+} and make it diamagnetic. In Fe^{2+}, all the $3d^5$ electrons are not paired up. One electron remains unpaired. So, it is paramagnetic.

Fe^{2+} in presence of CN^- in $K_4(Fe(CN)_6]$

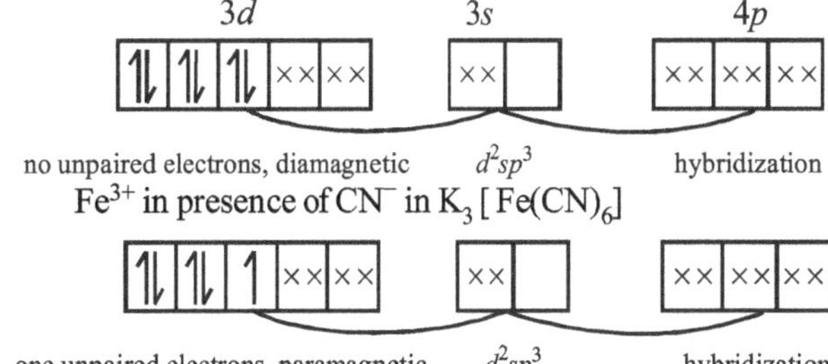

Crystal field splitting in ferrocyanide is less than in ferricyanide ion as higher the oxidation state of the metal, greater will be the crystal field splitting.　(2 Marks)

OR

(c) Oxidation state of Cr in $[Cr(H_2O)_6]^{2+}$ is + 2.

Electronic configuration of Cr = $[Ar]_{18} 4s^1 3d^5$

Electonic configuration of $Cr^{2+} = [Ar]_{16} 3d^4$

H_2O is a weak field ligand.

CFSE value $[-0.4n_{t_{2g}} + 0.6n_{e_g}]\Delta_0 + nP$

$= [-0.4 \times 3 + 0.6 \times 1]\Delta_0 + 0 = -0.6\,\Delta_0$

Oxidation state of Cr in $[Cr(H_2O)_6]^{3+}$ is +3

Electronic configuration of $Cr^{3+} = [Ar]_{16} 3d^3$

CFSE value of $\left[Cr(H_2O)_6\right]^{3+}$

$= \left[-0.4n_{t_{2g}} + 0.6n_{e_g}\right]\Delta_0 + nP$

$= [-0.4 \times 3 + 0]\Delta_0 + 0 = -1.2\,\Delta_0$ (2 Marks)

33. (a) Here $P_A^o = 70$ mm Hg. $P_B^o = 90$ mm Hg.

$X_A = 0{\cdot}3$

$\therefore\ X_B = 1 - X_A = 1 - 0{\cdot}3 = 0{\cdot}7$ (½ mark)

According to Raoult's Law, $P_A = P_A^o X_A$ (½ mark)

$= 70 \times 0{\cdot}3 = 21$ mm Hg.

$P_B = P_B^o X_B = 90 \times 0{\cdot}7 = 63$ mm Hg. (1 mark)

(b) (i) Liquid A will have higher vapour pressure at 80 °C. (1 mark)

(ii) When any solute, *i.e.,* glucose is dissolved in water, the surface of the solution is occupied of (non-volatile) molecules. Whereas in case of pure water whole surface is occupied by solvent molecules. Therefore, the number of solvent molecules escaping from the surface is correspondingly reduced as compared to the pure solvent and thus results in the decrease of vapour pressure. (2 marks)

OR

(a) Using Raoult's law equation of lowering of vapour pressure :

$$\frac{p_A^o - p_A}{p_A^o} = x_B$$ (½ mark)

or $$\frac{31.82 - 30.95}{31.82} = \frac{27/M_B}{100/18}$$ (½ mark)

or $$\frac{0.87}{31.82} = \frac{27}{M_B} \times \frac{18}{100}$$

or $$M_B = \frac{27 \times 18 \times 31.82}{0.87 \times 100} \text{ or } 177.75 \text{ g mol}^{-1}$$

Hence, molecular mass of the solute = 177.75 g mol^{-1}. (1 mark)

(b) (i) Non-ideal solutions are those solutions which do not follow Raoult's Law.

Also $\Delta H_{mix} \neq 0$ and $\Delta V_{mix} \neq 0$. (1 mark)

The force of attraction between A–A and B–B is not equal to that between A – B.

(ii) (1) In alcohol and acetone solution, force of attraction is less between alcohol and acetone molecules than in pure alcohol molecules as well as in pure acetone molecules, therefore, vapour pressure increases. (1 mark)

(2) In chloroform and acetone, force of attraction increases due to intermolecular H-bonding therefore, vapour pressure decreases. (1 mark)

34. (i) Positive test with 2, 4-DNP and negative tests with Tollen's reagent and Fehling's solution suggest that the compound [A] is a ketone. Since it responds to iodoform test (I_2/NaOH), it must be a methyl ketone (CH_3COR). (1 Mark)

(ii) The molecular formula suggests a high degree of unsaturation which is ruled out because it does not decolourise either bromine water or Baeyer's reagent. Thus, we may conclude that it is an aromatic compound and the side chain has – $COCH_3$ group. (1 Mark)

(iii) Thus, the compound [A] is $C_6H_5CH_2COCH_3$ (1-phenylpropanone).

The reactions involved are as follows :

$C_6H_5CH_2C(CH_3){=}O + H_2NNH{-}C_6H_3(NO_2)_2$ (2,4-D.N.P.) ⟶ $C_6H_5CH_2C(CH_3){=}NNH{-}C_6H_3(NO_2)_2$

1-Phenylpropanone [A] ($C_9H_{10}O$)

Orange red [B] ppt. (1 Mark)

C_6H_5COOH ⟵(H_2CrO_4, Oxidation)— $C_6H_5CH_2{-}C(CH_3){=}O$ [A] —(I_2/NaOH)⟶ $C_6H_5CH_2{-}C(=O){-}OH$ + CHI_3

Benzoic acid [E] ($C_7H_6O_2$) (Colourless)

2-Phenyl ethanoic acid [D] (Colourless)

Iodoform [C]

(1 mark)

OR

(a) (i) Schiff's reagent or Fehling's solution. (1 mark)
(ii) I_2/NaOH or Fehling's solution (1 mark)
(iii) I_2/NaOH. (1 mark)

(b) (i) Formaldehyde to acetaldehyde

$$\underset{\text{Formaldehyde}}{HCHO} \xrightarrow{CH_3MgBr} \underset{\text{Addition compound}}{CH_3CH_2OMgBr} \xrightarrow{H_2O}$$

$$\underset{\text{Ethyl alcohol}}{CH_3CH_2OH} \xrightarrow[K_2Cr_2O_7/H_2SO_4]{\text{Oxidation}} \underset{\text{Acetaldehyde}}{CH_3CHO}$$ (1 mark)

(ii) Acetaldehyde to formaldehyde

$$\underset{\text{Acetaldehyde}}{CH_3CHO} \xrightarrow{\text{Oxidation}} \underset{\text{Acetic acid}}{CH_3COOH} \xrightarrow[-H_2O]{NH_3/\text{Heat}}$$

$$\underset{\text{Acetamide}}{CH_3CONH_2} \xrightarrow{Br_2/KOH} \underset{\text{Methyl amine}}{CH_3NH_2}$$

$$\downarrow \text{HONO}$$ (1 mark)

$$\underset{\text{Methyl alcohol}}{CH_3OH}$$

35. (a) Size of trivalent lanthanoid cations decreases with increase in the atomic number. It is due to poor shielding effect of 4*f*-electrons. As effective nuclear charge increases, ionic size decreases. (1 mark)

(b) Ionic character of metal halide depends upon the electronegativity difference between the metal and halogen. F is more electronegative than Cl and Br, therefore, fluorides of transition metals are ionic whereas chlorides and bromides are covalent in nature. (1 mark)

(c) + 2 oxidation state of Mn is most stable. In this oxidation sate, it has exactly half-filled *d*-orbitals. (1 mark)

(d) Osmium, (Os) shows highest oxidation state in osmium tetraoxide (OsO_4). (1 mark)

(e) Osmium (Os) is the densest transition element. (1 mark)

1. (a) Gabriel phthalimide synthesis gives 1° amine in good yield.
2. (d) Sc^{3+} : $1s^2, 2s^2p^6, 3s^2p^6d^0, 4s^0$; no unpaired electron.
Cu^+ : $1s^2, 2s^2p^6, 3s^2p^6d^{10}, 4s^0$; no unpaired electron.
Ni^{2+}: $1s^2, 2s^2p^6, 3s^2p^6d^8, 4s^0$; unpaired electrons are present.
Ti^{3+} : $1s^2, 2s^2p^6, 3s^2p^6d^1, 4s^0$; unpaired electron is present
Co^{2+}: $1s^2, 2s^2p^6, 3s^2p^6d^7, 4s^0$; unpaired electrons are present
So from the given options the only correct combination is Ni^{2+} and Ti^{3+}.
3. (a) $\Delta T_f = K_f m$

$$\Delta T_f = K_f \frac{n_2 \times 1000}{w_1}; \ 14 = 1.86 \times \frac{n_2 \times 1000}{1000}$$

$n_2 = 7.5$ mol
4. (a) The complex chlorodiaquatriammine cobalt (III) chloride can be represented as $[CoCl(NH_3)_3(H_2O)_2]Cl_2$. (1 mark)
5. (c) For S_N2 reaction polar aprotic solvent is needed.
6. (d)
7. (b) In $H_2 - O_2$ fuel cell, the combustion of H_2 occurs to create potential difference between the two electrodes.
8. (d)
9. (a) As doubling the initial conc. doubles the rate of reaction, order = 1
10. (d) Aldehydes can reduce while ketones cannot reduce Fehling's solution. (1 mark)
11. (c) Aliphatic amines are more basic than aromatic amines. Resonance decreases the basic character due to delocalisation of shared pair of electrons on nitrogen within benzene nucleus. Further electron withdrawing if $(-NO_2)$ decreases basicity.
12. (a) $CH_3CH_2Cl > CH_2=CHCl > C_6H_5Cl$
13. (d) Electronic configuration of

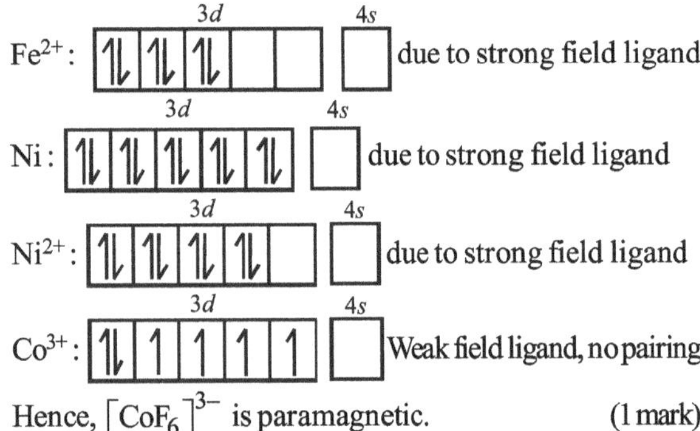

Hence, $[CoF_6]^{3-}$ is paramagnetic. (1 mark)

14. (a) Pyrolusite (It is MnO_2)
15. (b) (1 mark)
16. (c) Rate of a reaction does not remain constant during the course of reaction because rate depends upon the concentration of reactants which decreases with time. (1 mark)
17. (c) Isobutanal does not give iodoform test because it does not have $-COCH_3$ group. (1 mark)
18. (a) K_b of $H_5C_2-N<$ > $CH_3-\ddot{N}<$ + I effect of C_2H_5-group is more than CH_3- group.
N, N-Diethylethanamine
19. Osmotic pressures of different solutions can be calculated by using van't Hoff equation.

(i) $M = \frac{34.2}{342} = 0.1 \text{ mol L}^{-1}, \pi = iMRT = 1 \times 0.1\,RT = 0.1\,RT$ (½ mark)

(ii) $M = \frac{60}{60} = 1 \text{ mol L}^{-1}, \pi = iMRT = 1 \times 1RT = RT$ (½ mark)

(iii) $M = \frac{90}{180} = 0.5 \text{ mol L}^{-1}, \pi = iMRT = 1 \times 0.5\,RT = 0.5\,RT$ (½ mark)

The increasing order of osmotic pressure is (i) < (iii) < (ii) (½ mark)
20. Corrosion is basically a process of oxidation, so oxidation potential is considered here.
Oxidation potential of Fe = 0.44 V
Oxidation potential of X = 2.36 V
Oxidation potential of Y = 0.14 V
Since, A has a higher oxidation potential than that of iron, so it will oxidise faster than Fe. Therefore, A is better for coating. (2 marks)
21. (a) It is also called dipolar ion and its structure is as follows :

$$\ddot{N}H_2-CH_2-\overset{\overset{O}{\|}}{C}-OH \rightleftharpoons \overset{+}{N}H_3-CH_2-\overset{\overset{O}{\|}}{C}-\overset{-}{O}$$

(1 mark)

(b) Phenyl alanine hydroxylase is an enzyme. The deficiency of the enzyme causes disease phenyl ketonuria. (1 mark)

22. (a) Cr^{3+} exhibits paramagnetism due to the presence of unpaired electrons in 4*d*-orbitals.
$Cr^{3+} \Rightarrow 1s^2 2s^2 2p^6 3s^2 3p^6 3d^3$ (1 mark)
(b) $V (Z = 23) \Rightarrow 1s^2 2s^2 2p^6 3s^2 3p^6 4s^2 3d^3$
$Mn (Z = 25) \Rightarrow 1s^2 2s^2 2p^6 3s^2 3p^6 4s^2 3d^5$
Mn exhibits more number of oxidation states as it can loose upto seven electrons from both 4*s*-and 3*d*-orbitals, whereas V can loose maximum five electrons. (1 mark)

23. (a) **Ethanal to propanone:** CH_3CHO to CH_3COCH_3

$$\underset{\text{Ethanal}}{CH_3CHO} \xrightarrow{CH_3MgBr} CH_3\underset{\displaystyle OH}{\underset{|}{C}H}CH_3 \xrightarrow{CrO_3} \underset{\text{Propanone}}{CH_3COCH_3}$$

(1 mark)

(b) **Toluene to Benzoic acid:**

Toluene ($C_6H_5CH_3$) $\xrightarrow[\Delta]{\text{alk. } KMnO_4}$ $C_6H_5COO^-K^+$ $\xrightarrow{H^+}$ C_6H_5COOH (Benzoic acid)

(1 mark)

OR

(a) Aromatic carboxylic acids do not undergo Friedel crafts reaction. This is because the carboxyl group is an electron withdrawing group and hence deactivates the benzene ring towards Friedel crafts reaction. The catalyst (anhydrous $AlCl_3$) gets bonded to the carboxyl group thus preventing the desired reaction. (1 mark)

The Friedel-crafts alkylation may give polyalkylated products, so the Friedel-crafts acylation is a valuable alternative. The acylated products may easily be converted to the corresponding alkanes via clemmensen reduction or wolff-kishner reduction.

(b) pK_a value of 4–nitrobenzoic acid is lower than that of benzoic acid. This is because in 4-nitrobenzoic acid, nitro group being electron withdrawing in nature, makes the O–H bond in –COOH more polar, thus facilitating the release of H^+. Thus, 4-nitrobenzoic acid is more acidic. More is the acidity, lesser is the pK_a value. (1 mark)

Acid strength increases as we move to the right along a row of the periodic table, and as we move down a column.

24. (a)

$CH_3-CH(CH_3)-CH(Br)-CH_3 \longrightarrow CH_3-C(H)(CH_3)-\overset{\oplus}{C}H-CH_3 + Br^-$ (2° carbocation)

$\xrightarrow{1,2-H^- \text{ shift}} CH_3-\overset{+}{C}(CH_3)-CH_2-CH_3$ (3° carbocation) $\xrightarrow{CH_3\ddot{O}H}$

$CH_3-C(CH_3)(\overset{+}{O}(H)-CH_3)-CH_2-CH_3 \xrightarrow{-H^+} CH_3-C(CH_3)(OCH_3)-CH_2-CH_3$

(b) $C_6H_5C_2H_5$ $\xrightarrow{Br_2, Fe}$ (Electrophilic substitution reaction) (alkyl are ortho and para directing) $p\text{-}BrC_6H_4C_2H_5$ $\xrightarrow{Cl_2, \Delta}$ (benzylic halogenation) $p\text{-}BrC_6H_4CH(Cl)-CH_3$ $\xrightarrow{\text{alc. KOH}}$ (Elimination reaction) $p\text{-}BrC_6H_4CH=CH_2$

25. A chelate is a complex or coordination compound which is formed when a multi dentate ligand attaches to a metal ion. It is a five or six-membered ring that includes the central metal ion and atoms of the ligand.
A chelating agent is a multidentate ligand. It simultaneously attaches to two or more positions in the coordination sphere of a central metal, e.g., ethylenediamine.
(1 + 1 = 2 marks)

OR

$[Fe(CN)_6]^{3-}$ has one unpaired electron (d^2sp^3-hybridization of Fe^{3+}) while $[Fe(H_2O)_6]^{3+}$ has five unpaired electrons (sp^3d^2-hybridization of Fe^{3+}),

$[Fe(CN)_6]^{3-}$: 3*d* [⇅][⇅][1][••][••] 4*s* [••] 4*p* [••][••][••] — d^2sp^3

No. of unpaired e^- (n) = 1

Magnetic moment $= \sqrt{n(n+2)}$ B.M. $= \sqrt{3} = 1.73$ B.M. (1 mark)

$[Fe(H_2O)_6]^{3+}$

3d: 1 1 1 1 1 | 4s: •• | 4p: •• •• •• | 4d: •• •• _ _ _

sp^3d^2

No. of unpaired e^- (n) = 5

Magnetic moment

$= \sqrt{n(n+2)}$ B.M. $= \sqrt{5 \times 7} = \sqrt{35} = 5.92$ B.M. (1 mark)

26. (a) The presence of electron-withdrawing groups such as $-NO_2$, $-CN$, etc. at *o*-and *p*-positions (but not at *m*-position) w.r.t. the halogen greatly activates the halogen towards nucleophilic displacemnt. The NO_2 group at *o*- and *p*- positions withdraws electrons from the benzene ring and thus makes the ring electron deficient and facilitates the attack of the nucleophile (OH^-) on haloarenes. (1 mark)

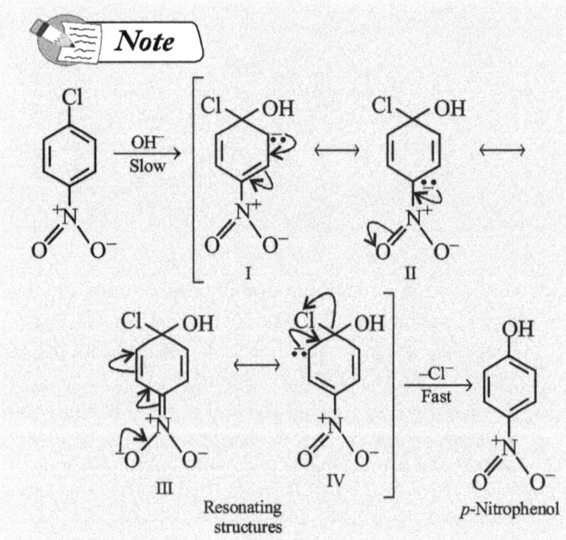

(b) *p*-Dichlorobenzene, being symmetrical, fits tightly in its crystal lattice. Thus the intermolecular forces of attraction in the *p*-isomer are stronger than those in the *o*-and *m*- isomers; which requires larger amount of energy to melt or dissolve the *p*-isomer than the *o*- and *m*-isomers. Consequently, the melting point of the *p*-isomer will be higher and its solubility lower than the corresponding *o*- and *m*-isomers. (1 mark)

(c) Thionyl chloride method is preferred over hydrogen chloride or phosphorus pentachloride method since both the by-products (SO_2 and HCl) in this reaction being gases escape leaving the chloro alkanes in almost pure state.

$$\underset{}{R-OH} + \underset{\text{Thionyl chloride}}{SOCl_2} \xrightarrow{\text{Pyidine}} \underset{\text{Haloalkane}}{R-Cl} + SO_2\uparrow + HCl\uparrow$$

(1 mark)

OR

(a) $$\underset{\text{1-chlorobutane}}{CH_3CH_2CH_2CH_2Cl} + NaI \xrightarrow{\text{acetone}} \underset{\text{1-Iodobutane}}{CH_3CH_2CH_2CH_2I} + NaCl\downarrow$$

(1 mark)

(b) 2-Bromo-2-methyl butane is most reactive towards elimination reaction.

$\underset{\text{1-Bromopentane}}{CH_3-CH_2CH_2CH_2CH_2-Br}$ 1° alkyl halide

$\underset{\text{2-Bromopentane}}{CH_3-CH_2-CH_2-\underset{}{\overset{Br}{CH}}-CH_3}$ 2° alkyl halide

$\underset{\text{2-Bromo-2-methylbutane}}{CH_3CH_2-\overset{Br}{\underset{CH_3}{C}}-CH_3}$ 3° alkyl halide

3° Alkyl halide is most reactive towards elimination reaction (E_1) due to the formation of more stable 3° carbocation which loses proton to form alkene.

$$\underset{\text{3° Carbocation}}{CH_3CH_2-\overset{+}{\underset{CH_3}{C}}-CH_3} \xrightarrow{-H^+} \underset{\text{Saytzeff's product}}{CH_3-CH=\underset{CH_3}{C}-CH_3}$$

(1 mark)

(c) 4-Bromo-4-methylpent-2-ene. (1 mark)

27. Paramagnetic substances are those substances which have unpaired electrons. They are attracted by magnetic field. (1 mark)

Transition metals having unpaired electrons are paramagnetic in nature. (1 mark)

Paramagnetic character increases from Ti to Cr because number of unpaired electrons increases and then decreases due to decrease in number of unpaired electrons. (1 mark)

28. (a) Sc loses all the three electrons ($3d^1\ 4s^2$) to show + 3 oxidation state to attain stable inert gas configfuration. (1 mark)

(b) $[PtCl(NH_3)_5]Cl_3$ (1 mark)

(c) Linkage isomer of $[Co\ (NH_3)_5\ ONO]Cl_2$ is $[Co\ (NH_3)_5NO_2]Cl_2$. Its IUPAC name is pentaamminenitrito-N- cobalt (III) chloride. (1 mark)

(d) Coordination isomerism. (1 mark)

29. (a) $C_6H_5N_2^+Cl^- \xrightarrow{CuCN} \underset{(A)}{C_6H_5CN} \xrightarrow{H_2O/H^+}$

$\underset{(B)}{C_6H_5COOH} \xrightarrow[\Delta]{NH_3} \underset{(C)}{C_6H_5CONH_2}$

(½ + ½ + ½ = 1½ marks)

(b) $C_6H_5NO_2 \xrightarrow{Sn+HCl} \underset{(A)}{C_6H_5NH_2} \xrightarrow[273K]{NaNO_2+HCl}$

$\underset{(B)}{C_6H_5N_2^+Cl^-} \xrightarrow[\Delta]{H_2O/H^+} \underset{(C)}{C_6H_5OH}$

(½ + ½ + ½ = 1½ marks)

30. (a) Osmotic pressure method is preferred for the determination of molar masses of macromolecules. This is because it is done around room temperature and molarity of solution is used instead of molality. As compared to other colligative properties, its magnitude is large even for very dilute solutions. This method is preferred for biomolecules as they are not stable at higher temperatures and polymers have poor solubility. (1 mark)

(b) Aquatic animals are more comfortable in cold water than in warm water. This is because as temperature increase, solubility of gases in water decreases (from Le-chatelier's principle). Thus, in warm water the amount of oxygen available decreases. As a result, aquatic animals are more comfortable in cold water. (1 mark)

(c) Elevation of boiling point for 1M KCl solution is nearly double than that of 1 M sugar solution. This is because elevation of boiling point depends on the value of '*i*'. KCl being a strong electrolyte completely dissociates in water to give K^+ and Cl^- ions. Thus, $i = 2$ for KCl. On the other hand, sugar does not dissociate/associate in water so $i = 1$ for sugar solution. Hence ΔT_b (KCl) = $2\Delta T_b$ (sugar) (1 mark)

31. (a) Acetaldehyde gives aldol condensation reaction because it contains α-hydrogen. (1 mark)

(b) Grignard reagents are highly reactive, so react with the hydroxyl group. (1 mark)

(c) RCOCl, $(RCO)_2O$ and RCOOR' all add two molecules of Grignard reagents to give 3° alcohols.

OR

$H_2C=O \rightarrow$ The central carbonyl carbon is hybridized

(2 marks)

32. (a) Disruption of the natural structure of a protein is called denaturation. (1 mark)

(b) When egg is cooked, the proteins present in egg gets denatured and it is evident from the change in colour and appearance of the egg. (1 mark)

(c) The primary structure of proteins remains intact during denaturation but the secondary and tertiary structures get disrupted.

In the formation of proteins, $-NH_2$ group of one amino acid condenses with –COOH group of other with the elimination of a water molecule to form a peptide bond.

OR

The isoelectric point, is the pH at which a molecule carries no net electrical charge or is electrically neutral. It is represented by pH(I) or pI.

At isoelectric point, amino acids are present zwitter ionic form, which is actually neutral. Therefore, the proteins donot migrate at isoelectric point under the influence of electric field. (2 marks)

33. (a) (i) Calculation of specific rate constant (*k*).

For the first order reaction, $k = \frac{2.303}{t} \log \frac{a}{a-x}$

a = 100% ; x = 20%; (a – x) = (100 – 20) = 80% ; t = 15 min

$k = \frac{2.303}{(15 \text{ min})} \log \frac{100}{80} =$

$\frac{2.303}{(15 \text{ min})} \log 1.25 = \frac{2.303}{(15 \text{ min})} \times 0.0969$

$= 0.015 \text{ min}^{-1}$ (1 mark)

(ii) Calculation of time in which 10% of original substance remains unreacted.

a = 100% ; (a – x) = 10% ; $k = 0.015 \text{ min}^{-1}$

$t = \frac{2.303}{k} \log \frac{a}{a-x} = \frac{2.303}{(0.015 \text{ min}^{-1})} \log \frac{100}{10}$

= 153.5 min (1 mark)

(iii) Calculation of time in which 20% of the reactant left to react after first 15 minutes.

a = 80% ; x = 80 × 20/100 = 16% ; (a – x) = (80 – 16) = 64% ; $k = 0.015 \text{ min}^{-1}$

$t = \frac{2.303}{k} \log \frac{a}{a-x} = \frac{2.303}{(0.015 \text{ min}^{-1})} \log \frac{80}{64}$

$= \frac{2.303}{(0.015 \text{ min}^{-1})} \log 1.25$

$= \frac{2.303}{(0.015 \text{ min}^{-1})} \times 0.0969 = 15 \text{ min}$ (1 mark)

(b) In the vapour state, the molecules of bromine have more kinetic energy than in the liquid state. Therefore, collisions with the molecules of other reactants in the vapour state will be faster than in the liquid state. Moreover, in the vapour state, the surface area available for the chemical reaction is more as compared to the liquid state. Hence, bromine in the vapour state reacts at a faster rate compared with the liquid state. (1 mark)

(c) The rate of reaction represents the change in molar conentration of reacting species taking part in the reaction per unit time. Since the change in molar concentration is not uniform, the rate of reaction does not remain constant. (1 mark)

OR

(a) Calculation of order with respect to A and B.
Let the rate law equation for the reaction be : rate = $k [A]^x[B]^y$.
The rates for the four experiments may be written as :
$0.096 = k[0.30]^x[0.30]^y$ .... (i)
$0.384 = k[0.60]^x[0.30]^y$ .... (ii)
$0.192 = k[0.30]^x[0.60]^y$ .... (iii)
$0.768 = k[0.60]^x[0.60]^y$ .... (iv) (½ mark)
Dividing eqn. (ii) by eqn. (i), we get

$$\frac{0.384}{0.096} = \frac{k[0.60]^x[0.30]^y}{k[0.30]^x[0.30]^y}$$ (½ mark)

or $4 = (2)^x$
$(2)^2 = (2)^x$ or $x = 2$ (½ mark)
Dividing eqn. (iii) by eqn. (i), we get

$$\frac{0.192}{0.096} = \frac{k[0.30]^x[0.60]^y}{k[0.30]^x[0.30]^y}$$

or $2 = (2)^y$
$y = 1$ (½ mark)
Order w.r.t. A = 2 ; B = 1
(b) Rate law expression ; Rate (r) = $k [A]^2 [B]^1$ (1 mark)
(c) Rate constant (k)

$$= \frac{\text{Rate (r)}}{[A]^2[B]^1} = \frac{0.096}{(0.30)^2 \times (0.30)} = \frac{0.096}{0.027} = 3.56$$ (1 mark)

(d) Rate of reaction in terms of A and C : Rate

$$= \frac{-d[A]}{dt} = \frac{1}{2}\frac{d[C]}{dt}$$ (½ + ½ = 1 mark)

34. (a) $\Lambda^{\infty}_{NH_4OH} = \lambda^{\infty}_{NH_4^+} + \lambda^{\infty}_{OH^-}$

$$\Lambda^{\infty}_{NH_4OH} = \lambda^{\infty}_{NH_4^+} + \lambda^{\infty}_{Cl^-} + \lambda^{\infty}_{Na^+} - \lambda^{\infty}_{OH^-} - \lambda^{\infty}_{Cl^-}$$

(1 mark)

$$\Lambda^{\infty}_{NH_4OH} = \Lambda^{\infty}_{NH_4Cl} + \Lambda^{\infty}_{NaOH} - \Lambda^{\infty}_{NaCl}$$
$= 129.8 + 248.1 - 126.4$
$= 251.5 \ ohm^{-1}cm^2mol^{-1}$ (1 mark)

(b) Degree of dissociation is given by: $\alpha = \frac{\Lambda}{\Lambda^{\infty}}$
(½ mark)

Evaluation of $\Lambda^{\infty}_{CH_3COOH}$,
$\Lambda^{\infty}_{CH_3COOH} = \lambda^{\infty}_{CH_3COO^-} + \lambda^{\infty}_{H^+} = 40.9 + 349.8 = 390.7$ $ohm^{-1}\ cm^2\ eq^{-1}$ (½ mark)
Evaluation of degree of dissociation at C = 0.1 M

$$\alpha = \frac{\Lambda}{\Lambda^{\infty}} = \frac{5.20}{390.7} = 0.013$$
$\alpha = 1.3\%$ (1 mark)
Evaluation of degree of dissociation at C = 0.001 M,
$$\alpha = \frac{\Lambda}{\Lambda^{\infty}} = \frac{49.2}{390.7} = 0.125 \text{ i.e., } 12.5$$
$\alpha = 12.5\%$ (1 mark)

OR

(a) The cell reactions are :

At anode : $Fe(s) \longrightarrow Fe^{2+}(aq) + 2e^-$

At cathode : $Cu^{2+}(aq) + 2e^- \longrightarrow Cu(s)$ (1 mark)
We know that :

$\Delta G^0 = -nFE^0_{cell}$; $n = 2$ mol

$$E^0_{cell} = [E^0_{(Cu^{2+}/Cu)} - E^0_{(Fe^{2+}/Fe)}]$$
$= (+0.34\ V) - (-0.44\ V) = +0.78\ V$ (1 mark)
$F = 96500\ C\ mol^{-1}$

$\therefore \quad \Delta G^0 = -nFE^0_{cell}$
$= -(2\ mol) \times (96500\ C\ mol^{-1}) \times (+0.78\ V)$
$= -150540\ CV = -150540\ J$ ($\because$ 1 CV = 1 J)
(1 mark)

(b) According to Faraday's first law of electrolysis :
The reaction at cathode :
$Cu^{2+} + 2e^- \longrightarrow Cu$ (½ mark)
63.5 $\quad 2 \times 96500$ C
The quantity of charge passed = I × t = (10 amp) × (1 × 60 × 60s) = 36000 C (½ mark)
2 × 96500 C of charge deposit copper = 63.5g
36000 C of charge deposit copper

$$= \frac{(63.5g)}{(2 \times 96500C)} \times (36000C) = 11.84g$$ (1 mark)

Thus, 11.84g of copper will dissolve from the anode and the same amount from the solution will get deposited on the cathode. The concentration of the solution will remain unchanged.

35. (a) In the acid catalysed dehydration of alcohols, the slowest step or the rate determining step is the formation of carbocation. Thus dehydration of tertiary alcohols will be fastest because tertiary carbocation is most stable. (1 + 1 = 2 Marks)

Note:

$$(CH_3)_3C{-}\ddot{O}H + H^{\oplus} \underset{}{\overset{\text{fast}}{\rightleftharpoons}} (CH_3)_3C{-}\overset{\oplus}{O}H_2 \overset{\text{slow}}{\rightleftharpoons}$$

t-butyl alcohol

$$H_2O + (CH_3)_3C^{\oplus} \underset{H^+}{\overset{\text{fast}}{\rightleftharpoons}} (H_3C)_2C{=}CH_2$$

It is an example of Reimer-Tiemann reaction. Reimer-Tiemann reaction is an electrophillic substitution reaction in which dichlorocarbene is generated in the first step and act as strong electrophile.

(b) (i) phenol (OH on benzene) $\xrightarrow[\text{aq.NaOH}]{CHCl_3}$ intermediate (O^-Na^+, $CHCl_2$ on benzene) $\xrightarrow{NaOH}$ (O^-Na^+, CHO on benzene) $\xrightarrow{H^+}$ salicylaldehyde (OH, CHO on benzene)

(1 mark)

It is an example of Williamson Synthesis. Williamson synthesis is S_N2 reaction. Nucleophile attacks from the back side which results in inversion of configuration at the site of the leaving group.

(ii) $H_3C-C(CH_3)_2-Cl + C_2H_5-O^-Na^+ \xrightarrow[-NaCl]{} H_3C-C(CH_3)_2-O-C_2H_5$

t-butyl chloride → t-butyl ethyl ether

(1 mark)

(iii) $\underset{\text{propene}}{6CH_3-CH=CH_2} + \underset{\text{diborane}}{B_2H_6} \longrightarrow 2(CH_3-CH_2-CH_2)_3B$

$(CH_3-CH_2-CH_2)_3B \xrightarrow{H_2O_2} \underset{\text{propanol}}{CH_3-CH_2-CH_2-OH} + \underset{\text{boric acid}}{B(OH)_3}$

(1 mark)

1. **(b)** $P = P_A^\circ x_A + P_B^\circ x_B = P_B^\circ + x_A(P_A^\circ - P_B^\circ)$

$[\because x_B = 1 - x_A]$

2. **(d)** The order of reactivity of alcohol with Lucas reagent is *tert.* > *sec.* > *pri.*

3. **(b)** The given reaction is known as Sandmeyer's reaction.

4. **(a)**

(i)	(ii)	(iii)
CHO	CHO	CH_2OH
H—C—OH	H—C—OH	C=O
CH_2OH	HO—C—H	HO—C—H
	H—C—OH	H—C—OH
	H—C—OH	H—C—OH
	CH_2OH	CH_2OH
(+)	(+)	(−)

When OH on lowest asymmetric carbon is written at right hand side, it is represented as D configuration and when OH is written on left hand side, it is represented as L configuration.

*4. **(b)** Glycosidic linkage is actually an ether bond as the linkage forming the rings in an oligosaccharide or polysaccharide is not just one bond, but the two bonds sharing an oxygen atom e.g. sucrose

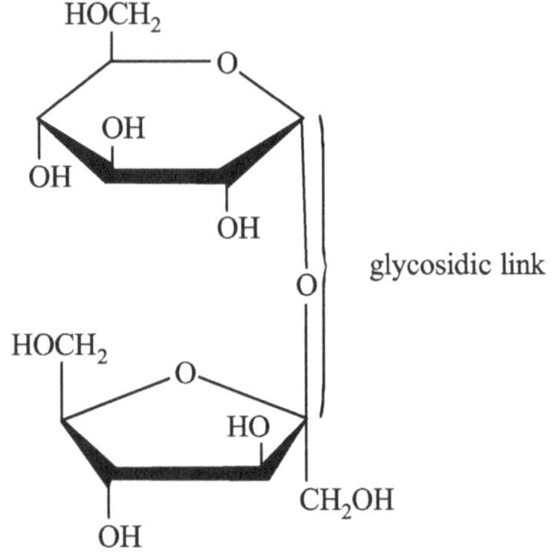

5. **(b)** The value of rate constant can be increased only by increasing the temperature.

6. **(b)** $AlCl_3 + Cl_2 \longrightarrow [AlCl_4]^- + Cl^+$

$C_6H_6 + Cl^+ \longrightarrow C_6H_5Cl$

Chlorobenzene

7. **(a)** Given: w = 10 g; Mol. mass = 40

Weight of solvent = 1250 × 0.8 g = 1000 g = 1 kg

$\therefore$ Molality $= \frac{10}{40 \times 1} = 0.25$

8. **(d)** $[Ma_3b_3]$ type complex shows facial and meridional isomerism.

So, the complex $[CO(NH_3)_3(NO_2)_3]$ will show fac and mer- isomers.

9. **(d)** *tert*-Alkyl halides undergo S_N1 reactions, hence they involve the formation of quite stable carbocations, and not the transition state. In S_N1 reactions, the nucleophile is not involved in rate determining (first) step, hence its stronger or weaker nature does not influence the reaction rate. In S_N1, the product has more percentage of the inverted configuration than the retained configuration, i.e. only partial racemization takes place, hence the product will be having some optical activity.

10. **(b)** $(CH_3)_3CBr + NaOC_2H_5$ can't be applied for synthesising the ether because sod. ethoxide, being a strong base, will preferentially cause elimination reaction.

$$(CH_3)_3CBr \xrightarrow{^-OC_2H_5} (CH_3)_2C = CH_2 + HBr$$

In isobutene + ethanol, isobutene will form *tert*-butyl cation which reacts with ethanol, a nucleophile to form ether.

$$(CH_3)_2C = CH_2 \xrightarrow{H^+} (CH_3)_2\overset{+}{C}CH_3$$

$$\xrightarrow[\text{(ii) } -H^+]{\text{(i) } CH_3CH_2OH} (CH_3)_3COCH_2CH_3$$

11. **(a)** Higher the value of reduction potential higher will be the oxidising power whereas the lower the value of reduction potential higher will be the reducing power.

12. **(a)** Highest O.S. by Mn (+7)

13. **(c)** Only aldehydes and ketones react with 2, 4-dinitrophenylhydrazine.

14. **(b)** $O_3 \xrightarrow{\text{Fast}} O_2 + O;\ O + O_3 \xrightarrow{\text{Slow}} 2O_2$

$k = \frac{[O_2][O]}{[O_3]}$ (I) Rate = $k'[O_3][O]$ put [O] from (I)

$$r = \frac{k'[O_3]K[O_3]}{[O_2]} = k[O_3]^2[O_2]^{-1}$$

Intermediates are never represented in rate law equation.

15. (a) In polar solvents, acetic acid will dissociate which loads to greater depression in freezing point. (1 mark)

16. (c) The correct reason is : The overall electron deficiency in *m*-nitroaniline is much less (due to –R effect of NO_2 group and +R effect of NH_2 group) than in *m*-dinitrobenzene (–R effect of the two NO_2 groups) and hence does not accept additional electrons from a weak reducing agent such as $(NH_4)_2S$ and thus further reduction is prevented. (1 mark)

17. (d) Br_2 water oxidized only –CHO not alcohol. Oxidation of glucose with Br_2 water produces gluconic acid. (1 mark)

18. (a) Benzyl cation $(C_6H_5\overset{+}{C}H_2)$ is more stable than methyl cation $(\overset{+}{C}H_3)$, so the products formed are $C_6H_5CH_2I$ and CH_3OH. (1 mark)

19. $CH_3COOH \rightleftharpoons CH_3COO^- + H^+$

$$\Lambda^\circ_{(CH_3COOH)} = \lambda^\circ_{(CH_3COO^+)} + \lambda^\circ_{(H^+)}$$

$= 40.9 + 349.6 = 390.5$

Now degree of dissociation (α)

$$\propto = \frac{\Lambda_m}{\Lambda^\circ} = \frac{39.05}{390.5} = 0.1 \quad \text{(1 mark)}$$

The degree of dissociation of acitic acid is 0.1.

20. In $[Co(NH_3)_6]^{3+}$, Co is in + 3 oxidation state, with the configuration $3d^6$. In the presence of NH_3, $3d$ electrons pair up leaving two *d*-orbitals empty. Hence, the hybridisation is d^2sp^3 forming an inner orbital complex. (1 mark)

In $[Ni(NH_3)_6]^{2+}$, Ni is in + 2 oxidation state with the configuration $3d^8$. In presence of NH_3, the $3d$ electrons do not pair up. The hybridisation involved is sp^3d^2 forming an outer orbital complex. (1 mark)

OR

(i) Since CO can form σ as well as π bond, whereas NH_3 has lone pair of electrons and can form σ bond only. Therefore, CO is better complexing reagent than NH_3. (1 mark)

(ii) Electronic configuraton of Ni in $Ni(CO)_4$:
$[Ar]\, 4s^2, 3d^8$

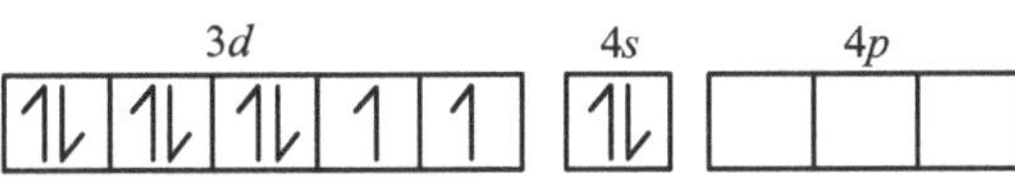

CO is a strong field ligand.

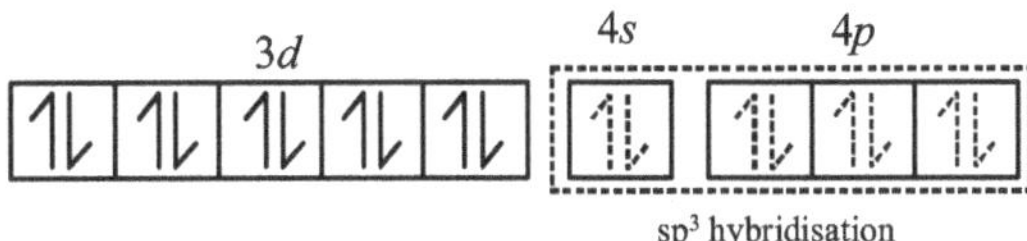

Thus $[Ni(CO)_4]$ has sp^3 hybridisation and has tetrahedral shape.

Electronic configuration of Ni in $[Ni(CN)_4]^{2-} = 3d^8\, 4s^0$

3d 4s 4p

the ligand involved here is strong i.e., CN^- ion.

Ni^{++} (after rearrangement)

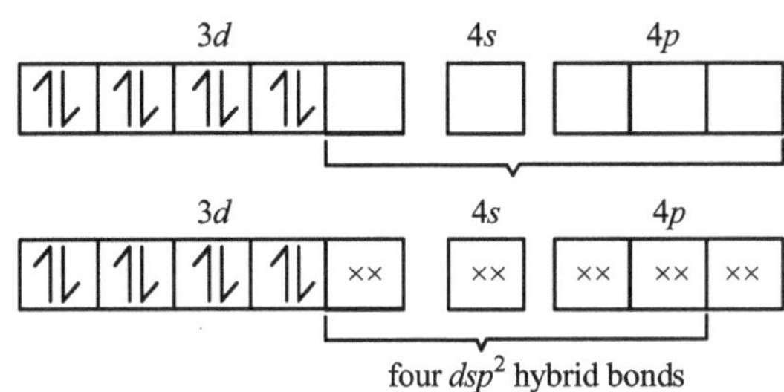

$[Ni(CN)_4]^{2-}$ has dsp^2 hybridisation and has square planar shape. (1 mark)

21. X is $CH_3-CH=CH_2$

Y is $CH_3-\underset{\displaystyle OH}{\underset{|}{C}H}-CH_3$, Z is $CH_3-\underset{\displaystyle Cl}{\underset{|}{C}H}-CH_3$

22. (a) Half-life calculation from the given graph: Concentration of reactant reduces from 0.8 to 0.4 in (20 – 10) = 10 seconds.

Again the concentration reduces to half (0.4 to 0.2) in (30 – 20) = 10 seconds.

Thus, the half-life of reaction remains constant or we can say that order of reaction is one.

(b) For a first order reaction, concentration never reduces to zero. For first order reaction $ln\,[A] = [A]_0\, e^{-kt}$ where $[A]_0$ is the initial concentration of the reactant. Mathematically, $[A] > 0$ for all $t < \infty$ (1 mark)

OR

(a) Rate law for the reaction (1 mark)
Rate $= k[H_2O_2]\,[I^-]$

(b) Order of reaction is 2. (½ mark)

(c) Step 1 is rate determining step because it is the slowest step. (½ mark)

23. (a) DNA, on hydrolysis, gives four nitrogenous bases, namely adenine, guanine, cytosine and thymine. (1 mark)

(b) An equimolar mixture of glucose and fructose is called an invert sugar. (1 mark)

24. (a) Fehling's reagent is composed by Fehling A and Fehling B. Fehling A is a blue-coloured aqueous solution of $CuSO_4$. Fehling B is colorless aqueous solution of potassium sodium tartrate ($KNaC_4H_4O_6.4H_2O$). (1 mark)

Note

Fehling reagent is used to test aldehydes. Ketones and aromatic aldehyde do not respond to Fehling's test.

(b) Structure of semicarbazone of ethanal

$$\begin{matrix}CH_3 \\ H\end{matrix}\rangle C=O + H_2N-NH-\overset{O}{\overset{\|}{C}}-NH_2 \longrightarrow NH-\overset{O}{\overset{\|}{C}}-NH_2$$

$$H_3C-\overset{H}{\overset{|}{C}}=N-NH-\overset{O}{\overset{\|}{C}}-NH_2$$

Semicarbazone (1 mark)

25. (a) Copper exhibits + 1 O.S. because after loss of one electron, it acquire $3d^{10}$ configuration and becomes fully filled and hence stable.

(b) V^{3+} ($3d^2$), Mn^{2+} ($3d^5$) ions are coloured in aqueous solution because they have unpaired electrons in *d*-subshell.

26. (a) Alcohols and amines combine with anhydrous $CaCl_2$ to form complexes. For example, with C_2H_5OH it gives a complex of molecular formula, $CaCl_2.3C_2H_5OH$. Therefore, it cannot be used as a drying agent. (1 mark)

(b) Grignard reagents form coordination complexes with ethers but not with benzene since the former has lone pairs of electrons but the latter does not. Grignard reagent and ether form a complex where Mg acts as a Lewis acid and ether act as a Lewis base. This makes Grignard reagent soluble in ether. (1 mark)

(c) This is because the nucleophile attack by the halide ion on the carbon of the benzene ring does not occur. Oxygen of ether is in resonance with ring. Also the C of ring is sterically more hindered. (1 mark)

OR

(a) $CH_3CH_2CH_2CH_2OH \xrightarrow[\text{Oxidation}]{[O]} \underset{\text{Butanoic acid}}{CH_3CH_2CH_2COOH}$

(1 mark)

(b)

$$\underset{\text{2-butanol}}{CH_3-\underset{OH}{\underset{|}{C}H}-CH_2CH_3} \xrightarrow[\text{Oxidation}]{[O]} \underset{\text{2-butanone}}{CH_3-\underset{O}{\underset{\|}{C}}-CH_2CH_3}$$

(1 mark)

(c)

$$CH_3-\overset{H}{\overset{|}{\underset{CH_3}{\underset{|}{C}}}}-CH_2OH \xrightarrow[\text{Oxidation}]{[O]} CH_3-\overset{H}{\overset{|}{\underset{CH_3}{\underset{|}{C}}}}-COOH$$

2-methylpropanoic acid

(1 mark)

27. Rate = $k[A]^\alpha[B]^\beta$

Divide $(Rate)_1$, and $(Rate)_4$

$$\frac{(Rate)_1}{(Rate)_4} = \frac{k(0.1)^\alpha(0.1)^\beta}{k(0.4)^\alpha(0.1)^\beta}; \frac{6\times10^{-3}}{2.40\times10^{-2}} = \left(\frac{0.1}{0.4}\right)^\alpha$$

$$\frac{1}{4} = \left(\frac{1}{4}\right)^\alpha; \alpha = 1$$ (½ mark)

$$\frac{(Rate)_2}{(Rate)_3} = \frac{k(0.3)^\alpha(0.2)^\beta}{k(0.3)^\alpha(0.4)^\beta} \Rightarrow \frac{7.2\times10^{-2}}{2.88\times10^{-1}} = \left(\frac{0.2}{0.4}\right)^\beta$$

$$\frac{1}{4} = \left(\frac{1}{2}\right)^\beta; \left(\frac{1}{2}\right)^2 = \left(\frac{1}{2}\right)^\beta; \beta = 2$$ (½ mark)

Rate = $k[A]^1[B]^2$

Order: $1+2=3$ (1 mark)

From experiment 1:

$6\times10^{-3} = k(0.1)^1(0.1)^2$

$k = 6\times10^{-3}/1\times10^{-3} = 6\ mol^{-2}\ L^2\ min^{-1}$ (1 mark)

28. (a) $[Ni(CN)_4]^{2-}$ has square planar geometry on account of dsp^2 hybridisation. (1 mark)

(b) $[Ag(NH_3)_2]^+Cl^-$ remains colourless in aqueous solution. The complex does not have unpaired electron in central cation, Ag^+ and thus d-d transition is not possible. Ag in + 1 oxidation state which has following electronic configuration:

The electronic configuration of $[Ag]^+$ is $[Kr]_{36}\ 4d^{10}\ 5s^0$. (2 marks)

29. (a) Aldehyde group is not free in glucose, it is involved in the formation of cyclic structure in glucose. Thus, it does not react with 2, 4-dinitrophenylhydrazine. (1 mark)

(b) The two strands in DNA are held together by hydrogen bonds between specific pair of bases (cytosine with guanine and adenine with thymine).

Thus, the two strands are complementary to each other. (1 mark)

(c) Starch contains α-D-glucose, while cellulose contains β-D-glucose as their monomers. (1 mark)

(d) When a protein, in its native form, is subjected to a physical change like change in temperature, or a chemical change like change in pH, the native conformation of the molecule is disrupted and proteins so formed are called **denaturated proteins**. (1 mark)

30. (a) $(CH_3)_3C—I$ is more reactive towards S_N1 than $(CH_3)_3C—Br$ because I^- is a better leaving group than Br^-. (1 mark)

(b) 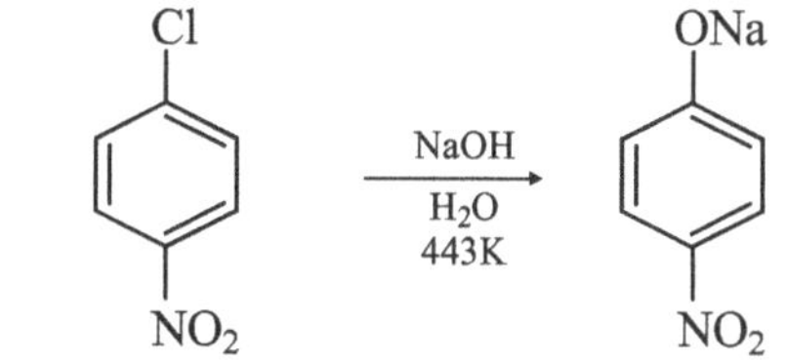 p-nitrochlorobenzene $\xrightarrow[H_2O,\ 443K]{NaOH}$ sodium p-nitrophenoxide (ONa, NO_2) $\xrightarrow[H^+]{\text{acidification}}$ p-nitrophenol (OH, NO_2) (1 mark)

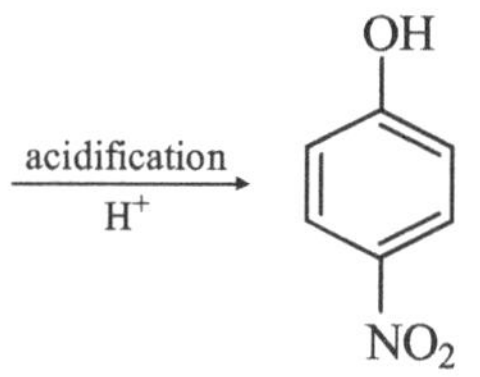

p-nitrochlorobenzene

p-nitrophenol

(c) Elimination reaction is highly favoured if

(i) Bulkier base is used

(ii) Higher temperature is used

Hence in given reaction, biomolecular elimination reaction provides major product.

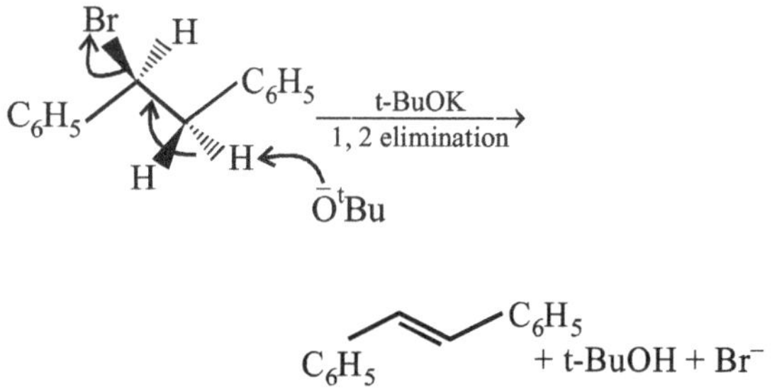

C_6H_5–CH(Br)–CH(H)–C_6H_5 + $\bar{O}^tBu$ $\xrightarrow[\text{1, 2 elimination}]{\text{t-BuOK}}$ C_6H_5–CH=CH–C_6H_5 + t-BuOH + Br^-

31. (a) Osmotic pressure.

Measurement of osmotic pressure is performed at room temperature and the concentration of the solution is taken in molarity. Biomolecules such as proteins are not stable at higher temperature. Therefore, osmotic pressure determination is the best method of finding out the molecular weight of macromolecules. (1 mark)

(b) Colligative properties depend on the number of solute particles. If the solute is an electrolyte then it will produce more number of particles in the solution and the magnitude of colligative property will be high. (1 mark)

(c) The rules of colligative properties obey in ideal or very dilute solutions. In these conditions, there is no interaction between particles. Hence, chemical properties do not depend on the chemical nature of solute particles. (2 marks)

OR

By measuring the relative lowering in vapour pressure, the elevation in boiling point, the depression in freezing point, the osmotic pressure.

All these phenomena are colligative properties of solution as they are dependent on the added solute particles in solution. (2 marks)

32. (a) Conversion of (iii) to (iv) involving rearrangement is the slowest step. Species (iii) is electron deficient (N has only 6 electrons), hence it has a tendency to get its octet completed by migration of alkyl group. (1 mark)

(b) $CH_3CH_2CH_2-\overset{O}{\overset{\|}{C}}-NH_2$ (1 mark)

(c) Since the reaction is intramolecular, no cross product will be formed.

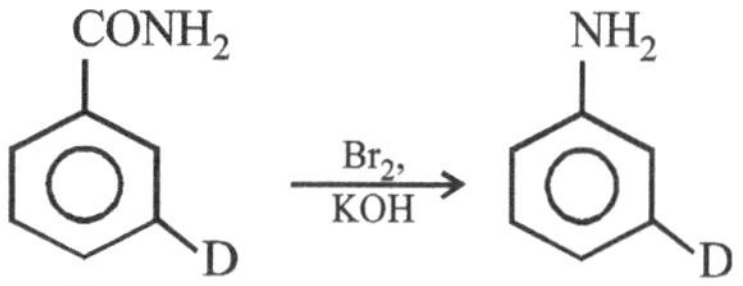

(i) $C_6H_4(D)CONH_2$ $\xrightarrow[KOH]{Br_2,}$ $C_6H_4(D)NH_2$

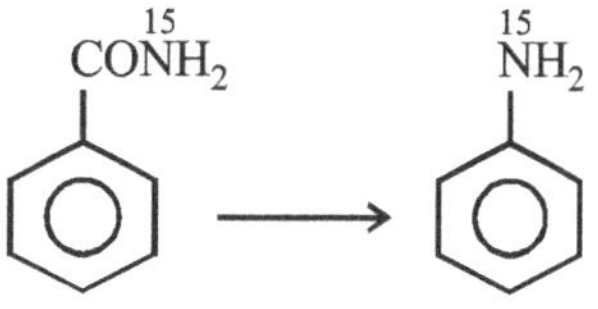

(ii) $C_6H_5\overset{15}{C}ONH_2$ ⟶ $C_6H_5\overset{15}{N}H_2$

OR

Amine (vi) is more basic than amide (i) because lone pair of electrons on nitrogen is in conjugation with C=O group in amides. (2 marks)

33. (a) (i) $\Lambda_m = \frac{1}{\rho}\cdot\frac{1000}{C} = \frac{1}{58\ \Omega\ cm} \times \frac{1000\ cm^3\ L^{-1}}{0.1\ mol\ L^{-1}}$

$= 172.4\ \Omega^{-1}\ cm^2\ mol^{-1}$

$$\text{(ii) } \Lambda_m = \kappa\frac{1000}{C} = \frac{2\times10^{-2}\,\Omega^{-1}\,\text{cm}^{-1}\times1000\,\text{cm}^3\text{L}^{-1}}{0.08\text{ mol L}^{-1}}$$

$= 250\ \Omega^{-1}\ \text{cm}^2\ \text{mol}^{-1}$ (1 mark)

Therefore, solution (ii) has larger molar conductance.

(b) A solution of an electrolyte can be stored in a particular vessel only in case there is no chemical reaction taking place with the material of the vessel.

Now if silver nitrate solution is to be kept in copper vessel, the probable reaction will be :

$$Cu\,(s) + 2\,Ag^+(aq) \longrightarrow Cu^{2+}(aq) + 2Ag(s)$$

Since copper is placed below silver in the activity series, this means that it is a stronger reducing agent and can lose electrons to Ag^+ ions and the chemical reaction will occur. Therefore, silver nitrate solution cannot be kept in copper vessel. Now, when copper sulphate solution is placed in silver vessel, the likely chemical reaction is :

$$2Ag\,(s) + Cu^{2+}(aq) \longrightarrow Cu\,(s) + 2Ag^+(aq)$$

Since Ag is placed above copper in the activity series, the chemical reaction will not take place. As a result, copper sulphate can be easily stored in silver vessel. (3 marks)

(c) Λ_m slightly decreases with increase in concentration of KCl. At higher concentration in strong electrolyte, there is large inter-ionic attraction. (1 mark)

OR

(a) (i) E° is an intensive property i.e., it does not depend on the amount of material in the system. Therefore, E° value for $2Ag^+/2Ag$ is the same as for Ag^+/Ag, i.e., 0.81V. (1 mark)

(ii) $E^\circ_{cell} = E_{right} - E_{left}$

$= 0.81\text{ V} - (-2.36\text{ V})$

$= 3.17\text{ V}$ (1 mark)

(b) $$E_{cell} = E^\circ_{cell} - \frac{0.0591}{n}\log\frac{[Mg^{2+}]}{[Ag^+]^2}$$

$$= 3.17 - \frac{0.0591}{2}\log\frac{(0.1)}{(0.0001)^2} = 2.96\text{ V}$$

(2 marks)

(c) (i) $Mg(s)\,|\,Mg^{2+}(0.10\text{ M})\,||\,Ag^+(0.0001\text{ M})\,|\,Ag(s)$ (½ mark)

(ii) Yes (½ mark)

34. (a) Compound B is an aldehyde having α-H atom as it gives positive Fehling's test and also forms iodoform. Compound C should be a methyl ketone as it forms iodoform and does not give Fehling's test. The reactions involved are given as:

$$CH_3-CH=\underset{\underset{CH_3}{|}}{C}-CH_3 \xrightarrow[\text{(ii) Zn/H}_2\text{O}]{\text{(i) O}_3}$$

2-Methylbut-2-ene (A)

$$H_3C-CHO + O=\underset{\underset{CH_3}{|}}{C}-CH_3$$

Ethanal (B) Acetone (C) (2 marks)

$$CH_3-\overset{\overset{O}{||}}{C}-H \xrightarrow{2NaOH\,+\,I_2} HCOOH + CH_3I + 2NaOH$$

(B) Iodoform

(½ mark)

$$O=\underset{\underset{CH_3}{|}}{C}-CH_3 \xrightarrow{2NaOH\,+\,I_2} CH_3COOH + CH_3I + 2NaOH$$

(C) Iodoform

(½ mark)

(b) The boiling point of butanol is higher than that of butanal because butanol has stronger inter-molecular H-bonding while butanal has weak dipole - dipole attraction. However, both of them form H-bonds with water and hence are soluble. (1 mark)

(c) It is because the NH_2 – group closer to the carbonyl group is deactivated, i.e., resonance stabilised compared with the other end NH_2 group.

$$H_2N-NH-\overset{\overset{:O:}{||}}{C}-\ddot{N}H_2 \longleftrightarrow H_2N-NH-\overset{\overset{:\ddot{O}^-}{|}}{C}=\overset{+}{N}H_2$$

(1 mark)

OR

(a) As the compound A gives negative Tollen's test but positive 2, 4-dinitrophenyl hydrazine test, it is a ketone (and not an aldehyde). It is further confirmed by the fact that it gives a carboxylic acid with lesser number of carbon atoms on vigorous oxidation. The sodium salt of acid (B) on electrolytic reduction gives a hydrocarbon. The reaction involved are:

$$\underset{\substack{\text{3-pentanone}\\(A)}}{\begin{matrix}CH_3CH_2\\CH_3CH_2\end{matrix}\!\!>C=O} + H_2N-NH-C_6H_3(NO_2)_2 \xrightarrow{-H_2O} \underset{\text{3-pentanone - 2, 4-dinitrophenyl hydrazone}}{\begin{matrix}CH_3CH_2\\CH_3CH_2\end{matrix}\!\!>C=N-NH-C_6H_3(NO_2)_2}$$

$$(A) \xrightarrow{\text{Alk. } KMnO_4} \underset{\text{Propionic acid}}{C_2H_5COOH} + \underset{\text{Acetic acid}}{CH_3COOH}$$

$$\underset{\text{Sodium salt of B}}{C_2H_5COONa} \xrightarrow{\text{Kolbe's electrolysis}} \underbrace{C_2H_5-C_2H_5 + 2CO_2}_{\text{At Anode}} + \underbrace{2\,NaOH + H_2}_{\text{At Cathode}}$$

(3 marks)

(b) (i) The reaction is an example of Rosenmund's reduction in which the acid chloride is reduced to an aldehyde.

$$\underset{\substack{\text{2-Methylpropanoyl chloride}\\[A]}}{CH_3-CH(CH_3)-C(=O)-Cl} + H_2(g) \xrightarrow{Pd/BaSO_4}$$

$$\underset{\text{2-Methylpropanal}}{CH_3-CH(CH_3)-C(=O)-H} + HCl$$ (1 mark)

(ii) This reaction is an example of iodoform reaction and proceeds as follows :

$$2\,\underset{\text{3,3-Dimethylbutan-2-one}}{CH_3-C(CH_3)_2-C(=O)-CH_3} + 8NaOI \longrightarrow$$

$$\underset{\substack{\text{Sodium-2,2-dimethylpropanoate}\\[B]}}{2CH_3-C(CH_3)_2-C(=O)-ONa} + \underset{\substack{\text{Iodoform}\\[C]}}{2CHI_3} + 6NaOH + I_2$$

(1 mark)

35. (a) $La(OH)_2$ is more basic than $La(OH)_3$. La^{3+} has smaller size than La^{2+} and due to this $La(OH)_2$ is more ionic and so more basic than $La(OH)_3$. (1 mark)

(b) (i) Because ionisation energies ($I.E_1$ and $I.E_2$) and sublimation energies of transition metals of 3*d*-series do not exhibit any regular trend, therefore there is no regular variation of reduction potentials. (1 mark)

(ii) These metals have completely filled *d*-orbitals with no unpaired electron that may be available for covalent bonding amongst the atoms of these metals which is responsible for high m.pt and b.pt. (1 mark)

(iii) Due to six unpaired electron in *d*-orbitals ($[Ar]\,3d^5 4s^1$) chromium possesses strong tendency of covalent bonding amongst its atoms whereas mercury has completely filled configuration ($[Xe]\,4f^{14}\,5d^{10}\,6s^2$) and have no scope for covalent bonding. (1 mark)

(iv) This is because $SnCl_2$ reduces $HgCl_2$ first to mercurous chloride (white) and then to mercury (block).

$$2HgCl_2 + SnCl_2 \longrightarrow \underset{\text{(White)}}{Hg_2Cl_2} + SnCl_4$$

$$Hg_2Cl_2 + SnCl_2 \longrightarrow \underset{\text{(Black)}}{2Hg} + SnCl_4$$ (1 mark)

1. **(d)** The aqueous solutions of diazonium salts are good conductors of electricity.
2. **(c)** Polypeptide chains, in fibrous proteins, are held together by disulphide and hydrogen bonds.
3. **(b)** For the given cell

$$E_{cell} = E^{\circ}_{cell} - \frac{0.059V}{2}\log\frac{[Zn^{2+}(aq)]}{[Cu^{2+}(aq)]}$$

The cell potential decreases with increase in $[Zn^{2+}(aq)]$ and increases with increase in $[Cu^{2+}(aq)]$.
4. **(a)** In graph (i), ln [Reactant] vs time is linear with positive intercept and negative slope. Hence it is 1st order In graph (ii), [Reactant] vs time is linear with positive intercept and negative slope. Hence, it is zero order.
5. **(a)** Density is directly related to molecular mass. Higher the molecular mass, higher will be the density of the compound. The order of molecular mass is benzene < chlorobenzene < dichlorobenzene < bromochlorobenzene
6. **(d)**
7. **(b)** $P_{Solution} = P^{\circ}_{solution}\, x_{Solvent}$

$$\frac{P^{\circ} - P}{P^{\circ}} = x_{solute}$$

8. **(a)** In $C_6H_5CH_2Br$ carbocation is $C_6H_5\overset{\oplus}{C}H_2$ which is stable due to resonance.
9. **(a)** Following are the three possible isomers of butanol

(i) $CH_3CH_2—CH_2—CH_2OH$

Butan-1-ol

no chiral carbon

(ii) $CH_3-CH_2-\overset{*}{C}H(OH)-CH_3$

Butan-2-ol

1-Chiral Carbon

(iii) $H_3C-C(CH_3)(OH)-CH_3$

2-methylpropan-2-ol

No Chiral Carbon

10. **(d)** $(CH_3)_2NH$ is a secondary amine.
11. **(b)** In DNA and RNA heterocyclic base and phosphate ester are at C_1' and C_5' respectively of the sugar molecule.

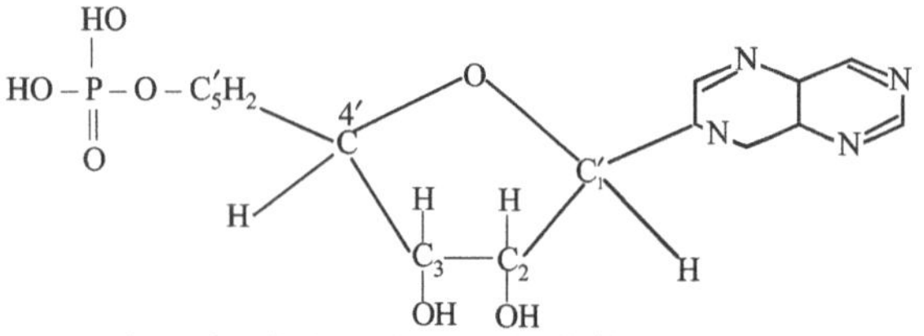

HO–P(=O)(HO)–O–$C_5'H_2$–C_4' ... O ... C_1'–(base); H, H, C_3, C_2, OH, OH, H

12. **(c)** Ni – Cd cells have longer half-life than lead-storage battery.
13. **(c)** The path of the reaction changes by decreasing the E_a.
14. **(b)** $PhNH_2 < NH_3 < Et_3N < Et_2NH$
15. **(a)**
16. **(a)** The element which can reduce itself acts as an oxidising agent.
17. **(a)** Ambidentate ligand like NO_2 has two different donor atoms i.e. N and O. Thus, it can form coordinate bonds through N and O both or we can say that it can form linkage isomers.
18. **(a)** Both carbanion (formed in presence of a base) and enol (formed in presence of an acid) act as nucleophiles and hence add on the carbonyl group of aldehydes and ketones to give aldols.
19. (a) $[Cr(NC)(H_2O)_5]^{2+}$ (b) $[PtBr_2(NH_3)_4]Cl_2$
20. (a) Chloromethane is more reactive towards nucleophillic substitution reaction since it is an alkyl halide.
    (b) Thionyl chloride method is preferred for preparing alkyl chlorides from alcohols because the by products of the reaction, *i.e.*, SO_2 and HCl being gases escape into thc atmosphcrc lcaving bchind alkyl chloridc in almost pure state. (½+1=1½ marks)
21. No. of moles of methanol (n_B)

$$= \frac{\text{Mass of } CH_3OH}{\text{Gram molar mass}} = \frac{(40\ g)}{(32\ g\ mol^{-1})} = 1.25\,mol \quad (¼\ mark)$$

No. of moles of ethanol (n_A)

$$= \frac{\text{Mass of } C_2H_5OH}{\text{Gram molar mass}} = \frac{(60\ g)}{(46\ g\ mol^{-1})} = 1.30\ mol \quad (¼\ mark)$$

Mole fraction of methanol (x_B)

$$= \frac{n_B}{n_B + n_A} = \frac{(1.25\ mol)}{(1.25\ mol + 1.30\ mol)} = 0.49 \quad (¼\ mark)$$

Mole fraction of ethanol (x_A)

$$= \frac{n_A}{n_A + n_B} = \frac{(1.30\ mol)}{(1.25\ mol + 1.30\ mol)} = 0.51 \quad (¼\ mark)$$

Vapour pressure of pure methanol $\left(P^{\circ}_B\right) = 88.7$ mm Hg

Vapour pressure of pure ethanol $\left(P^{\circ}_A\right) = 44.5$ mm Hg

Partial vapour pressure of methanol

$$(P_B) = P^{\circ}_B x_B = (88.7\ mm \times 0.49) = 43.46\ mm\ Hg$$

(¼ mark)

Partial vapour pressure of ethanol

$$(P_A) = P^{\circ}_A x_A = (44.5\ mm \times 0.51) = 22.70\ mm\ Hg$$

(¼ mark)

Since the solution is ideal in nature,
Total vapour pressure of solution

$$(P) = P_A + P_B = (22.70 + 43.46) = 66.16\ mm\ Hg$$

(½ mark)

22. (a) $CH_3-\underset{\underset{O}{||}}{C}-CH_3 + CH_3-MgI \longrightarrow CH_3-\underset{\underset{O\text{-}MgI}{|}}{\overset{\overset{CH_3}{|}}{C}}-CH_3$

$\xrightarrow[\text{(hydolysis)}]{H_2O} CH_3-\underset{\underset{OH}{|}}{\overset{\overset{CH_3}{|}}{C}}-CH_3 + Mg(OH)I$ (1 mark)

(b) $C_6H_6 + CH_3-\overset{\overset{O}{||}}{C}-Cl \xrightarrow{AlCl_3} C_6H_5-\overset{\overset{O}{||}}{C}-CH_3 + HCl$ (1 mark)

23. (a) Ammonolysis yields a mixture of primary, secondary, tertiary and quaternary salts. The separation of pure primary amines from ammonolysis of alkyl halide is a difficult process. (1 mark)

(b) Aniline does not give friedel-crafts reaction as it forms anilinium chloride salt which deactivates the ring for further acylation and alkylation reaction. (1 mark)

24. Calculation of cell constant (1 mark)

Resistance of KCl solution (R) = 100 ohm

Conductivity (specific conductance) (κ)

$= 1.29\times10^{-2}\ ohm^{-1}\ cm^{-1}$

Specific conductance (κ) $= \frac{1}{R}\times$ cell constant

Cell constant

$= \kappa\times R = \left(1.29\times10^{-2}\ ohm^{-1}\ cm^{-1}\right)\times\left(100\ ohm\right)$

$= 1.29\ cm^{-1}$, (½ mark)

Specific conductance of 0.02 M KCl solution

Resistance of KCl solution (R) = 520 ohm

Cell constant of the cell (l / a) = $1.29\ cm^{-1}$

Specific conductivity (κ) $= \frac{1}{R}\times$ cell constant

$= \left(\frac{1}{520}\ ohm^{-1}\right)\times\left(1.29\ cm^{-1}\right)$

$= 2.48\times10^{-3}\ ohm^{-1}\ cm^{-1}$ (½ mark)

Molar conductivity of 0.02 M KCl solution

Concentration (C)

$= 0.02\ M = 0.02\ mol\ L^{-1} = \frac{0.02 mol}{1L} = \frac{0.02\ mol}{1000\ cm^3}$

$= 2.0\times10^{-5}\ mol\ cm^{-3}$

Molar conductance (Λ_m)

$= \frac{\kappa}{C} = \frac{(2.49\times10^{-3} ohm^{-1} cm^{-1})}{(2.0\times10^{-5} mol\ cm^{-3})}$

$= 124.5\ ohm^{-1}\ cm^2 mol^{-1}$ (1 mark)

OR

(a) The cell reactions are (½ mark)

$Zn(s) \longrightarrow Zn^{2+}(aq) + 2e^-$(anode) (¼ mark)

$Cu^{2+}(aq) + 2e^- \longrightarrow Cu(s)$ (cathode)

(b) $E^\circ_{cell} = E_{cathode} - E_{anode} = 0.34-(-0.76)$
$= 0.34+0.76 = 1.10\ V$ (½ mark)

from Nernst equation

$E_{cell} = E^\circ_{cell} - \frac{0.059}{n}\log\frac{[Zn^{2+}]}{[Cu^{2+}]}$

$E_{cell} = 1.1 - \frac{0.059}{2}\log\frac{[2]}{[0.5]}$

$= 1.1 - \frac{0.059}{2}(\log 20 - \log 5)$

$= 1.1 - \frac{0.059}{2}\times 0.6021$

$= 1.1 - 0.0177 = 1.09\ V$ (1 mark)

25. (a) Two monosaccharides obtained on hydrolysis of lactose sugar are b-D-glucose and b-D-galactose.

(b) Vitamin C cannot be stored in our body because it is water soluble in nature so it repeatedly gets eliminated through urine.

OR

(a) When a base (purine or pyrimidine) get attached to 1′ position of a pentose sugar a nucleoside is formed. When a nucleoside is further linked to phosphoric acid at 5′ position of the sugar moiety, we get a nucleotide.

HOH2C5′ – O – Base (1′, 2′, 3′, 4′; H; OH OH)
Nucleoside

$^-O-\overset{\overset{O}{||}}{\underset{\underset{O^-}{|}}{P}}-O-H_2C^{5'}$ – O – Base (1′, 2′, 3′, 4′; H; OH OH)
Nucleotide

(1 mark)

(d) Enzymes are most reactive at optimum temperature. The optimum temperature for enzyme activity lies between 40°C to 60°C.

26. $Fe + 2H^+ \rightarrow Fe^{2+} + H_2$, n = 2 (½ mark)

$E_{cell} = E^\circ_{cell} - \frac{0.0591}{2}\log\frac{[Fe^{2+}]}{[H^+]^2}$

$= (0.44) - \frac{0.0591}{2}\log\frac{10^{-3}}{(1)^2}$

$= 0.44 + 0.0886 = 0.5286\ V$

27. (a) Salt bridge is used to complete the circuit so that current can flow. (1 mark)

(b) The energy difference between $(n-1)\,d$ and ns orbitals of transition metal atoms is very small, so the electrons from both these orbitals can participate in bonding and hence they show variable oxidation states. (1 mark)

(c) Due to Lanthanoid contraction, Hf has size similar to that of Zr. (1 mark)

Lanthanoid contraction is due to the poor shielding of one 4f electron by another in the same sub-shell. Lanthanoid contraction causes the radii of the members of the third transition series to be very similar to those of the corresponding members of the second series.

(d) The transition metals and their compounds behave as catalyst due to the presence of partly filled *d*-orbitals and exhibiting various oxidation states. They form unstable intermediate complex with reactants and thus lowering the energy of activation. They also provide a suitable surface for the reaction to occur. (1 mark)

OR

(b) $Cr_2O_7^{2-} + 6Fe^{2+} + 14H^+ \longrightarrow$

$2Cr^{3+} + 6Fe^{3+} + 7H_2O$ (1 mark)

(c) $2CrO_4^{2-} + 2H^+ \longrightarrow Cr_2O_7^{2-} + H_2O$ (1 mark)

(d) $2MnO_4^- + 5C_2O_4^{2-} + 16H^+ \longrightarrow$

$2Mn^{2+} + 8H_2O + 10CO_2$ (1 mark)

28. (a) Aniline, being a Lewis base, reacts with the Lewis acid ($AlCl_3$, catalyst for Friedel-Craft reaction) to form a salt. Thus the catalyst $AlCl_3$ is consumed. Moreover, the product has positive charge on N, which is deactivating for electrophilic substitution.

$\ddot{N}H_2$ (on benzene ring) + $AlCl_3$ $\longrightarrow$ $\overset{+}{N}H_2AlCl_3^-$ (on benzene ring)

Aniline (Lewis base) (having activating $-\ddot{N}H_2$ group) — Lewis acid — Salt (having deactivting $\overset{+}{N}H_2AlCl_3^-$ group)

(1 mark)

(b) Glucose:
- It is a aldohexose and contains aldehyde functional group. (½ mark)

Fructose:
- It is a ketohexose contains ketone functional group. (½ mark)

(c) The products of hydrolysis of lactose are b-D-glucose and b-D-galactose.(1 Mark)

29. The arrangement of ligands in order of their increasing field strengths, *i.e.*, increasing crystal field splitting energy (CFSE) values is called spertrochemical series. (1 mark)
The ligands with small value of CFSE (Δ_o) are called *weak field ligands* whereas those with large value of CFSE (Δ_o) are called *strong field ligands*. (2 marks)
In general, ligands can be arranged in a series in the order of increasing field strength as given below.

$$I^- < Br^- < S^{2-} < SCN^- < Cl^- < N_3^- < F^-$$
$$< urea < OH^- < C_2H_5-OH$$
$$< C_2O_4^{2-} < O^{2-} < H_2O$$
$$< NCS^- < gly < NH_3, Py < en, SO_3^{2-} < NH_2OH$$
$$< bpy, phen < NO_2^- < CH_3^- < C_6H_5^-$$
$$< R_3P < CN^- < CO$$

OR

(a) $[(Pt(NH_3)_2)Cl(NO_2)]$
IUPAC name : Diamminechloridonitrito-N-platinum (II)

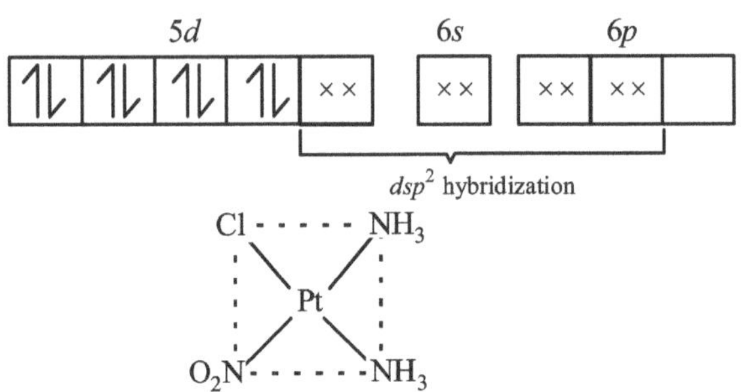

$[Pt(NH_3)_2Cl(NO_2)]$ has square planar shape and is diamagnetic in nature. (1½ marks)

(b) $[Ni(CO)_4]$
IUPAC name : Tetracarbonylnickel (0)
$Ni = 3d^8 4s^2$
CO transfers the 4*s* electrons into 3*d* orbitals and makes the 4*s* orbital available for bonding in $Ni(CO)_4$

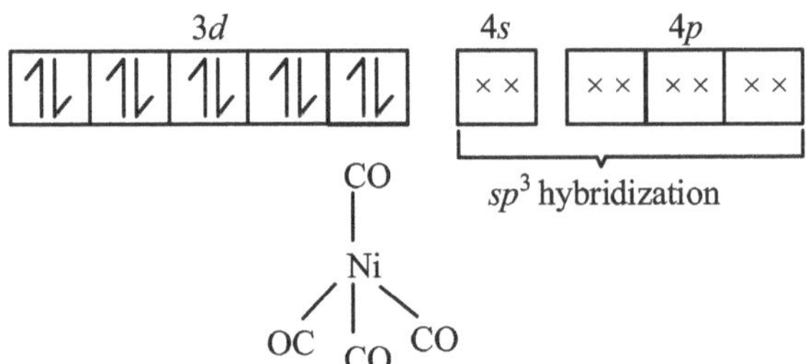

$Ni(CO)_4$ has tetrahectral shape and is diamagnetic in nature. (1½ mark)

30. Structure of the given compounds are :

$H_3C-CH_2-CH_2-CH_2-CH_2-Br$
1-Bromopentane
(A)

$H_3C-CH_2-CH_2-CH(Br)-CH_3$
2-Bromopentane
(B)

$H_3C-CH_2-C(Br)(CH_3)-CH_3$
2-Bromo-2-methylbutane
(C)

(a) As we can see in the above figures, (A), contains the least steric hindrance so towards the S_N2 reaction 1-bromopentane will be most reactive. (1 mark)

(b) 2-Bromopentane (figure B) contain chiral carbon in it. So, this compound is optically active. (1 mark)

(c) 2-Bromo-2-methylbutane will be most reactive towards the β-elimination since it will form most stable alkene (on account of highest no of α-hydrogens) (1 mark)

The identity of the nucleophile or base also determines which mechanism is favoured. E_2 reactions require strong bases whereas S_N2 reactions require good nucleophiles. Therefore, a good nueleophile (i.e., weak base) will favour S_N2 while a weak nucleophile (i.e, strong base) will favour E_2.

31. (a) $\overset{5}{CH_3}-\underset{OH}{\overset{4}{C}H}-\overset{3}{CH_2}-\underset{OH}{\overset{CH_3}{\overset{|2}{C}}}-\overset{1}{CH_3}$ (1 mark)

2-Methyl-2, 4-pentanediol.

(b) Secondary or tertiary alcohol is formed. (1 mark)

(c) Alcohols are versatile compounds. They react both as nucleophiles and electrophiles. (2 marks)

The lone pair of alcoholic 'o' attacks the moleophile when it acts as nucleophile and the O – H bond breaks.

$$R-\ddot{O}-H + C^+ \longrightarrow R-\underset{H}{\overset{\oplus}{O}}-C- \longrightarrow R-O-C-$$

The bond between C—O is broken when they react as electrophiles. Protonoted alcohol react in this manner.

$$R-CH_2OH + H^+ \longrightarrow R-CH_2-OH_2^+ \xrightarrow{Br^\ominus} R-CH_2-Br + H_2O$$

OR

$$\text{Salicylic ā (o-HO-}C_6H_4\text{-COOH)} \xrightarrow{NaHCO_3} \text{Enohes } CO_2$$

$$\text{Phenol } (C_6H_5OH) \xrightarrow{NaHCO_3} \text{No reaction}$$

correct order of basic character of—OH groups: A > B > C. stability of the carbocation is proportional to the basic nature of OH group. Leaving of $(OH)_A$ produces the carbocation which is stabilized by resonance with the π-orbitals of 3-membered ring. Leaving of $(OH)_B$ leads to tertiary carbocation and that of $(OH)_C$ forms the primary carbocation.

32. (a) Since the concentration of sample A is less, so it will show less depression in freezing point. Consequently, its freezing point will be higher than other solutions.(1 mark)

(b) When non-volatile solid is added to pure solvent the boiling point of solution increases and freezing point of solution decreases. (½ + ½ = 1 mark)

(c) A solute dissohies in a solvent if intermoleculer interactions are similar between solute and solvent or more than the individuals. Azcotropic mixture is a non-ideal solution which has the same composition in liquid phase and vapour phase. They less may have different boiling points either greater or than both the constituent components.

OR

Scuba divers must cope with high concentrations of dissolved gases while breathing air at high pressure underwater. Increased pressure increases the solubility of atmospheric gases in blood. When the divers come towards surface, the pressure gradually decreases. This releases the dissolved gases and leads to the formation of bubbles of nitrogen in the blood. This blocks capillaries and creates a medical condition known as bends, which are painful and dangerous to life. To avoid bends, as well as, the toxic effects of high concentrations of nitrogen in the blood, the tanks used by scuba divers are filled with air diluted with helium (11.7% helium, 56.2% nitrogen and 32.1% oxygen). (2 marks)

33. (a) (i)

$$C_6H_5-CH=O + CH_3-CH=O \xrightarrow[\text{aldol condensation}]{\text{dil. NaOH}} C_6H_5-CH=CH-\overset{O}{\overset{||}{C}}-H$$

(1 mark)

(ii)

$$C_6H_5-CH=O + H_2N-NH-C_6H_5 \xrightarrow{-H_2O} C_6H_5-CH=N-NH-C_6H_5$$

(1 mark)

(iii)

$$2\,C_6H_5-CHO \xrightarrow[\text{Cannizzaro reaction}]{\text{conc. NaOH } \Delta} C_6H_5-CH_2-OH + C_6H_5-COO^-Na^+$$

(1 mark)

(b) (i) $CH_3CH{=}CH-COCH_3$ and

$CH_3CH_2-CO-CH{=}CH_2$

can be distinguished by the iodoform test as the first compound contains a methyl ketonic group $(-\underset{O}{\underset{||}{C}}-CH_3)$ and undergoes iodoform test, whereas the other compound does not. (1 mark)

(ii) Benzaldehyde does not react with sodium bicarbonate ($NaHCO_3$) whereas benzoic acid evolves carbon dioxide upon reaction with $NaHCO_3$ because of its acidic character. (1 mark)

OR

(a) (i)

$$(CH_3)_2C=O \xrightarrow[\text{Conc.HCl}]{\text{Zn/Hg}} (CH_3)_2CH_2$$

(1 mark)

(ii) $C_6H_5-COONa \xrightarrow[\Delta]{NaOH\ CaO} C_6H_6 + Na_2CO_3$ (1 mark)

(iii) $CH_2=CH-CH_2-CN \xrightarrow[(b)\ H_3O]{(a)\ DIBAL-H} CH_2=CH-CH_2-\underset{\underset{O}{\|}}{C}-H$ (1 mark)

(b) $C_6H_5-\underset{\underset{O}{\|}}{C}-CH_3 < CH_3-\underset{\underset{O}{\|}}{C}-CH_3 < CH_3-\underset{\underset{O}{\|}}{C}-H < H-\underset{\underset{O}{\|}}{C}-H$ (1 mark)

(c) $CH_3-\underset{\underset{H}{|}}{C}=O + H_2N-\underset{\underset{H}{|}}{N}-C_6H_3(NO_2)_2$

Acetaldehyde 2, 4 – DNP

$\xrightarrow{-H_2O} CH_3-\underset{\underset{H}{|}}{C}=N-\underset{\underset{H}{|}}{N}-C_6H_3(NO_2)_2$

2, 4 – DNP derivative of acetaldehyde (1 mark)

34. (a) (i) It is a zero order reaction (1 mark)

(ii)

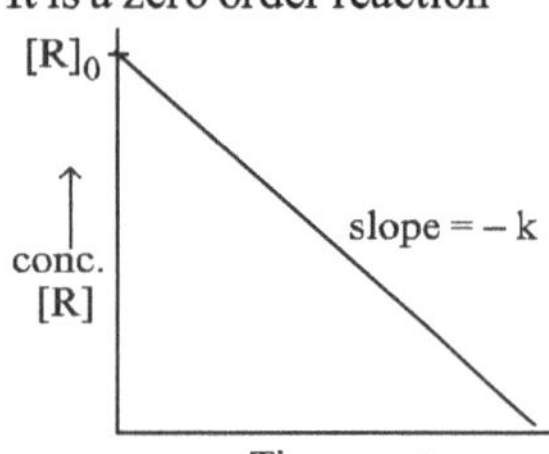

$R=-kt+[R]_0;\ y=mx+c$

The slope of the curve is negative which means concentration of reactant is decreasing with time. (1 mark)

(b) $T_1=293\,K$; $k_1=k$

$T_2=313\,K$; $k_2=4k$

$$\log\frac{k_1}{k_2}=\frac{E_a}{2.303R}\left[\frac{1}{T_2}-\frac{1}{T_1}\right]$$ (1 mark)

$$\log\frac{1}{4}=\frac{E_a}{2.303\times8.314}\left[\frac{1}{313}-\frac{1}{293}\right]$$

$$-0.6020=\frac{E_a}{2.303\times8.314}\left[\frac{293-313}{(313)(293)}\right]$$ (1 mark)

$$E_a=\frac{-0.6020\times2.303\times8.314\times313\times293}{-20}$$

$E_a=52854.55\ J\ mol^{-1}=52.854\ kJ\ mol^{-1}$ (1 mark)

OR

(a) $k=Ae^{-E_a/RT}$ (Arrhenius equation)

$$lnk = lnA-\frac{E_a}{RT}$$

$y = c+mx$

$y = lnk;\ x=1/T$

$c = lnA$ and $m=-E_a/R$

A plot of lnk v/s $\frac{1}{T}$ for a chemical reaction is as straight line. (1 mark)

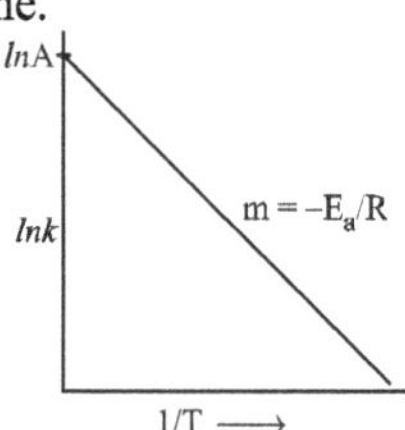

The intercept represents lnA, where A = frequency factor or pre-exponential factor.

$$slope=\frac{-E_a}{R};\ E_a=-(slope\times R)$$ (1 mark)

High temperature and low activation energy favour larger rate constant, and therefore speed up the reaction. Arrhenius equation is generally a combination of the concepts of activation energy and the Maxwell-Boltzmann distribution.

(b) For first order reaction

$$k=\frac{2.303}{t}\log\frac{a}{a-x}$$ (1 mark)

20% compound has been decomposed in 30 min. i.e. 80% compound is left.

$$k=\frac{2.303}{30}\log\frac{100}{100-20}=\frac{2.303}{30}\log1.25$$

$$=\frac{2.303}{30}\times0.0969=0.0074\ min^{-1}$$ (1 mark)

$$t_{1/2}=\frac{0.693}{k}=\frac{0.693}{0.0074}=93.64\ min$$ (1 mark)

35. (a) (i) Zn^{2+} with configuration [Ar] $3d^{10}$ has all filled *d*-orbitals. Therefore, its salts are colourless. Ni^{2+} with configuration [Ar] $3d^8$ has some half-filled *d*-orbitals. Therefore, its salts are coloured. (1 mark)

(ii) In copper sulphate pentahydrate, $CuSO_4\cdot5H_2O$, Cu^{2+} ion has unpaired electron in $3d$-orbital. Due to this, Cu^{2+} ion can have $d-d$ transition when exposed to visible radiation. (1 mark)

(iii) The electronic configuration of both the ions are: Mn^{2+} : $[Ar]3d^5$; Fe^{2+} : $[Ar]3d^6$

The Mn^{2+} ion has more symmetrical configuration than Fe^{2+} ion and therefore, it is more stable. (1 mark)

Thus, + 2 oxidation state of manganese is quite stable while that of iron is not.

(b) (i) The most stable oxidation state is + 3, *i.e.,* Cr^{3+}. (1 mark)

(ii) The most oxidising state is + 6, *i.e.,* Cr^{6+} state. In $K_2Cr_2O_7$, Cr is in + 6 oxidation state and during oxidation it changes to + 3 state.

$Cr^{6+}+3e^-\longrightarrow Cr^{3+}$ (1 mark)

www.ingramcontent.com/pod-product-compliance
Lightning Source LLC
LaVergne TN
LVHW070736170726
843469LV00090B/2297